DRYWALL

3RD EDITION

COMPLETELY REVISED & UPDATED

DRYWALL

PROFESSIONAL TECHNIQUES
FOR GREAT RESULTS

MYRON R. FERGUSON

The Taunton Press

TO MY FAMILY, ESPECIALLY MY PARENTS, AL AND THERESA FERGUSON

 The Taunton Press

The Taunton Press, Inc., 63 South Main Street, PO Box 5506, Newtown, CT 06470-5506
e-mail: tp@taunton.com

Editor: Matthew Teague
Copy editor: Seth Reichgott
Indexer: Jay Kreider
Jacket/Cover design: Renato Stanisic
Interior design: Renato Stanisic
Layout: Renato Stanisic
Illustrator: Chuck Lockhart

Library of Congress Cataloging-in-Publication Data
Ferguson, Myron R.
  Drywall : professional techniques for great results / Myron Ferguson. -- >3rd ed., rev. and updated.
     p. cm.
  Includes index.
   ISBN 978-1-56158-955-5
  1. Drywall construction--Amateurs' manuals. I. Title.

TH2239.F47 2007
693'.6--dc22

                                   2007029604

Printed in the United States of America
10 9 8 7 6 5 4 3

ACKNOWLEDGMENTS

Prior to writing the first edition of this book, most of what I learned throughout my years in the drywall trade was from my family—many of whom are in the contracting business—and through trial and error. In the 25-plus years I have been in business, many new tools, materials, and techniques have emerged. I have also discovered how well some of the older tools, materials, and techniques still perform. I really try to stay open minded and study and then put into use anything new and old that I can get my hands on.

Nowadays, I spend more and more time training and being trained—and I don't know when I learn more! So thanks to all the people who have supported me along the way. I would also like to thank the people I have gotten to know and become friends with from the many great companies out there.

Finally I would like to thank my family. As a fourth-generation building contractor, I know I wouldn't be where I am today without all I have learned and continue to learn from them every day.

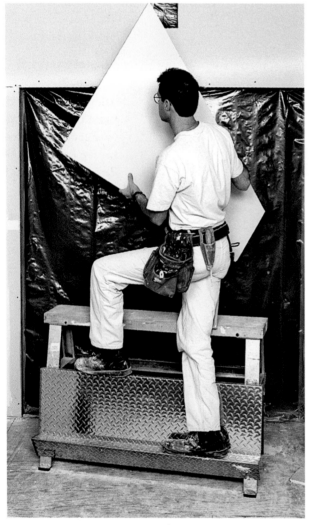

CONTENTS

INTRODUCTION

Drywall, wallboard, Sheetrock®, gypsum board—call it what you will, this material is on more walls and ceilings than any other material in new construction. Drywall covers approximately 80 percent of the visible interior of a typical home, and it holds more than a 90 percent market share of interior finish materials. Properly installed

and finished, drywall can add real beauty to a home or business. Improperly attached or finished, it can be a major eyesore. In this book, I'll teach you how to do it right, with techniques and materials used by the pros. Remember that the best drywalling job goes completely unnoticed.

My first drywalling job was on my own house quite a few years ago. I'd heard a lot of negative things about the chore of installing drywall, but to my surprise I found that I liked the work. Hanging the panels provided me with the physical work that I enjoy, while taping and finishing drywall proved to be an interesting test of my patience and skill. When I started out in the business in 1980, I had a bare minimum of tools and a pretty limited knowledge of the drywall trade. But over the years, I've experimented with different kinds of drywall, joint tape, and joint compounds; added numerous tools to my drywalling arsenal; and studied the work of many professional hangers and tapers.

I'm still learning. Each year manufacturers bring out new materials, such as the variety of corner beads and tapes now on the market. These products not only improve productivity, they also enhance the

finished look of the project. Hangers and tapers are always developing and honing installation techniques, and a whole rash of new application tools makes the work go more quickly and smoothly. My experiences, including countless hours spent hanging and taping drywall, as well as training and talking to people out in the field, have enabled me to develop techniques that virtually guarantee success when drywalling.

If you've ever watched a professional hanger or taper in action, the work probably looked deceptively simple—panels are attached and joints taped in a graceful rhythm. But don't be deceived; working with drywall is not without its frustrations. Getting the perfect finish on the final coat of joint compound can be maddening, and finding a 4-ft.-wide butted seam on a ceiling that is only visible when the sun is setting and shining in the window can all but reduce you to tears. Drywalling requires care and attention to detail every step of the way. Drywall work is just one piece in the

construction puzzle; it should be done at the proper time and under the proper conditions.

Drywalling is a very linear process, and I've organized the book in roughly the order I handle a typical job—from planning the layout to hanging, taping, and sanding drywall to finishing the walls and ceilings (with paint, textures, or wall coverings). I've also included a chapter on special installations (such as curved walls and double-layer applications) and another on drywall repairs. It's a complete course in drywalling.

You may also appreciate the new chapter that I have added detailing the basics of sound control. Whether he knows it or not, the drywall contractor is often involved in some form of sound control. Even the act of installing drywall adds mass to the assembly, which helps reduce sound transmission. But there can be much more than this, so I am offering a brief introduction to sound control. Basic sound control can become an offshoot of any drywall business. In these competitive times, setting yourself apart and establishing another niche market can reap big benefits.

1

Drywall Basics

During the 1940s and 1950s, prefabricated drywall panels gradually replaced plaster as the material of choice for finishing interior walls and ceilings. The earliest drywall panels were used to replace the lath backing in plasterwork; they were narrow (16 in. wide) and only $^3/_8$ in. thick. Today, drywall comes in a wide variety of lengths, thicknesses, and special-use materials. The low cost and the large, easy-to-attach panels make drywall the preferred choice over conventional plaster.

A sheet of drywall consists of a hardened gypsum core sandwiched between two layers of paper—a strong, smooth-finished paper on one side (the face) and a rougher, "natural" paper on the back (see the drawing "End View of a Drywall Panel," on p. 6). The face paper is folded around the long edges, which are tapered slightly to accommodate joint tape and compound after the panel is installed. The ends of the panel are cut square and finished smooth, leaving the gypsum core exposed.

Choose your panels Drywall panels are available in a number of sizes and thicknesses. The larger panel shown here is 54 in. wide.

A heavy load Drywall panels stacked on a truck wait to be unloaded.

easy to decorate and serves as a good base for paint, wallpaper, paneling, textured finishes, decorative fabric, and vinyl wall coverings. The generic term drywall refers to a number of different types of panels, each with characteristics that make it suitable for specific residential and commercial applications.

TYPES AND USES OF DRYWALL

When most people think of drywall, they probably picture the standard 4x8 panel that has been in use since drywall first became popular. But this is by no means the only size or type of drywall available today. Panels come in lengths of up to 16 ft. and in 48-in. and 54-in. widths. A wide variety of special-use drywall is also available, including moisture-resistant, mold-resistant, fire-resistant, and abuse-resistant panels; 1/4-in. flexible panels; 1/2-in. high-strength ceiling panels; and foil-backed panels. In this section, I'll guide you through the various types and their uses, the thicknesses and lengths available, and the framing specifications for each one. With this information, you'll be able to make the right decision about which type of drywall to order when it comes time to plan a job.

Plaster-and-lath construction adds a lot of moisture to a building, and plastered surfaces are traditionally left to dry for up to two weeks (depending on humidity, temperature, and airflow) before being decorated. By comparison, drywall has a low moisture content and the joint compounds used to finish the panels cover only a portion of the exterior, rather than the entire surface, so they dry in 24 hours or less—hence the name "drywall." Drywall is known by many other names, as well, such as Sheetrock (a brand name), gypsum board, plasterboard, wallboard, and gypsum drywall.

Drywall provides excellent sound control, structural integrity, and fire resistance. It is

END VIEW OF A DRYWALL PANEL

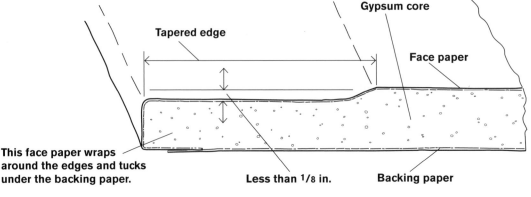

Gypsum core

Tapered edge

Face paper

This face paper wraps around the edges and tucks under the backing paper.

Less than 1/8 in.

Backing paper

WHY USE DRYWALL?

Regardless of the type, all drywall panels have common characteristics that make them more suitable for wall coverings than plaster, plywood, and other materials.

- Panels are available at most lumber stores in a variety of lengths.
- Panels are easy to cut and install.
- When properly reinforced with tape and joint compound, panels are highly resistant to cracks.
- Panels readily accept paint and most other decorating materials.
- Drywall eliminates excessive moisture during construction—a common problem with plaster.
- The noncombustible gypsum core provides fire protection.
- The dense panels provide more effective sound control than do lighter materials, such as plywood and fiberboard.

A room full Half-inch-thick drywall is the most commonly used drywall in residential construction. It works great in most areas and is even rated for 24 in. o.c. spacing on ceiling joists.

Regular drywall

Regular drywall panels are 48 in. wide and come in a variety of lengths, ranging from 8 ft. to 16 ft. (see the chart on p. 8). Panels are available in four thicknesses—5/8 in., 1/2 in., 3/8 in., and 1/4 in.—and each one has specific applications and framing requirements.

Five-eighth-in. regular drywall Five-eighth-in. regular drywall is the thickest regular drywall available. It also provides the best single-layer application over wood and metal framing on walls and ceilings. These panels have greater fire resistance and better sound control than the other thicknesses, and because the panels are stiffer they are more resistant to sagging. This drywall can be used on walls and ceilings with framing members (wall studs and ceiling joists) spaced up to 24 in. on center (o.c.). If you install (or "hang") the panels parallel to the ceiling joists, the joists should be no farther apart than 16 in. o.c. to prevent sagging. It you hang 5/8-in. panels perpendicular to the

REGULAR DRYWALL

THICKNESS	COMMON USES	AVAILABLE LENGTHS	MAXIMUM FRAMING SPACING
5/8 in.	Walls and ceilings	8 ft., 9 ft., 10 ft.,12 ft., 14 ft.	24 in. o.c.; 16 in. o.c., if textured or hung parallel to ceiling joists
1/2 in.	Walls and ceilings (most common	8 ft., 9 ft., 10 ft.,12 ft., 14 ft., 16ft.	24 in. o.c.; 16 in. o.c., if textured or hung parallel to ceiling joists
3/8 in.	Remodeling, mainly on walls	8 ft., 10 ft., 12 ft.	16 in. o.c.
1/4 in.	Remodeling over solid surfaces or curved surfaces with long radii	8 ft., 10 ft.	16 in. o.c. as double layer or as single layer over solid surfaces

Pick panels for convenience
Fifty-four-in. panels provide flexibility on the job. You can use them in combination with 48-in. panels on 8-ft. 6-in. walls or with other 54-in. panels on 9-ft. walls.

ceiling joists, a water-based textured coating can be applied only if the ceiling joists are 16 in. o.c. or closer (again, to avoid sagging.)

Half-in. regular drywall Half-in. regular drywall is the most commonly used drywall in both new construction and remodeling. It is usually used as a single layer over wood or metal framing; however, it can be installed in two layers (with staggered seams) to increase fire resistance and sound control. The framing requirements for 1/2-in. drywall are the same as for 5/8-in. panels. If the framing is farther apart than the recommended spacing, wood or metal furring strips can be attached across the framing to create the specified o.c. spacing.

Three-eighth-in. regular drywall Three-eighth-in. regular drywall was initially used to replace wood lath as a backing for plaster. When drywall first became popular, 3/8-in. panels were widely used on walls and ceilings in new construction, but it was eventually replaced by the more durable 1/2-in. drywall. Today, 3/8-in. drywall is used mainly to cover existing surfaces in repair and remodeling work or to provide a backing for paneling. It is also used in double-layer applications. The maximum distance between framing members on walls and ceilings is 16 in. o.c. For installation on studs and joists that are more than 16 in. o.c. apart, install furring strips. Use a double layer of 3/8-in. drywall with adhesive applied between the two layers (for more on this process, see p. 147).

Quarter-in. regular drywall Quarter-in. regular drywall is a lightweight panel commonly used to cover old walls in remodeling jobs or to provide sound control in double-layer or multilayer applications. When hanging 1/4-in. drywall over old plaster or drywall, use adhesive in combination with screws between the old surface and the new drywall to strengthen the panels and for a more solid attachment. These thin panels are too weak to install in a single layer over bare studs or joists without a backing.

Regular 1/4-in. drywall is easily bent and can be used to form curved surfaces with long radii (5 ft. or more) if applied dry or shorter radii (3 ft. or more) if applied wet. A better choice for curved surfaces, however, is 1/4-in. flexible drywall, which is discussed later in this chapter (see p. 13).

Fifty-four-in.-high drywall One of the main goals of hanging drywall is to have as few seams as possible. That's fine when you're hanging 4-ft.-wide sheets on walls with 8-ft. (or lower) ceilings, because the panels can be hung horizontally with just one seam (see p. 19 for an explanation of why I prefer to hang drywall horizontally rather than vertically). But more and more homes are being constructed with 9-ft.-high ceilings, which means that 4-ft.-wide drywall creates two horizontal seams on each wall. The way to avoid the extra seam is to use 54-in.-wide drywall panels, which were introduced in the early 1990s for use on 9-ft.-high ceilings. Fifty-four-in. drywall comes in regular 1/2-in. and 5/8-in. fire-resistant panels. Sheets are readily available in 12-ft. lengths, but lengths anywhere from 8 ft. to 16 ft. long can be ordered. Fifty-four-in. drywall has the same framing specifications as those for regular 4-ft.-wide panels.

Moisture-resistant drywall

This drywall, which has a light to dark green paper face to distinguish it from other types

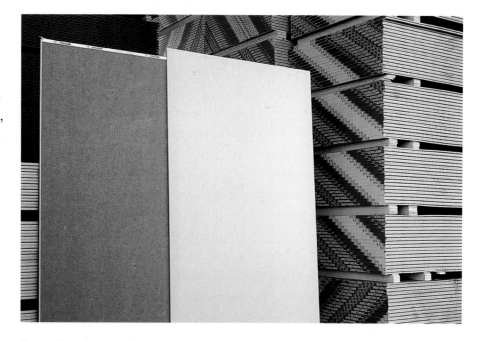

Drywall and water Moisture-resistant drywall has a distinctive green face paper and a darker, moisture-resistant backing paper.

of drywall (hence the name greenboard), is designed to minimize moisture problems. The panels are moisture-resistant all the way through and are made to withstand high humidity and low levels of moisture. Moisture-resistant drywall is mainly used to cover bathrooms, the bottom 4 ft. of a laundry or utility room, or the wall behind a kitchen sink. It is an excellent base for ceramic, plastic, and metal tile applied with an adhesive, as well as for other nonabsorbent finishes, such as paint and wallpaper.

Moisture-resistant drywall should not be used in a wet or high-moisture area, such as a shower enclosure or the wall just above a tub. In addition, moisture-resistant drywall should not be installed over a vapor retarder if it will later be finished with another vapor-retarder material, such as ceramic tile, vinyl tub surround, vinyl wallpaper, or oil-based paint. The objective here is to avoid creating a double vapor retarder, which could eventually deteriorate the drywall if moisture were to become trapped by a water-resistant finish. Rather, moisture-resistant drywall

If mold is a problem Relatively new to the market, mold-resistant drywall is specially treated to resist mold growth. Because these panels are also moisture resistant, they're a good choice for bathrooms.

MOISTURE- AND MOLD-RESISTANT DRYWALL

THICKNESS	COMMON USES	AVAILABLE LENGTHS	MAXIMUM FRAMING SPACING
1/2 in.	Bathrooms; damp areas	8 ft., 10 ft., 12 ft. (up to 16 ft. as special order)	16 in. o.c. on walls; 12 in. o.c. on ceilings
5/8 in.	Bathroom ceilings; fire walls in damp or high-humidity areas	8 ft., 10 ft., 12 ft. (up to 16 ft. as special order)	16 in. o.c. on walls; 16 in. o.c. on ceilings
MOLD-RESISTANT DRYWALL			
1/2-in. regular or firecode	Bathrooms and damp areas	8 ft., 10 ft., 12 ft. (up to 16 ft. as special order)	16 in. o.c. on walls; 12 in. o.c. on ceilings
5/8-in. firecode	Bathroom ceilings; fire walls in damp or high-humidity areas	8 ft., 10 ft., 12 ft. (up to 16 ft. as special order)	16 in. o.c. on walls; 16 in. o.c. on ceilings

should be attached directly to the framing. In areas that are not covered with tile or other wall coverings, moisture-resistant drywall can be taped and painted just like other types of drywall.

Moisture-resistant drywall, which is available in ½-in. regular or ⅝-in. fire-resistant panels, is used mainly as a wall covering over 16-in. o.c. framing. If you plan to install it on a ceiling, use ⅝-in. panels over 16-in. centers and ½-in. panels over 12-in. (or less) centers. (If the ceiling is insulated, make sure that unfaced insulation was used to avoid creating a double vapor barrier.)

Mold-resistant drywall

It seems that we are hearing more and more about mold lately—with all the damage caused by storms and flooding, dealing with mold and preventing mold growth are on a lot of people's minds. The truth is mold is more prevalent today, particularly in struc-

tures built during the past 25 years. Focusing on improving energy efficiency resulted in more airtight homes that do not "breathe" like older homes.

Also, homes are now built year-round, which was not the norm many years ago, so these structures are subjected to the elements during all phases of construction. Add to this the more complex home designs and you have created increased potential for moisture intrusion: WATER + OXYGEN + NUTRIENTS = MOLD.

Moisture trapped in walls and ceilings often results in mold growth on the drywall itself. Some drywall manufacturers have decided to do what they can to help reduce the mold problem. On the market today are mold resistant types of drywall. Most offer resistance to moisture, mold, and mildew. I have started using mold-resistant drywall in all the places I previously would have chosen moisture-resistant drywall. I figure, why not offer the customer the added benefit of using a mold-resistant panel that is also moisture-resistant?

Mold-resistant drywall is available with treated paper-faced panels or in paperless panels—instead of being faced with paper, the front and back are covered with an inorganic fiberglass mat that does not promote mold growth. Both types are available in 1/2-in. or 5/8-in. panels and they come in lengths of 8 ft. or 12 ft.

Fire-resistant drywall

As a dense, noncombustible, mineral-based material, drywall in all its forms is a better fire barrier and a more efficient sound absorber than lighter materials, such as plywood. Even better, fire-resistant drywall has a gypsum core with special additives and glass fibers that are particularly effective in containing fire. This drywall is a little harder to cut than regular drywall, because the gypsum core is tougher.

On the surface, these panels look the same as regular drywall, except for a stamp indicating that they are fire resistant. The term fire resistance means the ability of a constructed assembly (a wall or a ceiling covered with drywall) to contain a fire. The fire-resistance rating for each thickness of

drywall is measured in intervals of time: 45 minutes for 1/2-in. fire-resistant drywall, 60 minutes for 5/8-in. panels, and 120 minutes for 3/4-in. panels. The panels can be layered to increase the fire rating.

One-half-in. fire-resistant drywall Many building codes specify fire-resistant drywall for attached garages, furnace or utility rooms, and ceilings and walls separating dwelling

In case of fire Fire-resistant drywall panels have gypsum cores with glass fibers that help contain fire.

FIRE-RESISTANT DRYWALL

THICKNESS	COMMON USES	FIRE RATING	AVAILABLE LENGTHS	MAXIMUM FRAMING SPACING
1/2 in.	In areas where butted against regular 1/2 in.	45 min.	8 ft., 10 ft., 12 ft.	24 in. o.c.
5/8 in.	Garages; over 24-in. o.c. ceilings (most commonly used thickness)	60 min.	8 ft., 10 ft., 12 ft. (14 ft. as special order)	24 in. o.c.
3/4 in.	Where high fire rating is required	120 min.	8 ft., 9 ft., 10 ft., 12 ft.	24 in. o.c.

A more rugged option
A garage wall is an ideal place for abuse-resistant drywall.

units in apartment and condominium complexes. The two most commonly used fire-resistant panels are 1/2 in. and 5/8 in. One-half-in. panels are convenient when you need to cover only part of a wall or ceiling with fire-resistant drywall and finish the rest with regular 1/2-in. panels (the most common standard thickness). For example, a garage ceiling might be finished with two types of drywall. Typically, only the first 5 ft. of the ceiling adjacent to a wall needs to be fire resistant. Using the same thicknesses of fire-resistant and regular drywall allows you to make a smooth transition at the joint. If you use different thicknesses (say, 5/8-in. fire resistant and 1/2-in. regular), you'll create a seam that's difficult to hide during the taping process.

Five-eigth-in. fire-resistant drywall For fire resistance, 5/8-in. panels are the most commonly used size. They have the one-hour fire rating that many building codes require.

Because most garage-ceiling joists are 24 in. o.c., 5/8-in. panels work best because they are approved for 24-in. spacing. Although manufacturers approve 1/2-in. panels for joists 24 in. o.c., they are more likely to sag, especially in a garage that is exposed to extremes in temperature and humidity. Because of the extra thickness and stronger core, 5/8-in. fire-resistant drywall stands up better to denting and other types of abuse than 1/2-in. drywall does. Because garages often suffer a lot of abuse from car doors, bikes, and tools, I prefer to cover the entire surface with 5/8-in. drywall.

Three-quarter-in. fire-resistant drywall This type of drywall has a two-hour fire rating or a four-hour rating when the layers are doubled. It is used where a high fire rating is a must, such as to separate apartments or to divide offices from a garage or factory. The extra thickness and fire rating mean fewer layers, cutting down on the cost of materials and labor.

Abuse-resistant drywall

Abuse-resistant drywall is tougher than other types of drywall. It has a high-strength reinforced gypsum core sandwiched between smooth but thick abrasion-resistant paper on the face and heavy liner paper on the back. These products are called by a variety of different names, including abuse-resistant, impact-resistant, and high-impact-resistant drywall. There are some advertisements that

ABUSE-RESISTANT DRYWALL

THICKNESS	COMMON USES	AVAILABLE LENGTHS	MAXIMUM FRAMING SPACING
1/2 in.	As an upgrade to regular drywall in high-traffic areas	8 ft., 10 ft., 12 ft.	24 in. o.c.
5/8 in.	As a fire wall in commercial and apartment buildings in high-traffic areas	8 ft., 10 ft., 12 ft.	24 in. o.c.

WORK SMART
One-quarter-in. flexible drywall is worth a little extra per sq. ft. because it bends more uniformly than other types of 1/4-in drywall, which means a smoother finished surface.

claim the panels are as tough as concrete. That's overdoing it, but they are tougher than both regular and fire-resistant panels. Despite their toughness, abuse-resistant panels can be finished like other types of drywall.

Abuse-resistant drywall holds up well in areas where regular drywall may be easily damaged, such as in mudrooms, workshops, garages, and other high-traffic areas. It is also more resistant to cracking and warping. This extra strength means long-term savings on repairs and replacement costs. Abuse-resistant drywall is available in 1/2-in. panels and 5/8-in. fire-resistant panels. The 5/8-in. fire-resistant panels are ideal in garages, utility rooms, and commercial work areas, where a high fire rating is necessary.

Quarter-inch flexible drywall

This drywall is designed for use on curved walls, archways, and stairways. It works well on both concave and convex surfaces. Flexible drywall has a heavier face paper and a stronger liner paper than regular 1/4-in. drywall does, and it is easier to bend and more resistant to cracking caused by structural changes. It is usually applied in double layers, with staggered seams where possible.

Not all curved surfaces have the same radius—some are tighter than others—and they must be treated slightly differently. For curved surfaces with a short radius (32 in. or

less), it may be necessary to wet the drywall before trying to attach it. Use a sponge or roller to wet the surface to be compressed; this helps the drywall mold around the curve without breaking. (For more on this procedure, see Chapter 6.)

For curved surfaces Flexible drywall panels are designed for use on archways and curved walls.

TYPE OF CURVE	WET OR DRY	MINIMUM RADIUS	MAXIMUM STUD SPACING
Inside curve (concave)	Dry	32 in.	9 in. o.c.
Inside curve (concave)	Wet	20 in.	9 in. o.c.
Outside curve (convex)	Dry	32 in.	9 in. o.c.
Outside curve (convex)	Wet	15 in.	6 in. o.c.

WORK SMART

Cement board is a better choice than moisture-resistant dry-wall for wet areas, like those around tubs and shower enclosures.

WORK SMART

The use of moisture-resistant drywall in wet areas is no longer an accepted practice. There are simply better materials on the market today available for little or no additional cost.

One-half-in. high-strength ceiling panels

One-half-in. high-strength ceiling panels have a reinforced gypsum core that increases resistance to sagging, a common problem when using regular ¹/₂-in. drywall on widely spaced framing or when applying water-based textured coatings over drywall. High-strength drywall is rigid enough to hang over 24-in. o.c. joists (rather than 16-in. o.c. joists, as I recommend for regular ¹/₂-in. drywall) and can be textured without fear of sagging. Half-in. high-strength drywall is available in lengths of 8 ft. and 12 ft. (lengths of up to 16 ft. can be specially ordered).

Foil-backed drywall

This drywall has aluminum foil laminated to the back of the panel. The foil creates an effective vapor barrier and adds to the insulating value of the drywall. It is used mainly in cold climates to help prevent interior moisture from entering wall and ceiling cavities.

Foil-backed drywall can be used over wood and metal framing, over furred masonry, or as the base layer for multilayer applications. It should not be used as a base for tile or highly moisture-resistant wall coverings, such as vinyl wallpaper, because the core could absorb and trap moisture and eventually damage the drywall. Foil-backed drywall is also not recommended for use in hot, humid climates. Panels are available in ³/₈-in., ¹/₂-in., and ⁵/₈-in. thicknesses and in the same lengths as those for regular drywall.

Cement board

Cement board is a high-strength tile backer that serves as a water-durable and mold-resistant base for walls and ceilings. It will not swell, soften, or delaminate when exposed

Right: Cement board under tile Cement board, which has one smooth side and one rough side, is used primarily as an underlayment for tile in areas exposed to water.

to moisture, but it is not a vapor barrier. Moisture can travel through cement board, so a barrier may be necessary behind the board.

Designed for areas exposed to water or high levels of moisture, cement board is an excellent base for tiled walls and floors and bathtub and shower enclosures. Unlike the materials discussed up to this point, cement board is not a gypsum product; it has a cement core covered with fiberglass mesh. One side is rough, the other is smooth (see the photo on the facing page). The rough side, designed for mortar application of tile, increases bonding and decreases tile slippage. The smooth side is designed for mastic application of tile.

Cement board is commonly available in ¼-in. and ½-in. panels. Standard widths are 32 in., 36 in., and 48 in.; the standard length is 5 ft., although 8-ft. panels are also available. The maximum stud spacing for cement board is 16 in. o.c. Panels should be attached with special screws or galvanized roofing nails, not with drywall screws or nails. (For more on installing cement board, see p. 149.) Cement board is quite fragile, so it should be stored flat to prevent warping and handled as carefully as possible.

Gypsum-core tile backer

This type of drywall consists of a silicone-treated core covered with a glass mat on both sides for added strength. The face also has an acrylic coating that provides a water barrier to stop moisture from penetrating into the wall, ceiling, or floor. It acts as a vapor barrier, so be careful not to create a double vapor barrier. These panels, available in ½-in. and ⅝-in. thicknesses, are strong, lightweight, and easy to cut, snap, and fasten. Gypsum-core tile backer is recommended for residential and light commercial use as an underlayment for ceramic tile. It is used in many of the same areas as cement board. Although not as durable as cement board,

gypsum-core tile backer is easier to work with and is available in larger sizes (4x8 and 5x8). Framing specifications are the same as those for cement board.

PLANNING THE JOB

Planning a drywall job involves more than just selecting the right type of drywall. You'll also need to estimate materials, make sure the materials (especially the longer-length panels) are available when needed, plan access for

Above: An easier option Gypsum-core tile backer, which is used as an underlayment for tile, has a silicone-treated core sandwiched between layers of glass mat and an acrylic coating on the face.

DEALING WITH WET AREAS

- Use a material that prohibits mold growth and holds together even after getting wet.

- Drywall, even moisture- or mold-resistant, is not approved for installation in most wet areas.

- You still need to try and contain water. There should be no water leaking in through gaps and cracks. Proper maintenance is important.

- Installing a waterproof membrane behind the backer board may be necessary.

- Be careful not to install double vapor barriers.

- Consult the tile contractor or general contractor to make sure the assembly meets his approval.

FROM FRAME TO FINISH

Everything that happens from the time the framing starts until the finish work is complete affects the quality of the finished product. And it may even go back further than that. For example, if I get a complaint about drywall work I may be able to blame the excavator: Maybe he overdug the footings and when he backfilled he didn't tamp down the dirt enough. So, the floor settles and then the ceiling joist is low and I cover it with drywall. Now there is a bump along the edge and of course the crown molding does not fit the ceiling properly. See how one thing leads to another. To prevent such problems, I like for the general contractor to have a carpenter at the jobsite when we hang the drywall. This way, any questionable framing issues discovered during hanging can be addressed. The end result is a better job overall.

Keep it flush The framing was not aligned flush to this opening. When the drywall was attached it cracked, leading to an unnecessary repair.

Check the framing These firestops are located where a horizontal seam will fall. It seems like a good location, but blocks and nails often stick out past the framing and create a ridged seam.

the drywall, and make sure you have enough help on the job site to maneuver the cumbersome panels. But before you start figuring out a material list for the job, there are some basic layout principles that you should keep in mind.

General layout guidelines

No two drywall projects are exactly alike, and each presents a unique set of challenges. But I've found that keeping the following items in mind helps just about any job go smoothly.

Always think of ways to eliminate unnecessary joints when planning the layout of a room. Use the longest panels possible; remember that most types of drywall are available in lengths of up to 14 ft. or 16 ft. You may be tempted to use all 8-ft. lengths

because they are lighter and easier to handle (and often cheaper), but don't. Using all 8-ft. panels creates too many seams that are difficult to hide. Keep in mind that fewer seams means less taping.

Ceiling panels can be attached either perpendicular to the ceiling joists (my preference) or parallel to the joists. Make sure that the type of drywall you intend to use is approved for the stud or joist spacing; drywall is stronger in the long direction (see "Grain Orientation in Drywall," on p. 71). In addition, the framing spacing may affect the direction in which the drywall is hung.

Always try to avoid butted seams A butted seam is a joint created when two untapered panel ends are joined together on the same framing member. If you have to use butted

Smart layout When possible, attach drywall panels perpendicular to the ceiling joists and cover the span with one length of drywall whenever possible.

WHY AVOID BUTTED SEAMS?

Below are some of the reasons butted seams create trouble spots for the drywaller:

- Framing members are often too narrow. If the edge of one panel isn't exactly centered on the framing, the next panel won't fit correctly. The result is a poor attachment to the framing.

- Screws have to be installed close to the edge of the drywall, damaging the core of the panel and resulting in a weak attachment.

- Structural movement or lumber shrinking or expanding will cause butted seams to ridge or crack because they are the weakest points in the wall or ceiling.

- Unlike the sides of drywall panels, the ends of panels are not tapered to create a recess. At the finishing stage, this means you're concealing a bump rather than filling a recess.

Positioning screws The screws tying the end of this panel to the framing are too close to the edge of the panel. The result is a damaged core and weak attachment.

PLACEMENT OF BUTTED SEAMS

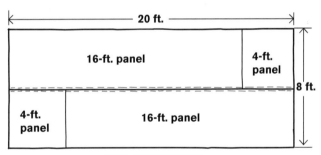

THE RIGHT WAY
Butted seams (at the panel ends) are on different studs as far as possible from the center of the wall.

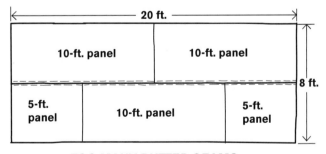

TOO MANY BUTTED SEAMS
Butted seams are staggered but there are too many, and one is in the center of the wall.

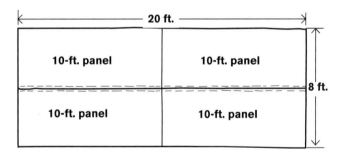

POORLY PLACED BUTTED SEAMS
Butted seams are on the same stud and in the center of the wall.

HORIZONTAL VS. VERTICAL LAYOUT

Hanging drywall horizontally reduces the number and length of the seams.

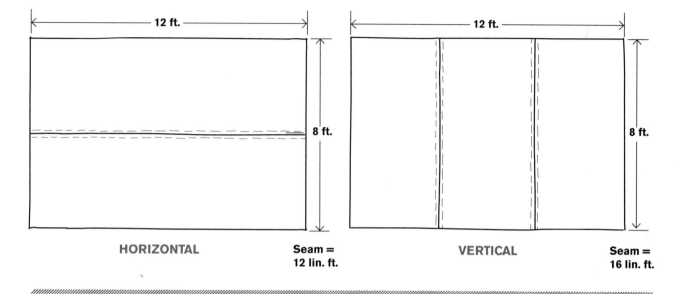

12 ft.   **8 ft.**

HORIZONTAL   Seam = 12 lin. ft.

12 ft.   **8 ft.**

VERTICAL   Seam = 16 lin. ft.

seams, stagger them as far as possible from the center of the wall. For example, if a wall is 8 ft. high by 20 ft. long, it is not a good idea to use four 10-ft. panels (see the drawing on p. 18). You'll end up with more than two butted seams on one wall or with seams on the same stud in the center of the wall. Instead, order two 16-ft. panels and one 8-ft. panel, and arrange them as shown in the drawing on the facing page. This way, there are only two butted seams on the wall and they're away from the center, where they are easier to hide when taping and finishing. For information on how to avoid potential problems with butted seams, see p. 142.

On walls that are more than 4 ft. wide and no higher than 8 ft., hang the drywall horizontally (perpendicular to the studs). This technique reduces the linear footage of joints and also places the horizontal joints at a good height for taping (see the drawing above).

For walls that are more than 8 ft. high, consider using 54-in.-wide drywall panels, which can greatly reduce the linear footage of seams. Fifty-four-in.-wide drywall is only available in lengths of up to 12 ft. That could be a problem in larger rooms or areas where the walls are over 9 ft. high. In those cases, it may be better to install the drywall vertically. The goal is to use whichever method produces the fewest seams (measured in linear feet) to tape.

ESTIMATING MATERIALS

On most drywalling jobs, I figure out a rough material list from the blueprints and job specifications. I use this information to estimate the cost of the job. Once the building is framed, I obtain my exact material list by measuring the actual walls and ceilings.

Measuring the walls and ceilings makes it easier to visualize how to hang the drywall, decide which lengths and types to use, and figure out where to hang them. As I measure each room, I write down exactly what I'll need on a material list, using a separate list for each story of the building (see the sample

Avoid seams when possible
On walls 4 ft. wide or less, hang the panels vertically. Not only does this cut down on finishing, but it often avoids having to blend the seam into the outside corner bead.

SAMPLE MATERIAL LIST

DATE: _____

JOB NAME: _____

LOCATION: ☐ DOWNSTAIRS ☐ UPSTAIRS ☐ GARAGE ☐ OTHER _____

REGULAR DRYWALL 1/2 IN.

length	total
8 ft.	
10 ft.	
12 ft.	
14 ft.	
16 ft.	

FIRE-RESISTANT DRYWALL 5/8 IN. 1/2 IN.

length	total
8 ft.	
10 ft.	
12 ft.	
14 ft.	

CORNER BEAD

length

total

8 ft.	
10 ft.	

MOISTURE-RESISTANT DRYWALL 1/2 IN.

length

total

8 ft.	
10 ft.	
12 ft.	
14 ft.	

OTHER   **THICKNESS**

length	total
8 ft.	
10 ft.	
12 ft.	
14 ft.	

SPECIAL INSTRUCTIONS

_____

_____

_____

_____

_____

When filling out a material list, there are many ways to keep a tally of the number of sheets of drywall you'll need. I like to use the "dot tally" method—it takes up little space and doesn't require erasing if you make mistakes. Here's the key to the dot-tally system:

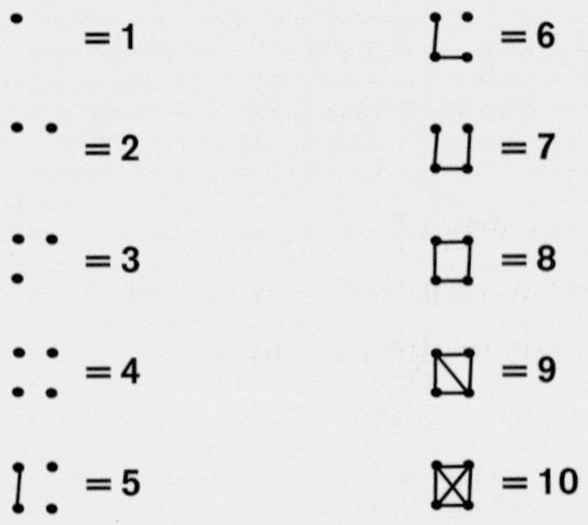

If you put a dot in the wrong place, simply circle it. For example,

indicates 9 instead of 10.

• = 1		= 6
• • = 2		= 7
• • = 3		= 8
• • = 4		= 9
• = 5		= 10

Create a game-plan There are a lot of framing transitions to consider before hanging the first sheet of drywall on a wall like this.

material list on p. 20). The material list makes it easy to calculate the square footage of drywall, which helps me estimate the cost for the entire job (I usually estimate a job by the square foot). From the square footage, I can calculate the approximate amount of screws, nails, joint tape, joint compound, and paint needed to complete the job (see the sidebar on p. 52).

Sometimes figuring materials for a larger wall or ceiling with a lot of framing issues is difficult. I study the area and as always think about ways to reduce seams, especially butted seams. I am also concerned with seam location more than ever—a seam placed at a transition point in the framing can result in a ridged seam that will be difficult to conceal and may crack as settling and structural movement occur. Don't simply start at the bottom and work your way up with drywall; you may have to start with a ripped piece so that an upper seam falls in the best location. Remember that on highly visible areas any little bump, ridge, or defect will be on display after the drywall is painted.

When working up the material list, I usually round lengths of walls and heights

of ceilings to the next highest 2-ft.-length panel. For example, if a wall is 12 ft. 9 in. long, I order a 14-ft. panel (see the drawing on p. 22). In this example, the lower 4 ft. of the wall is broken up by a doorway, so I

Avoid butted seams When the final sheets are attached to this wall, the seams will be quite visible—any defects in the finishing will be on display.

SAMPLE WALL LAYOUT

The most efficient way to drywall on this wall is to use one 14-ft. panel (top) and one 10-ft. panel (bottom). Hanging the drywall horizontally requires the fewest seams and produces the best-looking job.

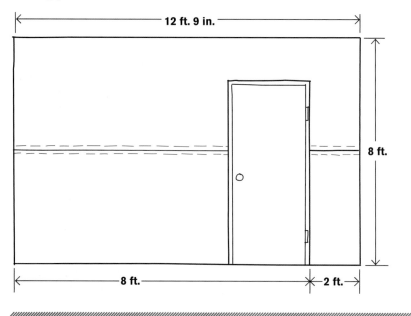

mum length possible for each wall. If a room is 12 ft. by 16 ft., I mainly use 12-ft.- or 16-ft.-long panels—unless a doorway allows me to use a shorter length.

As I walk through a house, I note any rooms that will require special treatment. In the example shown in the plans on pp. 26–27, the upstairs master bedroom has a cathedral ceiling, so I need to allow extra drywall for the ceiling and the gable ends. It's not a good idea to plan a butted seam directly under the ridge beam on the ends of a cathedral ceiling—there could be structural weight and some movement or settling, which would eventually cause the seam to crack—so I figure on spanning the end wall with 16-ft. panels.

In addition, cement board or tile backer will need to be used in the shower area of the master bathroom. I would also plan for the rest of the bathroom walls to be covered with $1/2$-in. moisture-resistant drywall—or my new preference, mold-resistant drywall—and the ceiling to be covered with $5/8$-in. moisture- or mold-resistant panels.

The garage ceiling joists are 24 in. o.c., so I would estimate the entire ceiling using $5/8$-in. fire-resistant drywall. All the garage walls adjacent to the house will need $5/8$-in. fire-resistant drywall, too; for the rest of the garage I could switch over to regular $1/2$-in. drywall. The garage walls are 10 ft. high, so I'd stand 10-ft. panels on end to avoid butted seams and to keep the linear footage of seams to a minimum (see p. 18).

After tallying the number and types of drywall panels needed, the next step is to calculate the total square footage of drywall required. Multiply the number of panels needed for each length by the square footage in one panel, and then add all the totals together. For example, the total square footage of drywall needed for the house shown in the plans is displayed in the chart on the facing page.

WORK SMART

If you are planning to hang drywall vertically on the walls, the on-center spacing of the framing has to be correct and care must be taken not to attach a seam to a crooked stud. This is much more critical than when you're hanging the drywall horizontally.

would order a 10-ft. panel to complete each side of the doorway with a minimum amount of waste. Keep in mind that the idea is to use panels that span the entire length of the wall or ceiling whenever possible.

The drawing on p. 23 shows how I estimate drywall for an entire room. In this particular example, I can use one length (16 ft.) for the wall with the window, because the window doesn't go all the way to the ceiling or the floor and the wall is less than 16 ft. long. On the ceiling, I can use either three 16-ft. panels or four 12-ft. panels. In this example, I'd choose the four 12-ft. panels, because it's preferable to attach the panels perpendicular to the ceiling joists (see p. 70) and the shorter lengths are easier to handle.

Estimating materials for an entire house
When I'm working up a material list for a job, I usually don't need to figure out a separate list for each room—I know to use the maxi-

Rough estimating a house A quicker but less accurate way to estimate the amount of drywall needed for a house is to multiply the square footage of the living-area floor space for each story by 3.5 (for a home with 8-ft.-high ceilings). I use this method to give a rough estimate over the phone, for example. In the house in our example, multiplying the square footage of the upstairs and downstairs living areas (1,984 sq. ft.) by 3.5 gives a rough drywall total of 6,944 sq. ft. We also need to add the total for the garage. Multiply the total length of the garage walls by the height (112 ft. x 10 ft. = 1,120 sq. ft.), and then add the ceiling (approximately 700 sq. ft.): 1,120 + 700 = 1,820 sq. ft.

Using the rough estimating method, the total square footage of drywall needed for this house works out to be 8,764 sq. ft. (6,944 + 1,820). This figure is reasonably close to the actual square footage needed (9,128 sq. ft.) and a lot quicker to calculate.

For a house with 9-ft.-high ceilings, use 3.82 as the multiplier. Many houses have 8-ft.-high ceilings upstairs and 9-ft.-high ceilings downstairs. In those cases, calculate each floor separately and then add the totals together to obtain the rough estimate.

PLANNING ACCESS FOR MATERIALS

When calculating a material list for any building, you need to consider which lengths you can get into the building and the best way to get them inside (ideally, the contractor should start thinking about this before the framing begins).

For a normal single-story building, access is generally not a concern. For anything over one story, however, you may need to make some special arrangements.

SAMPLE ROOM ESTIMATE

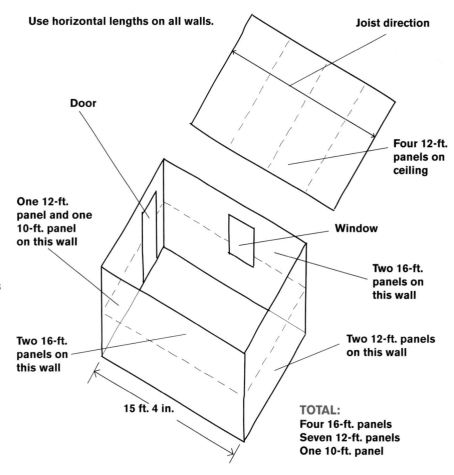

Use horizontal lengths on all walls.

Joist direction

Door

Four 12-ft. panels on ceiling

One 12-ft. panel and one 10-ft. panel on this wall

Window

Two 16-ft. panels on this wall

Two 16-ft. panels on this wall

Two 12-ft. panels on this wall

15 ft. 4 in.

TOTAL:
Four 16-ft. panels
Seven 12-ft. panels
One 10-ft. panel

CALCULATING TOTAL SQUARE FOOTAGE

LENGTH	# PANELS NEEDED		SQUARE FOOTAGE OF EACH PANEL		TOTAL SQUARE FOOTAGE
8 ft.	40	X	32	=	1,280
10 ft.	90	X	40	=	3,600
12 ft.	39	X	48	=	1,872
14 ft.	31	X	56	=	1,736
16 ft.	10	X	64	=	640
					9,128 sq. ft.

Here are some ways to help plan for the best access:

- Measure and inspect the job site before the rough framing is complete.

- If necessary, ask the builder to leave out a window, a door, or even a section of plywood on an exterior wall to allow access for long panels.

- Make note of overhead wires that could get in the way of a boom-truck delivery.

- Look for freshly covered ditches or septic tanks, which may not support a heavy truck.

- Note good areas to stack the drywall once it is delivered.

If you need to make special arrangements for access, watch the timing. And if you must special-order materials, do it early so the job is not held up. Also, check out the job site to make sure there are appropriate areas to place all the drywall panels. When I receive a drywall delivery, I like to distribute the panels in neat piles throughout the building to spread out the weight and speed up the hanging process. The panels can be laid flat on the floor, which is the safest way, or on edge against a wall. If you stand them on edge, make sure they are almost straight, so that they don't develop a bow, but not so straight that they will topple.

Some time ago, my crew and I were drywalling the upstairs ceilings and walls in an old farmhouse. The only room finished upstairs was the master bedroom. Because the stairs were crooked and steep, the only

Save your back If there is a large enough opening in an exterior wall, a drywall boom truck can make quick work of a second- or third-story delivery.

WORK SMART
When possible, stack drywall panels on the floor to keep them straight and flat.

Or carry it up If you don't have the luxury of an upper-story access, the drywall's journey upstairs can be a little more circuitous.

length I was able to maneuver up them was an 8-ft. panel. But I didn't want to use only 8-ft. panels. The walls and ceilings were crooked and patched up, and there was quite a bit of loose plaster; if I'd used all 8-ft. panels, I'd have ended up with a lot of difficult seams. The only way to get longer panels upstairs was through a large window in the finished master bedroom.

Going through a finished room can be a customer's worst nightmare, so to avoid any damage to the master bedroom I covered the room with drop cloths and plastic and removed the window sashes. It took five of us approximately two hours to unload the truck and hand the panels through the window, but it was well worth it in the long run. It sounds like a lot of trouble, but I ended up with a minimum number of seams. As a result, the customer got the best job possible.

Storing drywall Standing large amounts of drywall on edge is convenient for cutting and marking, but the weight is distributed better lying flat. Also, panels laid flat never fall over.

SAMPLE HOUSE ESTIMATE

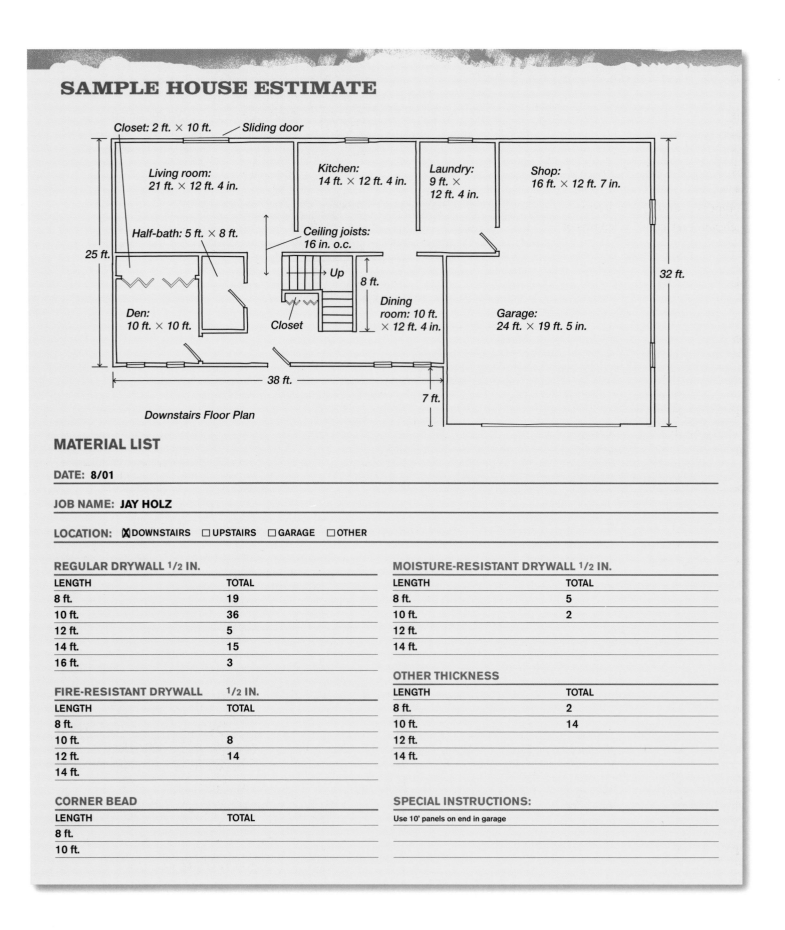

Closet: 2 ft. × 10 ft. — Sliding door

Living room:
21 ft. × 12 ft. 4 in.

Kitchen:
14 ft. × 12 ft. 4 in.

Laundry:
9 ft. ×
12 ft. 4 in.

Shop:
16 ft. × 12 ft. 7 in.

Half-bath: 5 ft. × 8 ft.

Ceiling joists:
16 in. o.c.

25 ft.

Up

8 ft.

32 ft.

Den:
10 ft. × 10 ft.

Closet

Dining
room: 10 ft.
× 12 ft. 4 in.

Garage:
24 ft. × 19 ft. 5 in.

38 ft.

7 ft.

Downstairs Floor Plan

MATERIAL LIST

DATE: 8/01

JOB NAME: JAY HOLZ

LOCATION: ☒ DOWNSTAIRS ☐ UPSTAIRS ☐ GARAGE ☐ OTHER

REGULAR DRYWALL ¹/₂ IN.

LENGTH	TOTAL
8 ft.	19
10 ft.	36
12 ft.	5
14 ft.	15
16 ft.	3

FIRE-RESISTANT DRYWALL ¹/₂ IN.

LENGTH	TOTAL
8 ft.	
10 ft.	8
12 ft.	14
14 ft.	

CORNER BEAD

LENGTH	TOTAL
8 ft.	
10 ft.	

MOISTURE-RESISTANT DRYWALL ¹/₂ IN.

LENGTH	TOTAL
8 ft.	5
10 ft.	2
12 ft.	
14 ft.	

OTHER THICKNESS

LENGTH	TOTAL
8 ft.	2
10 ft.	14
12 ft.	
14 ft.	

SPECIAL INSTRUCTIONS:

Use 10' panels on end in garage

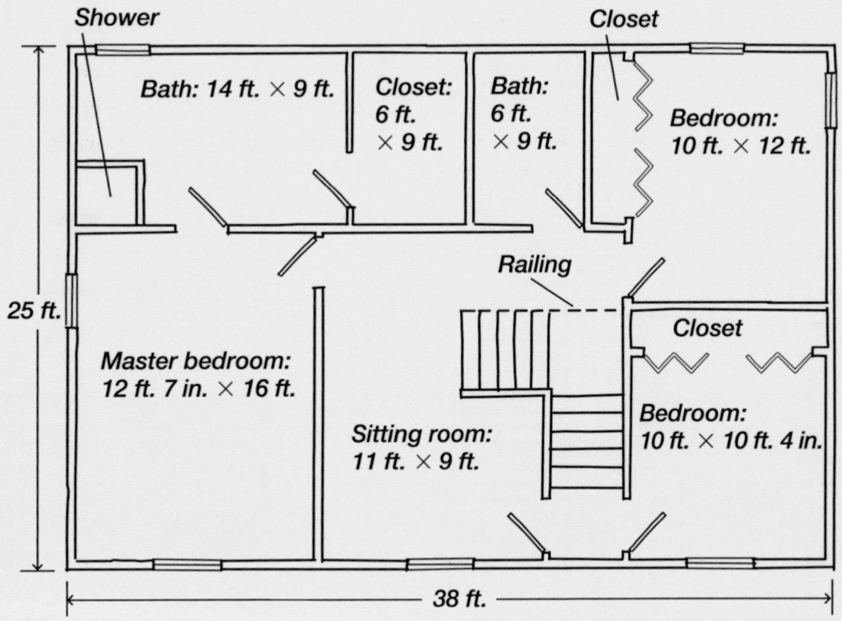

Shower

Closet

Bath: 14 ft. × 9 ft.

Closet: 6 ft. × 9 ft.

Bath: 6 ft. × 9 ft.

Bedroom: 10 ft. × 12 ft.

Railing

25 ft.

Master bedroom: 12 ft. 7 in. × 16 ft.

Closet

Sitting room: 11 ft. × 9 ft.

Bedroom: 10 ft. × 10 ft. 4 in.

38 ft.

Upstairs Floor Plan

MATERIAL LIST

DATE: 8/01

JOB NAME: JAY HOLZ

LOCATION: ☐ DOWNSTAIRS   ☒ UPSTAIRS   ☐ GARAGE   ☐ OTHER

REGULAR DRYWALL 1/2 IN.

LENGTH	TOTAL
8 ft.	13
10 ft.	18
12 ft.	17
14 ft.	13
16 ft.	7

FIRE-RESISTANT DRYWALL 5/8 IN. 1/2 IN.

LENGTH	TOTAL
8 ft.	
10 ft.	
12 ft.	
14 ft.	

CORNER BEAD

LENGTH	TOTAL
8 ft.	
10 ft.	

MOISTURE-RESISTANT DRYWALL 1/2 IN.

LENGTH	TOTAL
8 ft.	1
10 ft.	7
12 ft.	3
14 ft.	3

OTHER MOISTURE-RESISTANT DRYWALL

THICKNESS 5/8"

LENGTH	TOTAL
8 ft.	
10 ft.	5
12 ft.	
14 ft.	

SPECIAL INSTRUCTIONS:

Master bedroom (cathedral ceiling):
use 16' lengths
Bring baker's scaffold
Bathroom ceiling: 5/8" M.R.
Bathroom shower: get (3) 36" X 5' cement boards
1/2" thick

CHAPTER

2

Tools and Materials

When I started out in the drywall business, I could easily carry in my arms all the tools that I needed to hang, tape, and sand a drywalling job. My basic set of tools consisted of a T-square, a utility knife, a screw gun, a prybar, a utility saw, a wooden bench, four trowels, and a hand sander. With these few basic tools, I was limited to relatively simple jobs—drywalling single rooms and small additions, repairing cracks, and doing some minor remodeling—and I had to work pretty hard to get results that I was happy with.

As I gained experience and improved my techniques, I began to take on more challenging jobs, such as drywalling entire houses, working on high ceilings, and hanging drywall on curved surfaces. These more difficult jobs required that I add tools (and manpower) to my drywalling arsenal, including a greater assortment of taping knives, adjustable workbenches, and scaffolding. In addition to using new tools, I have always tried to keep up with the latest

The drywaller's toolset Using the right tools speeds the drywall process and helps deliver better results.

For good measure A tape measure can be used to scribe short, straight measurements. Pinch the tape at the desired dimension, and then scribe a line with a utility knife as you ride the tape along the edge of the panel.

developments in drywalling materials. Over the years, the types of fasteners, joint tapes, and joint compounds have changed and new ones have been developed for specific uses.

You can do a pretty good drywalling job with only the basic tools, but you'll get much better results—whether you're a professional or a homeowner—if you have the right materials and equipment. I've organized this chapter roughly in the order in which each tool or material is needed, starting with tools for measuring and marking on through tools for sanding. Rather than listing all the tools first and then listing the materials, I've combined the two categories. For example, you'll find screws and nails with the discussion of screw guns and hammers. I've also included some specialized tools (such as a drywall router, a self-feeding screw gun attachment, and a corner crimper) that can make the job easier or faster. Keep in mind that many of these tools can be rented at most rental equipment stores.

HANGING TOOLS

There are probably more tools required for hanging drywall than for any other step in the process. Later in this chapter I write that when I first went into the drywall business I could fit all my taping tools into a 5-gal. bucket. Well that was not true for my hang-

ing tools; even in the beginning, I needed quite a few hanging tools. Of course I needed the basics tools, such as t-squares, saws, utility knives, and a few stepladders. Larger tools like drywall lifts and scaffolding I rented from my local tool rental store. I eventually purchased many of these tools as well as drywall routers and cordless screw guns.

Measuring and marking tools

Taking accurate measurements is a very important part of drywalling. If you measure a panel too short, you'll have to do some extra patching at the taping stage (see the sidebar on p. 105). If you measure a panel too long and force it into place, the ends will break apart, again requiring additional patching. For accurate measurements, I rely on a 25-ft. tape measure. For calculating materials for large rooms, you'll need a tape at least that long. A 25-ft. tape is a little wider and stiffer than shorter-length tapes, so it extends farther before it bends or sags, making it easier to measure long lengths without a helper. Regardless of length, tape measures are also useful for scribing short, straight measurements, as shown in the photo above.

A 4-ft. aluminum T-square, which is used for both marking and cutting drywall, is one tool that you really can't do without. The top edge of the square is butted against the long tapered edge of the drywall panel and the 4-ft. piece hangs down along the face of the panel at 90 degrees (the square can also be used as a straightedge for angled cuts). The edges of the square are calibrated in inches. When marking straight, narrow pieces of drywall, locate the measurement you want on the top edge of the T-square and line it up with the panel edge (see the left photo on the facing page). Then mark the panel with a pencil or score it with a utility knife. ("Scoring" means cutting through the paper surface of the panel.)

A 24-in. framing square also comes in handy for marking and cutting drywall. I use this square mostly for transferring measurements when cutting out small openings (for electrical boxes, heat-duct openings, and so forth) after a panel has been attached (see the photos on p. 66).

A chalkline is used for marking straight lines, primarily ones that are difficult to scribe with a tape measure and a knife or ones that are too long to mark with a 4-ft. square. To mark a line between two points, hook the end of the chalkline over the mark on one end of the panel and stretch the line to the other mark. Pull the line tight, then with your other hand lift the string straight up from the surface a few inches and release it. The colored chalk from the string will leave a mark on the surface.

Similar to a drafting compass, a scriber is used to fit out-of-plumb walls or to mark round openings (see p. 67), and to fit

irregular surfaces. When fitting an uneven surface, such as a very wavy ceiling, hold the drywall panel as tightly as possible against the surface, place the metal point of the scriber against the surface at a right angle, and then follow along the contour. As you slide the scriber along the ceiling, the pencil end will leave a mark on the panel. Cut along the pencil line with a utility knife or a saw.

Cutting tools

It's not often that you hang a piece of drywall without having to make some sort of cut. You may need to cut the panel to length or width or make an opening for an electrical outlet box, a window, or a door. On some panels, you may

TOP: Pulling a line When you mark an angled line with a chalk line, use a pointed anchor attachment to hold the end of the line in place and then stretch the line to the other mark.

ABOVE: When cuts are out of square To cut drywall for an out-of-plumb corner, run a scriber along the edge of the panel so it will fit tight against the adjacent wall once cut.

LEFT: Keep it square A metal T-square is good for marking short strips of drywall and for squaring up the end of a panel. The measurements of the square come in handy when sizing panels.

can be used to cut along the mark left by a chalkline. To cut a panel using a utility knife, follow these steps:

1. Mark the length of the panel, and then cut through the face paper and into the gypsum core (see the photo below left).

2. Snap the panel away from the cut line and make a second cut along the crease on the back of the panel.

3. Snap the panel forward again, so that the two pieces separate cleanly.

The sharper the knife blade and the more consistent the depth of the cut, the smoother

Cutting panels **There is seldom a drywall panel that goes up that doesn't need to be cut or have an opening cut out of it.**

have to make more than one cut. The tools described in this section will help you make clean, accurate cuts in any type of drywall.

The most commonly used cutting tool is a utility knife. It is typically used in combination with a 4-ft. square to make cuts across the full width of a panel, though it

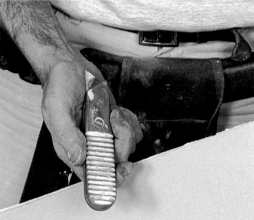

ABOVE: Score the panel To make a cut across the full width of a panel, score the paper with a utility knife along the edge of a T-square.

RIGHT TOP: Keep it sharp A dull blade in a utility knife can leave a jagged cut edge.

RIGHT: A versatile tool The author uses a utility knife that has a serrated edge in the handle. Make the cut with the blade and use the handle as a rasp.

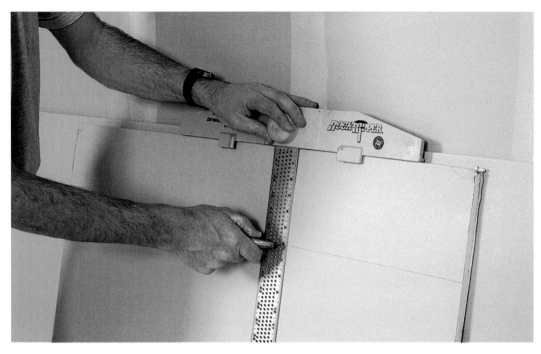

the cut edge will be. If the knife is sharp, one stroke on each side of the panel will be sufficient. A dull blade will create a jagged cut that may leave the panel a little longer than measured (see the top right photo on the facing page). The jagged edge can be trimmed off with a utility knife, or for a better job, smoothed out with a drywall rasp. I use a utility knife that has a serrated section built into the handle. After making the cut, I use the rough area as a drywall rasp (see the bottom right photo on the facing page).

One type of scribing square lets you score the drywall as you measure. The long edge of the tool has small slots that hold the blade of the knife in place as you slide the top of the square along the edge of the panel (see photo above).

Saws Customers are sometimes surprised to see me using a saw to cut drywall, but in certain instances it's faster and easier to use than a utility knife. The teeth in drywall saws have more "set" in them than standard wood-cutting handsaws. (The set is determined by the amount the teeth are bent out in each direction; the wider the set, the wider the kerf

taken out with the saw.) The wide-set teeth rip through the paper and gypsum core quite easily, and the wide kerf also helps prevent damage to the paper surface when the blade is drawn back.

There are two types of saws for cutting drywall. I use a smaller drywall utility saw to cut openings for electrical outlets, pipes, and ducts and to cut square pieces out of panels. This saw has a sharp pointed end, making it easy to start a cut in the center of a panel. I use a larger drywall saw, which is stiffer than an ordinary woodcutting saw, to cut along a door or window opening after the drywall has been hung over the opening and tacked in place. (Make this cut only if the door or window jambs have not been installed; otherwise, you'll damage the jambs.)

The larger drywall saw also works well for trimming panels that run a little long at the outside corners or at the edge of a doorway. Another use for this rigid saw is to make beveled cuts, which are sometimes necessary for a good fit at corners that are greater than 90 degrees. The saw is a little faster to use than a utility knife.

ABOVE LEFT: A better square
This scribing square has calibrated notches along the blade. To score a panel, insert the knife blade into the proper notch, and then slide the square along the edge of the drywall panel. The result is a quick, clean cut.

ABOVE: Keep a good saw
A drywall utility saw fits in your tool bag and is very handy for making quick cuts.

A multi-use tool A drywall saw has many uses, one of which is to cut the attached panel along a doorway opening (always cut from the face side to avoid damaging the finish side).

Drywall router A drywall router is a specialized tool that's great for cutting out small openings in drywall panels. A specially designed router bit cuts through the drywall as it follows along the edge of an electrical box or a heat-duct opening. Cutting openings with a router requires less accurate measurements than does cutting with a saw, because you need to find only one edge and follow it around (see p. 63). A drywall router is a powerful tool—be careful not to apply too much pressure or you risk cutting into the electrical box or framing.

Lifting tools

All drywall panels have to be lifted into place before they are attached. Sometimes they may have to be held only about 1/2 in. off the floor; other times, they may need to be hoisted to the top of a cathedral ceiling.

When hanging drywall on a wall horizontally (my preferred method of working), the top panel can be lifted into place by hand and nailed or screwed home. The bottom panel is then set into place and lifted up, usually less than 1 in. off the floor, to butt against the bottom of the panel above it. You can use a small prybar to hold the panel off the floor, but this tool usually requires using one or both hands. I prefer to use a panel lifter that is operated by foot, leaving both hands free to attach the panel.

On flat ceilings, a T-support is a handy tool for holding a panel in place, freeing up your hands for fastening. This simple prop can be made out of a furring strip or a 2x4 with a 4-ft.-long furring strip screwed to the top. It's best to make the T-support on the job to fit the height of the ceiling (I make mine about 1/2 in. longer than the ceiling

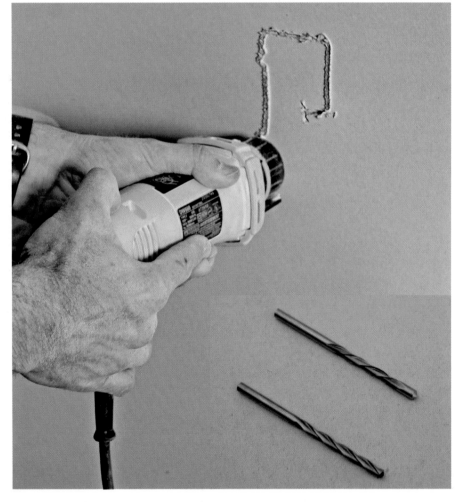

The drywall router A drywall router is a specialized tool used to cut holes for electrical boxes and other small openings. It uses a special bit with a guide tip that follows the outside edge of the opening.

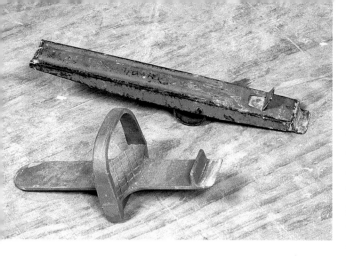

height so it will fit snugly). One option is to buy a T-support like the one shown in the bottom right photo below. Known as a "stiff arm," this support is made of metal and is adjustable to accommodate different ceiling heights.

Hanging drywall is usually a job for two or more people, but a drywall lift (available from rental tool stores) makes it possible for one person to hang drywall alone. The lift adjusts to various heights of walls and ceilings (sloped as well as flat) and to panels of different lengths. The panel is placed finished face toward the lift. For ceilings, begin by roughly positioning the panel, with one end tilted up slightly. Position the panel into its exact place as you crank up the lift, and leave the lift in place until the edges of the drywall are fastened.

Step-up benches or trestles are typically used for reaching ceilings up to 10 ft. high. These stable aluminum benches are about 4 ft. long and 10 in. wide and are adjustable in height from about 18 in. to 32 in. Optional legs bring the bench height up to 48 in. The

Raising a panel A foot lift is a handy tool for raising a drywall panel an inch or so off the floor. Controlling the lift with your foot frees up your hands to guide the panel into position.

ABOVE: An improved T-support A modern version of a T-support adjusts to different heights and holds a panel firmly in place with hydraulic pressure.

RIGHT: Keep the panel in place A simple T-support can really help when you need a free pair of hands for fastening.

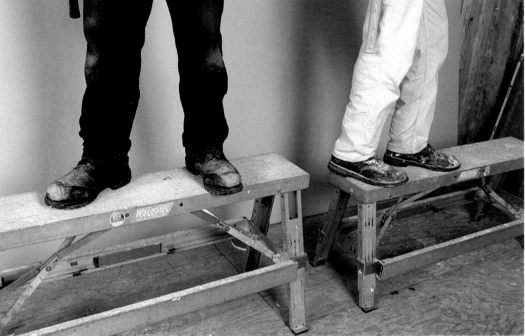

ABOVE LEFT: Mechanical help A drywall lift is a specialized tool used both to raise drywall and to position it on ceilings and upper walls.

ABOVE RIGHT: A stable base A fully extended bench can be wobbly, but you can purchase an attachment that provides stability and an additional step at a comfortable height.

RIGHT: Two legs up Drywall benches provide a stable platform for working on ceilings and upper walls. Most benches are adjustable for different height people and ceiling heights. Leg extensions provide even more height.

horizontal supports can be used as a step when climbing onto the bench with a drywall panel (see the top right photo above) or as a support for a short plank stretched between two benches. The bench should be adjusted to a height that places your head close to the ceiling. After the panel is lifted into place, it can be held there with light head pressure, leaving both hands free to attach the panel.

For ceilings that are too high for benches, a room-to-room type scaffold provides a

stable, adjustable platform (see the top photo on the facing page). These scaffolds are available in 6-ft., 8-ft., and 10-ft. lengths and are adjustable up to 6 ft. high. Some styles can be stacked two sections high. A single section can be guided through most doorways, so it doesn't need to be disassembled if you want to move it from room to room.

For higher ceilings or walls, a wider stable platform is a must. The scaffold should be at least 4 ft. wide and 10 ft. long, and it should

LEFT: Convenient scaffolding An adjustable scaffold provides stable support when installing and taping drywall up to heights of 12 ft. A single height section fits through most doorways.

BELOW: Heavy-duty scaffolding A larger drywall scaffold should be strong and stable a nd have crossbars at least every 15 in. at the ends.

than 9 ft. high. They make it easy to apply long lengths of joint tape and to finish an entire seam at one go, thereby helping to increase productivity and the quality of the job. (Note that safety regulations in some states do not allow the use of stilts, and many insurance policies do not cover workers who are injured while working on stilts.)

be adjustable at least every 15 in. or so. It should also have horizontal end supports, so that you can run planks at different heights (see the bottom photo above). Working on any type of scaffolding demands attention to safety; the sidebar at right lists some important precautions.

Stilts I use stilts primarily when I'm taping and sanding, but some pros like to use them when hanging drywall, too. Stilts provide a lot of mobility and eliminate the need for benches and scaffolding on ceilings less

SAFETY PRECAUTIONS WHEN WORKING ON SCAFFOLDING

- The floor supporting any scaffolding should be sound, rigid, and capable of carrying the load without settling or displacement. Any scaffold that is damaged or weakened should be repaired immediately.

- Scaffolds between 4 ft. and 10 ft. high should have standard guardrails on all open sides and ends of the platform. Guardrails should be made of lumber no smaller than 2x4 and installed 42 in. above the platform surface, with a midrail of 1x6 lumber.

- Any platform over 10 ft. high should have toeboards as well as guardrails on all open sides and ends. Toeboards should be at least 4 in. high and extend around the perimeter of the platform.

- Scaffold planks should extend at least 6 in. over the end supports and should be placed with the edges close together.

- If you are working in an area where there is any risk of head injury, wear an approved hard hat.

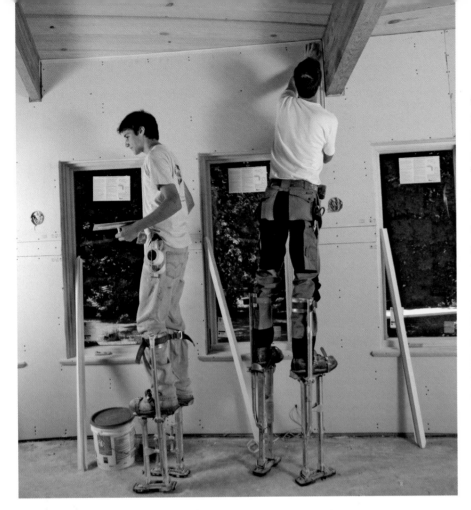

convex face, which leaves a shallow dimple in the front of the drywall without tearing the face paper (a standard carpenter's hammer has a flat face, which can easily tear the paper). The dimple is concealed with joint compound during the taping process.

Nowadays, most professional drywallers use screws rather than nails, and the drywall screw gun has replaced the hammer as the tool of choice for attaching panels. A screw

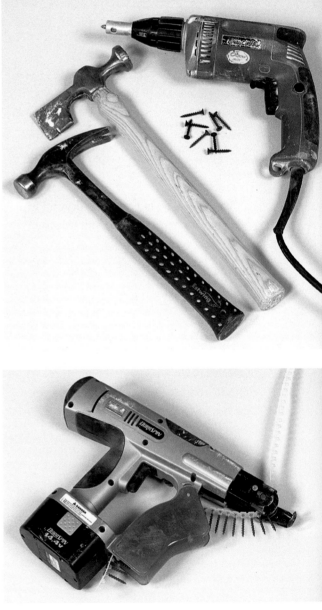

ABOVE: Walking tall Most stilts are adjustable for different heights. The stilts seen here have joints that flex with ankle movement.

RIGHT TOP: Screw or nail A drywall screw gun and a drywall hammer are the best tools for fastening panels. To minimize the risk of tearing the face paper, use a convex-faced drywall hammer (center) rather than a standard flat-faced carpenter's hammer (left).

RIGHT: Step up the pace A cordless, self-feeding screw gun saves a lot of time and energy when attaching panels.

When I bought my first pair of stilts, it took me a few weeks to summon up the courage to use them. I was afraid I'd make a fool of myself in front of a customer (and in front of my workmates!). But when I finally tried the stilts, it didn't take too long to get the hang of them. It's so much easier (and faster) to work on stilts than to drag around benches and ladders. And as long as you keep all work areas clean, using stilts is probably safer, too. Now I use stilts not only for taping and sanding but also for insulating ceilings and for cutting in with a paintbrush along ceiling edges.

Fastening tools and materials

Drywall can be hung with nails or screws. If you use nails, you'll need a drywall hammer, which looks a little like a hatchet. The blade end is tapered (but not sharp), so it can be used for prying or lifting. The hammer has a gun installs a screw with a bugle head just below the surface of the drywall paper. The nose of the screw gun pushes the drywall panel against the framing as the screw is installed. It has a positive clutch that is engaged when pressure is applied to the Phillips bit. When using a screw gun, the depth of the screw bit can be modified; when properly adjusted, the screw gun sets the screw just below the surface without tearing the face paper. Both corded and cordless models are available.

Screwing is faster than nailing, but having to place every screw onto the bit by hand is time-consuming (and tedious). A self-feeding screw gun solves that problem. Or you can buy a self-feeding attachment for your current screw gun. A string of screws feeds into the nosepiece as each screw is used, greatly increasing productivity. Self-feeding screw gun attachments are available to fit most brands; they accept screws from 1 in. to 1¾ in. long.

Screws and nails Fastening drywall with screws is preferred over nailing, because

screws are faster to install than nails, they do less damage to the drywall panel, and they hold the drywall tighter against the framing. Screws for wood framing should be long enough to penetrate the framing at least 5/8 in. (see the chart above). Screws for light-gauge metal framing have finer threads than wood framing screws; they should penetrate at least 3/8 in. Use self-tapping screws for heavier gauge metal. (Note that you should always use screws in metal studs—nails will not hold.)

FASTENER SPECIFICATIONS

FASTENER TYPE	DRYWALL THICKNESS	MINIMUM FASTENER LENGTH
Wood screws (coarse thread)	3/8 in., 1/2 in., 5/8 in.	1 in., 1 1/8 in., 1 1/4 in.
Screws into metal studs or furring (fine thread)	3/8 in., 1/2 in., 5/8 in.	3/4 in., 7/8 in., 1 in.
Ring-shank nails (wood studs only)	3/8 in., 1/2 in., 5/8 in.	1 1/8 in., 1 1/4 in., 1 3/8 in.

WORK SMART

No matter which type of fastener you use be sure the panel is tight against the framing and that the fasteners are properly set. Always use fasteners of the recommended length.

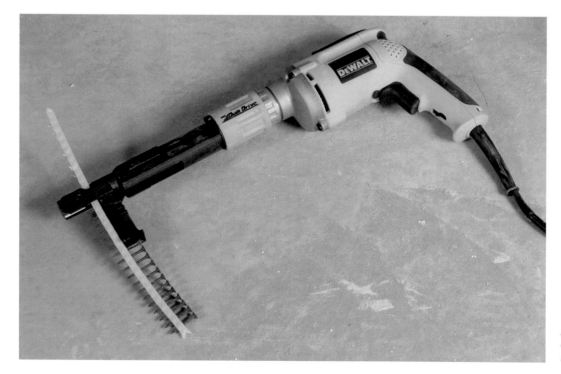

Retrofit your drill
A self-feeding attachment can be purchased to fit most any screw gun.

FASTENERS

Drywall can be attached using either nails or screws. If you're using screws, choose the thread type based on the framing behind the drywall.

Multiple options for screws
Drywall screws are available in lenghts starting at 1 in. They're sold loose, for regular screw guns, or collated, for self-feeding screw guns.

Designed for metal studs
Screws for attaching drywall to metal framing feature a fine thread and often have a drill-point tip for easy penetration of the metal.

Choose the correct threads
Coarse-thread screws are used for wood framing; fine-thread screws are used for metal framing.

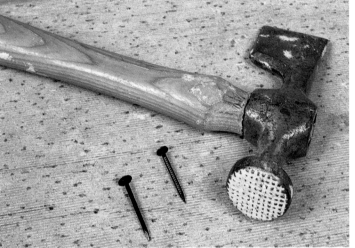

Opt for stronger nails
Ring-shank drywall nails, such as the one on the right, have 25 percent more holding power than the smooth-shank nail on the left.

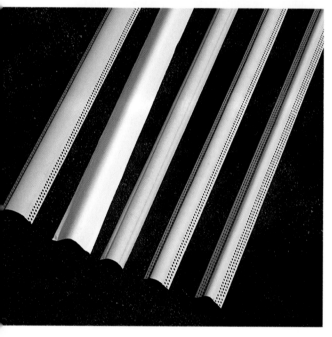

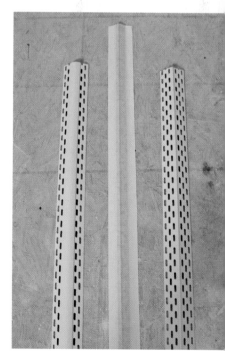

LEFT: Adhesive adds strength Used in conjunction with mechanical fasteners, drywall adhesive not only strengthens the bond to the framing but also reduces fastener pops.

FAR LEFT: Bullnose corner beads Bullnose corner beads are quite popular because they provide an easy way to add an elegant look to a room. They are available in many materials and radii, ranging from 3/8 in. to 1½ in.

BELOW: Corner beads for odd angles Off-angle beads are available pre-shaped for 135-degree outside corners, even in bullnose styles (at left). At center is a paper-faced bead and on the right is a vinyl bead.

Adhesive acts as a supplement to the screws and even reduces the number of screws you need to use. The drywall adhesive adds shear strength to the structure and greatly reduces fastener pops and loose panel.

Outside corner beads

Whether on a wall or on a soffit, outside corners must be covered with corner bead. The material protects the surface and has a slightly raised beaded edge, which keeps the corner straight and acts as a screed while taping.

It wasn't too long ago that square-edged metal corner bead was the most commonly used corner bead, and it may still be today, but the other options really are worth looking into. Today, you have your choice of metal, vinyl, plastic covered with paper, or metal covered with paper. Some types are available in 100-ft. rolls. Bullnose beads are also available in a variety of sizes and have become very popular because they offer an elegant look and are just as easy to install as regular bead. For more on bullnose beads and other available styles, see Chapter 6.

Archway bead For years, I used metal corner bead to finish the edges of archways. The only way to install it was to snip the bead at 1-in. intervals and push each piece into place

If you do use nails, they should penetrate the wood framing at least 3/4 in. Ring-shank nails are preferred over plain-shank nails because they have 25-percent greater holding power. (The holding power is greatly diminished if the drywall face is damaged, so be careful not to tear the paper or sink the nail too deep, which can severely damage the gypsum core.)

Whenever drywall is attached directly to wood I like to use drywall adhesive as well.

METAL CORNER BEAD

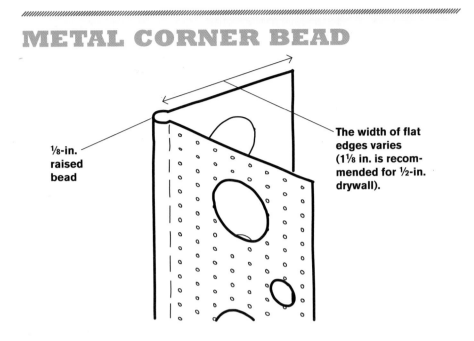

⅛-in. raised bead

The width of flat edges varies (1⅛ in. is recommended for ½-in. drywall).

Beads for arches Flexible archway beads are the easiest option for handing curved corners. They are also available in bullnose form.

along the curve of the arch. This method worked, but it cannot be compared to the simplicity and quality you get with new products designed specifically for archways. There are three basic types of flexible corner bead made for arches:

• Flexible wire bead has a plastic beaded edge and is nailed in place.

• Vinyl bead has a pre-snipped edge that is glued and stapled in place.

• Composite bead has a PVC core and a paper surface and is embedded in joint compound.

The PVC material comes in rolls up to 100 feet long and is now available in stick form with a wire reinforced edge. The wire and vinyl beads come in lengths of up to 10 ft. and the composite bead comes in lengths of up to 100 ft. Vinyl bullnose corner bead, which is flexible, is available to match the outside and inside corner bullnose beads.

If you are using bullnose corner bead on your 90-degree corners then you will most likely want bullnose on the archways. The vinyl bead companies make archway beads in all the bullnose radii. There are even bullnose beads made for off-angle inside and outside corners, (135-degree corners only).

Inside corner beads

On most inside corners, I use paper tape embedded in joint compound, which is then covered with compound and feathered to a smooth edge. This method works great for inside corners that are around 90 degrees.

When I first saw a 90-degree inside corner bead I really couldn't see why anybody would use it. I am a professional and I get great results with paper tape so I wouldn't spend the money on a bead for a 90-degree inside corner. But after using the different types of bead I can see where they would be used:

• You don't have to coat the very inside edge with compound. Therefore, both sides of the corner can be coated at once—as opposed to waiting for one edge to dry and then coating the other.

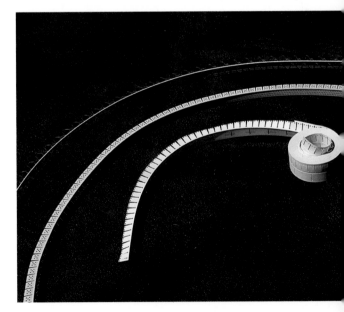

SECURING CORNER BEADS

Among many contractors, nailing or crimping a standard metal corner bead in place is gradually being replaced by beads that are attached using adhesive only. With these beads the adhesive is simply sprayed onto the drywall along the entire length of the bead. All corner beads should be installed in one piece, unless the length of the corner exceeds the standard corner-bead lengths of 6 ft. 10 in., 8 ft., 9 ft., and 10 ft. For more on installing corner beads, see Chapters 3 and 4.

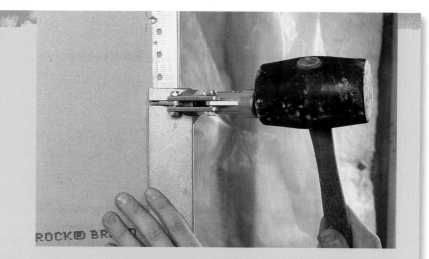

Metal beads One blow with a rubber mallet on a corner crimper every 4 to 6 in. attaches standard metal corner bead to an outside corner. This style bead can also be attached with drywall nails.

Paper-covered plastic Corner beads are available in a variety of styles. Pictured here is a paper-covered plastic outside corner bead that is attached with joint compound.

Compound secures the bead A special tool is used to coat the back side of tape-on corner beads with joint compound. The compound works as an adhesive to hold the bead in place.

Glue it in place Some beads, like this vinyl bead, are attached with spray adhesive and staples. The staples penetrate only the drywall—not the framing.

Beads for inside corners **Special tapes for inside corners provide excellent and long-lasting results. The one on top has a flexible center.**

• When sanding you can sand the inside edge clean and straight, because you don't have to leave any compound in the corner.

• All this adds up to a great looking inside corner, especially for the less experienced taper.

• The end result is a very strong and straight inside corner.

If an inside corner is much wider than 90 degrees, a specialized product is a must for achieving the straight lines that define these corners. Fortunately, there are a

J-TRIM AND L-BEAD

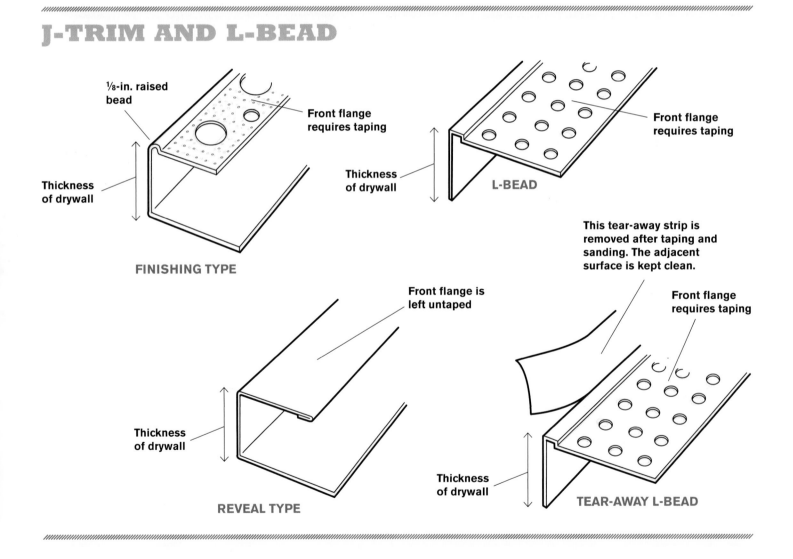

FINISHING TYPE
- ⅛-in. raised bead
- Front flange requires taping
- Thickness of drywall

L-BEAD
- Front flange requires taping
- Thickness of drywall

REVEAL TYPE
- Front flange is left untaped
- Thickness of drywall

TEAR-AWAY L-BEAD
- This tear-away strip is removed after taping and sanding. The adjacent surface is kept clean.
- Front flange requires taping
- Thickness of drywall

number of products that can handle these off angles. Some work on both inside and outside corners; others are more specialized and designed for application on specific-angle corners. For off-angle inside corners, there is even a product that has a rubber center groove, which flexes if the structure moves slightly, greatly reducing costly callbacks. Inside corner beads are also available in bullnose styles to match bullnose outside corners. These products cost more than regular paper tape and compound, but you easily make up the extra cost in time saved and improved quality.

Trim beads

Metal, plastic, and paper-covered metal J-trims are caps used to cover the edges of drywall panels. Typically, they are applied against a shower stall, a window jamb, or a brick wall; around an opening that is left un-trimmed; or on the exposed end of a panel. J-trim is available in different thicknesses to fit different sizes of drywall. It can be installed before the panel is hung or after the panel is loosely attached. It is held in place by driving a nail or screw through the face of the drywall and through the longer back flange of the J-trim. Some types need to be finished with joint compound, whereas others do not require any finishing at all (see the drawing on the facing page).

An L-bead finishes the edges of drywall that butt up against something, such as a suspended ceiling, a window, or a paneled wall. The drywall is cut so that the short edge of the L-bead can be inserted between the drywall and the abutting material. The exposed edge of the bead is then finished with joint compound. Many of these L-beads have a removable strip that protects the abutting surface from compound and some can be left on to protect the surface from paint. Trim beads are available in lengths of up to 12 ft. long and for 1/2-in.- and 5/8-in.-thick

drywall. I prefer L-beads over J-beads in most applications, as L-beads are easier to install—especially on longer runs—because they are attached after the drywall.

Expansion joints

Expansion joints, which are made of metal or vinyl, are installed between drywall panels. They are not covered with joint compound, as other typical drywall joints are, but they can be filled with a flexible caulk. Expansion joints are designed to compensate for the expansion and contraction of building materials and for the normal settling of a building, so that drywall seams don't become cracked or ridged. They are used when there is a large expanse of ceiling or wall. On ceilings, they run from wall to wall; on walls, they run from ceiling to floor. In high stairway walls, they are installed from wall to wall.

TAPING TOOLS AND MATERIALS

It used to be that a trowel, a couple of taping knives, a roll of paper tape, and a pail of joint compound were all that you needed to do a typical taping job. Nowadays, there are many

A toolset for finishing A quality hand taping job depends on a variety of taping tools.

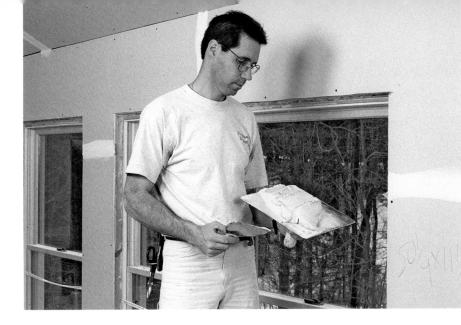

ABOVE: Working with com-
pound A hawk is used to hold
large amounts of joint compound when you're taping with
a knife or trowel.

RIGHT: Keep it contained
A mud pan is handy for holding compound and as a mixing
container.

types and sizes of trowels, various options
for reinforcing seams, and so many different
kinds of joint compounds that you may not
know where to begin when deciding which
one to use.

Hand Taping Tools

There are a variety of trowels and taping
knives that I use for taping, all of which are
available in different sizes for different applications. As I discuss each tool, I'll mention
the size that I use most often and, where appropriate, explain what features to look for
when purchasing a trowel. I'll explain how to
use each trowel in greater detail in Chapter 4.

Taping knives, which are available in
widths from 1 in. to 6 in. (in 1-in. incre-
ments), are used for taping seams and corners
and covering fasteners. The wider widths
often have a metal end on the handle for
resetting nail heads. Narrower widths come
in handy for taping tight areas (for example,
the often-narrow space between a doorframe
and a corner). I use a 6-in. knife more than
any other size. Whatever the width of the
knife, it should be fairly stiff (not too flexible).

When buying a taping knife, look for
one that has a little curve in the blade when
viewed from head on. If you can't find one,
you can put a slight curve in the blade by
bending it over a rounded surface, such as
a pipe. I use the convex side of the blade

when taping. Because the curve helps keep
the corners of the blade slightly away from
the taping surface, the result is a smooth
surface without the tool marks created by a
flat knife blade. The knife blades are available
in blue steel or stainless-steel. It's a matter
of personal preference, but I have used both
and, if anything, I prefer the stainless-steel
because they seem to last longer.

A square-cornered taping knife cannot
reach into a corner very well if the corner
is less than 90 degrees (for example, at the
intersection of a sloped ceiling and a wall or
at the top of a cellar stairway). In these areas,
I use a pointed trowel, which can easily be
made by cutting off the sides of an old 6-in.
taping knife. A small pointed mason's trowel
also works well for this purpose.

Hawks are used to hold large quantities of
joint compound when working with a taping
knife. These tools have a square aluminum
top with circular grooves to help prevent the
joint compound from sliding off, and a short,
straight handle centered on the underside.
Hawks are available in sizes from 8 in. to
14 in. square. I prefer to work with the

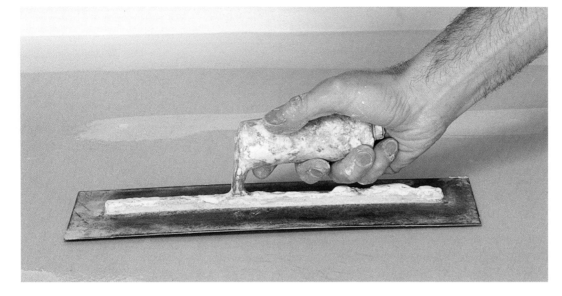

largest size only because it saves a few trips back to the compound bucket. A pan is commonly used instead of a hawk—especially when compound of a thin consistency is used. A pan also comes in handy as a mixing container.

Curved or beveled trowels have a slight curve in the blade that is about 5/32 in. deep. They are available in lengths from 10 in. to 14 in. and in widths of 4 in. and 4 1/2 in. I prefer to use a curved trowel rather than a flat trowel because the curve allows more control of the amount of compound I want to leave or remove. I usually like to leave a very slight crown in the compound, which will disappear when the compound shrinks a little and is finish sanded.

I use the 4 1/2-in. by 14-in. curved trowel for feathering and finishing most seams, as well as for holding joint compound while applying it with a taping knife. It has many uses, and I always seem to have a curved trowel and a 6-in. taping knife in my hand while taping.

Wide straight-handled taping knives are much the same as narrow taping knives, except they have a metal reinforcing strip at the back of the blade. I like to use this style knife that is 8 in. wide to embed the tape on seams when I am using automatic taping tools. I use a wider 10-in. or 12-in. version when applying and smoothing out the final coats of joint compound on seams and outside corners, as well as for smoothing out large areas and seam intersections. Straight-handled taping knives are available in widths from 10 in. to 24 in. As with regular taping knives, they should have a slight curve in the blade and the corners should be rounded with a file. I use a 12-in. knife for most applications.

WORK SMART

Use adjustable-angle knives to finish inside corners that are not 90 degrees. They work well for embedding the tape and feathering the joint compound.

TROWEL CARE

- While working, keep trowels free of dry compound to avoid marks or scratches when trying to smooth the compound. Use another trowel (or the edge of the hawk) to scrape off any excess compound. When you've finished a taping session, clean trowels with warm water.

- Use trowels for taping only. Don't scrape floors or apply adhesive or grout with your taping tools.

- Protect edges from nicks or scratches; any nicks should be sanded or filed smooth.

- Round any sharp corners on a new trowel with a file (sharp corners can rip the joint tape).

ABOVE LEFT: Bending the knife Even a straight taping knife can be bent so that it has a crowned or convex side. With the convex side against the compound, the knife edges lift slightly off the compound surface to reduce tool marks.

ABOVE RIGHT: Wider knives cover more ground Wider taping knives are very useful during later coats in the finishing process.

LEFT: Mechanical taping tools As an alternative to hand taping, you can buy or rent a variety of mechanical taping tools. An automatic taper is shown at top left. The three boxes to the right are used to apply different widths of joint compound over seams.

Automatic taping tools

Automatic tools are quite popular today because they cut down on labor and there are mechanical tools available for each step in the taping process. Mechanical taping tools are expensive, but the cost of the tools is soon recouped because of the increased productivity and quite often increased quality of work. You can also rent these tools. I use them mostly when I'm taping larger jobs, but they also come in handy when I'm working on two or three smaller jobs at once.

Joint tape

Joint tape is used to reinforce seams and corners and to repair cracks and holes in drywall and plaster. There are two types of tape: pre-creased paper tape and fiberglass-mesh tape.

Paper tape Not long ago, paper tape was the only tape you could buy. It is still the most widely used tape and is a good all-around tape for seams, cracks, and small holes. Available in rolls 2 in. wide and 250 ft. or 500 ft. long, paper tape has a light crease down the center, which helps it fold easily for

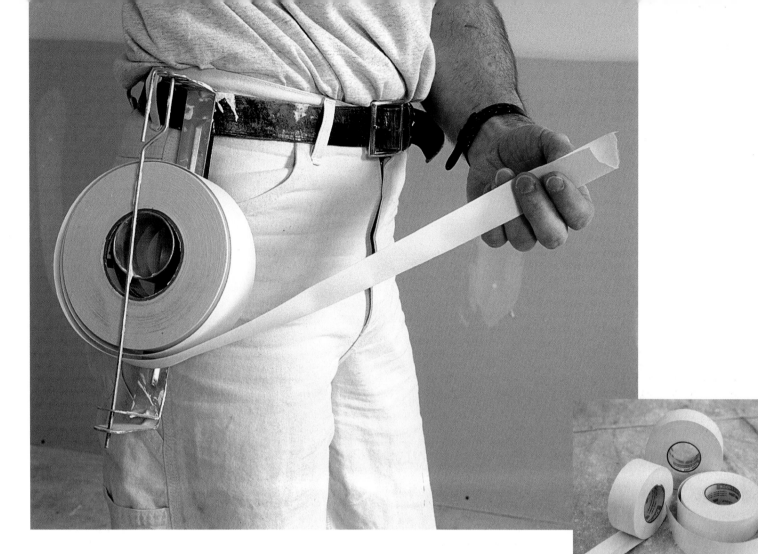

use on inside corners. Paper tape has a number of advantages and uses over mesh tape:

- It is stronger than most types of mesh tape and not as likely to be torn by taping tools.

- It resists stretching and wrinkling more effectively than mesh tape does.

- It is easier to install in corners because the crease makes it easy to keep the tape centered and straight.

- It is less expensive than mesh tape.

On the downside, paper tape is more time consuming to apply (it has to be embedded in a coat of compound) and is prone to bubbling if you don't apply enough compound or embed it tight enough.

Fiberglass-mesh tape This tape is commonly used for taping tapered seams and for patching cracks and small holes. It is also used to reinforce gaps between panels or corners that are more than ¼ in. wide. Mesh tape can be used on regular inside corners, but it is hard to keep centered and straight. A few companies, however, are now making a tool that creases and places the mesh tape in the corners, so mesh is becoming more widely used to tape inside corners as well.

Fiberglass-mesh tape comes in rolls that are 2 in. or 2½ in. wide and 300 ft. or 500 ft. long. There are two types: self-adhesive tape, which is simply pressed in place over a seam, and non-adhesive (or plain) tape. In addition, there are two types of self-adhesive mesh tapes. One is traditional leno-weave mesh, which, when used with a drying-type joint compound, is subject to cracking and

Applying paper tape Paper tape is stronger than most fiberglass mesh tapes and the creased center allows you to use it on inside corners. A tape holder is a handy dispenser for paper tape.

Rolling out fiberglass mesh tape Fiberglass self-adhesive mesh tape is foolproof for taping seams and small patches. In most cases, it is applied to the seam before the compound. Dispensers are now available which crease and the tape and make it easier to apply to corners.

THINK AHEAD

Always store open rolls of self-adhesive mesh tape in a plastic bag between uses to prevent the tape from drying out and losing its adhesiveness.

stretching when a joint is under stress. The other is a newer tape with a cross-fiber design that adds greater strength and crack resistance to joints than the older style. Non-adhesive tape is less expensive but not as easy to work with as the self-adhesive varieties (it has to be stapled in place over a seam). All types of mesh tape can be cut with a utility knife or the sharp edge of a trowel.

Mesh tape does have it's advantages over paper tape:

- When taping by hand, mesh tape is faster to embed than paper tape.

- It can be as strong as paper if it's embedded in a setting compound.

- Unlike paper tape, mesh tape is not prone to developing air bubbles under the surface of the tape.

If you're taping a lot of seams, a handy tool to have at your side is a tape reel (also known as a tape holder). The reel, which attaches to your belt, can hold up to a 500-ft. roll and works with both paper and mesh tapes. The tape rolls off the reel for quick and easy tear off. For fiberglass mesh tape, I prefer a roll-on tape dispenser, which works like a tape dispenser for packaging tape, allowing you to apply the tape directly from the dispenser to the wall (see photo at left).

Joint compound

There are so many types and brands of joint compound that it can be difficult to know which ones to use. The most important distinction is between *drying-type compounds* and *setting-type compounds*. In this section, I'll describe some of the most popular types within each of these categories.

Drying-type joint compound Drying-type joint compound is the type most commonly used. Available in both premixed and dry (powdered) forms, drying-type joint compound makes up the bulk of what you see in buckets and boxes at your local hardware store.

Most drying-type compounds are vinyl based and dry as the water evaporates. They require an application temperature of at least 55°F (this includes air, surface, and compound temperatures). The compound must dry thoroughly between coats, and the drying time is greatly affected by temperature, humidity, and airflow. (Under good conditions, drying-type compounds dry within 24 hours.)

Premixed drying-type joint compound comes in 1-gal. and 5-gal. buckets and boxes. The 1-gal. size is good for patching small jobs; the 5-gal. bucket is enough to tape an average 12-ft. by 12-ft. room.

Using the premixed compounds offers a few advantages:

- It is ready to use right out of the bucket.

- The consistency of the mix is factory controlled, and most brands are equal in quality.

- Also, there is little waste with premixed compound—the bucket can be resealed and used again later.

There are a few cautions to remember when using premixed compounds. First, the fresher the better. To preserve freshness, keep buckets out of direct sunlight and don't allow the compound to freeze. Also remember, premixed compound will not keep indefinitely—especially after it has been opened; at room temperature, a previously open bucket of compound will start to go bad in about a month.

Powdered drying-type joint compound has all the same working characteristics as the

CHOOSING THE RIGHT JOINT COMPOUND

When deciding which type of joint compound to use, consider the following factors:

- The size of the job (for a small job, it is less convenient to use two or three types of compound).

- The drying and heating conditions (temperature, airflow, and humidity).

- The availability of materials, including water, at the job site. Taping compound and some of the fast-drying setting-type compounds are available only at larger drywall-supply stores.

- The amount of time you have to complete the job (use setting-type compounds if time is short).

- The recommended combination of products (for example, most mesh tapes should be embedded in a taping compound or in a setting-type compound).

- Personal preferences (such as the convenience of the premixed drying type versus the strength and better bonding of the setting type).

Pick your compound A wide range of joint compounds are available in both dry and premixed forms. Always match the compound to the job at hand.

WORK SMART

Be aware that the setting time of joint compound can be adversely affected by overmixing or under-mixing, mixing a compound that has been in the sun or cold, and using dirty water (and equipment) or water that is too warm or cold.

APPROXIMATE COVERAGE OF MATERIALS

SCREWS AND NAILS

The number of fasteners used to attach drywall depends on framing spacing, fastener spacing, panel length, and panel orientation. For rough estimating, I usually figure around 1,000 fasteners per 1,000 sq. ft. of drywall.

JOINT TAPE

It usually takes about 370 linear ft. of joint tape to finish 1,000 sq. ft. of drywall.

JOINT COMPOUND

The amounts figured here are estimates for a complete taping job (three coats):

- Premixed drying-type joint compound: 11 gal. per 1,000 sq. ft. of drywall.

- Powdered drying-type compound: 80 lb. mixed with water per 1,000 sq. ft. of drywall. (Powdered compound is usually sold in 25-lb. bags.)

- Setting-type joint compounds vary in weight by types. A rough guide is to figure about 3 bags of setting compound per 1,000 sq. ft. of drywall.

WORK SMART

Regardless of the type of compound you use on the first two coats, use a drying-type compound for the final coat—it's easier to work with and sand.

premixed compound. The major difference is that it comes in dry form and must be mixed with water. A compound in dry form can be stored and transported at any temperature, (though it should always be brought to room temperature before mixing). Once mixed the compound is treated and stored just like the premixed compound.

I use three kinds of drying-type joint compound on a regular basis, (each is available premixed or dry):

- *Taping compound* is used to embed the joint tape for the first coat and as filler for the second coat (see Chapter 4). It is a strong compound, has little shrinkage as it dries, and has excellent bonding and resistance to cracking.

- *Topping compound* is used for a thin finishing coat. It is easy to work with, feathers out nicely, dries quickly, and sands smooth. Topping compound can be used over taping compound or over all-purpose joint compound.

- *All-purpose compound* can be used for all stages of the taping process—to embed the tape—as a filler coat—and as a finish coat. Because it's more convenient to deal with just one type, all-purpose compound is the most commonly used compound. However, it doesn't have the same strength, bonding qualities, or stability as the taping and topping combination.

Setting-type joint compounds Whereas drying type compounds are vinyl-based and dry as the water evaporates, setting-type compounds harden by chemical reaction. The great advantage of setting-type compounds, which are only available in powdered form, is that they harden faster than drying-type compounds. Unlike drying-type compounds, setting-type compounds actually harden before the joint is completely dry. When first mixed, setting compound is smooth and as easy to use as drying compound.

Setting times vary from 20 minutes to 6 hours, depending on the type used. I prefer a product that sets in 3 to 4 hours, which gives me enough time to apply the compound to the seams. I know that it will be ready for another coat of compound by the next day, even in humid or cool conditions (air, surface, and compound temperatures can be as low as 45°F). Furthermore, setting compound can be given a second and third coat as soon as it sets up—you don't have to wait until it is completely dry. Other benefits include better bonding qualities, less shrinkage and cracking, and a harder finish.

Given that setting-type compounds have so many advantages, you may wonder why

anyone would use anything else. But there is a downside: The stuff is much harder to sand, which means that you have to get it as smooth as possible while taping. (However, there is a lightweight setting-type compound that is easier to sand than the stronger, standard type.) Also, you should mix only as much compound as you can use before it sets up. Unlike powdered drying-type compound, it cannot be stored and reused at a later date.

When using fiberglass mesh tape or when I am trying to get a little ahead on a job, I like to use a setting-type compound to embed the tape (first coat). I'll often use the same type of compound for the second fill coat making sure to take the time to get the compound as smooth as possible. For the third and final coat, I use a drying-type compound, either an all-purpose compound or a topping compound.

Mixing tools

Joint compound can be mixed with a powered paddle or by hand (see the photo above and the discussion on pp. 90–92). For thorough mixing and textured finishes, use a mixing paddle with a heavy-duty electric drill. You can use a hand mixer for ready-mixed compounds that have sat too long or have been thinned with water for easier application.

SANDING TOOLS AND MATERIALS

Sanding is the final stage in the drywalling process. You can sand joint compound with a piece of folded sandpaper; however, there are a number of tools that help make this unpleasant (but important) task a little more efficient.

Sanders

I use a pole sander for most sanding work. It has a pivoting head designed to hold precut sanding screens or drywall sandpaper. The 4-ft.-long handle helps you reach along the top edge of a wall or near the floor without having to stretch or bend too much. Most low ceilings can also be reached with a pole sander. Grasp the handle with both hands for better leverage.

For areas that are easy to reach or that are too tight for a pole sander, a hand sander is a good alternative. It's the same size as a rectangle-shaped pole sander (with a 4-in. by 8-in. head) but without the pole. In addition, I recently purchased a triangular sander with a replaceable sandpaper pad that I use as a hand sander or as an attachment for a pole sander. Its pointed shape and beveled edges allow me to get into tight spaces that nothing other than folded sandpaper can reach.

For the extra-fine sanding work that is necessary after sanding with a pole or a hand sander, I like to use a dry sanding sponge. The small, dense sponge, which is 1 in. thick and coated with grit, is available in sizes ranging from 3 in. by 4 in. to 4 in. by 8 in. Dry sanding sponges are available in fine, medium, and coarse grit; I prefer the fine grit for touch-up sanding. Don't confuse this sanding sponge with the drywall sponge that is used wet.

To get into tight spots that even a sanding sponge can't reach, use a folded piece of sandpaper. Sandpaper allows the best control of any sanding method and works especially well for touching up inside corners.

For jobs where clouds of dust are unacceptable, a wet drywall sponge is the answer. The sponge shown in the photo on the facing page is a high-density polyurethane sponge that is soft and nonabrasive. These sponges are good for blending the edges of taped areas and for smoothing small defects, but they are not as effective for sanding ridges or built-up areas. You can also use an all-purpose household sponge or even a smooth, soft cloth for wet sanding small areas. However, if you intend to finish-sand with a wet sponge, you really must do a good taping job.

Sanding materials

You can sand joint compound with regular sandpaper, but sanding materials specifically made for drywall are more effective. (The problem with regular sandpaper is that the fine, dusty white powder quickly fills up the

RIGHT: Sanding tools **Tools for sanding drywall include a triangle-shaped hand sander, a rectangle-shaped pole sander, a round pole sander, a rectangle-shaped hand sander, and a dry sanding sponge. The author's favorite is the round pole sander.**

Cut down on dust Using a wet sanding sponge minimizes the amount of dust produced during the sanding process.

WORK SMART

I choose a taping knife or bend one so that it has a crowned or convex side. This is the side I work with. The edges of the knife are lifted slightly off the compound surface, which reduces tool marks.

grit of the paper, making it ineffective.) Drywall-specific sanding materials usually come precut to fit drywall sanding tools.

Drywall sandpaper, which has a paper back and a black carbide-grit surface, is available in 80 to 220 grit. The higher the grit number, the finer the sandpaper (and the smoother the finish). The 220 grit provides the smoothest finish, but it takes longer to sand down high areas or ridges. A good, universal sandpaper is the 120 grit. The only time I use the 80 or 100 grit is for rough sanding between second and third coats of joint compound (see Chapter 4).

Sanding screens, sometimes referred to as sanding cloths, are an alternative to sandpaper. Both sides of the screen are covered with carbide-grit-coated fiberglass mesh. When one side gets dull, the screen can be turned over and used again. Because of the holes in the screen, dust buildup is seldom a problem.

Sanding screens are available in grits from 120 to 200. The 120 grit is a good all-around screen; 150 and finer grits work well for finish sanding. Sanding screens are usually more expensive than sandpaper, but you get more life out of them. Also, a screen cuts through joint compound faster than sandpaper does.

Sanding screens and papers Cartridge sandpaper, a sanding screen, and a sanding pad can be purchased precut to fit pole and hand sanders.

CHAPTER

3

Hanging Drywall

Hanging drywall has the reputation of being a difficult, strenuous job; if done improperly, it certainly can be. But with the right attitude and the right techniques, it's not a job you need to approach with trepidation. A job can be as simple as covering a short partition wall or as difficult as hanging a 24-ft.-high cathedral ceiling. However big the job, hanging drywall is more than just cutting a panel and nailing it in place. Joints have to fit properly and be kept to a minimum. Holes for electrical boxes and other openings have to be cut out accurately. Fasteners have to be properly placed and properly set.

A good hanging job provides the foundation for a quality taping job. When I hear someone say that there's no need to be fussy because the tapers can fix it, I know that the finished job will suffer. A good hanger understands the taping process and has respect for the taper.

Hang ceilings first Whenever possible, cover the entire length of the ceiling with a single panel.

Inspect the walls Use a straightedge, such as a 4-ft. level, to check framing that you suspect is out of line.

Drywall panels can be attached in single or multiple layers. In this chapter, I'll deal with single-layer applications, though most procedures are the same for hanging two or more layers. Multilayer applications are discussed in detail in Chapter 6.

BACKING MATERIALS

For a quality finish, drywall must be attached to a flat, stable surface. There's not much structural strength in drywall, so if the framing or backing is weak or of poor quality, the drywall will probably crack or come loose. Drywall can be attached over most surfaces, but it's most commonly applied over wood or metal framing (see "Attaching Drywall to Metal Framing" on p. 78).

Wood framing

When installing drywall over wood framing, make sure that the framing members are aligned in a straight plane. A visual inspection is usually enough to detect badly bowed or twisted studs, though you can hold a straightedge across the studs, if you prefer. If a framing member is bowed or twisted more than 1/4 in., it should be straightened or replaced

(see "Straightening a Bowed Stud" below). Renailing sometimes straightens out twisted framing.

A bowed ceiling joist may have to be replaced, but wavy or irregular ceilings can be straightened using 1x3 furring strips nailed across the joists. Make minor adjustments with shims driven between the joists and the furring.

It's very important that the framing lumber be dry. If you're working in a cold climate, make sure the framing has been in a heated environment long enough to get the dampness out of the wood.

Solid backing

On remodeling jobs, I often attach drywall directly over old plaster or paneling. If you're drywalling over a solid backing, be sure to use fasteners that are long enough to provide firm attachment to the framing. Using drywall adhesive helps reduce the number of screws needed (for more on this process, see "Adhesive Cuts Down on Fasteners" on p. 74). Drywall can also be hung over rigid urethane insulation. On ceilings with rigid insulation, add 1x3 furring strips before

THINK AHEAD

Before any work starts, the temperature and humidity in the house has to be right. This not only applies to the air but also to the framing and drywall. Bring the drywall in a couple of days before you hang so that it has time to acclimate.

STRAIGHTENING A BOWED STUD

A bowed stud can be straightened by sawing a partial kerf into the concave side. Simply drive a wedge into the kerf, and then nail a 2-ft. or longer stud alongside the existing stud to keep it straight.

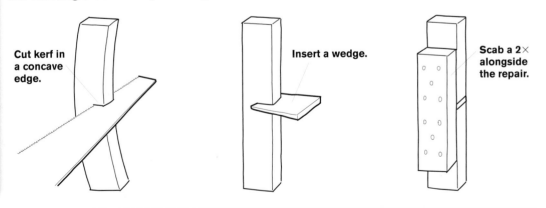

Cut kerf in a concave edge.

Insert a wedge.

Scab a 2× alongside the repair.

CARRYING DRYWALL

Carrying a drywall panel is a two-person job. Both carriers should be on the same side of the panel, with the same hand under the bottom edge and the other hand steadying the top. They should hold the panel 1ft. or more in from each end and let the panel lean against their shoulders. Working together like this is the least strenuous way to carry drywall. However, if you are forced to work alone, there are a number of specialized carrying tools available (see the photos below).

Sometimes it is easier to use a low carry position, with each person on the same side and at the ends of the panel.

A drywall cart works well for carrying single or multiple sheets.

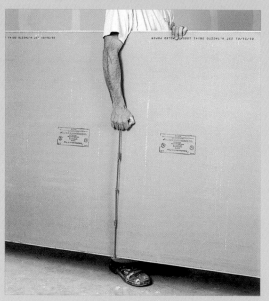

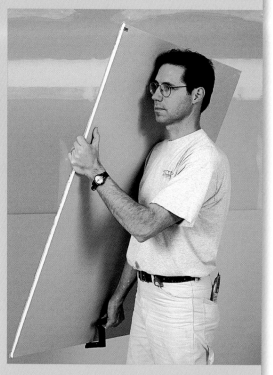

Special tools for carrying drywall make working alone less strenuous. The longer extendable carrier (left) is called The Troll, by Telpro Inc.® The smaller carrier (above) is a pocket Kart, by Diversified Tools, Inc.®

hanging drywall. From experience, I know that the insulation can expand a little over time, especially with the high temperatures common in attics. Expanding insulation will cause the fasteners to dimple—they'll probably still be tight, but they will need to be re-coated with joint compound.

Cut panels to fit Forcing an oversized panel into place can cause the edge to break apart. When it happens, cut off the broken section with a utility knife.

Check the corners Use a 24-in. framing square to make sure that the corners are square. If not, cut your panels accordingly.

MEASURING AND CUTTING DRYWALL

Once you're sure that the backing material is sound, you can begin taking measurements for the first sheet of drywall. When measuring the length of a wall or ceiling, I usually take two measurements—one where each edge of the panel will be. If the measurements are close, I usually go with the smaller measurement. If there's quite a difference, say 5/8 in. or more, I use both measurements and cut the panel out of square. Check for square by placing a 24-in. framing square in each corner, as shown in the photo below left.

Drywall panels should be cut to length so that they fit loosely into place. A good rule is to cut the panels about 1/4 in. short. On ceilings, split the 1/4 in. on each end. On walls, keep the panel edge tight against the panel that is already hung. Avoid cutting panels so long that they have to be forced into place—the ends will break and have to be repaired during taping.

Cutting panels

Cutting drywall is probably the easiest part of the whole job. If you're cutting with a utility knife, use the "score and snap" method (see "Cutting Drywall: The Score and Snap Method" on the facing page). When using a utility knife, it doesn't matter whether you cut the face or the back of the panel first. I prefer to score each panel on the face side first, but because the panels are packaged face to face in pairs, I cut every other panel from the back. If the cut is a little ragged or you've cut the panel a little long, use a drywall rasp for smoothing and light shaping.

In some cases, it is easier to cut drywall with a drywall utility saw or a drywall saw. When sawing, always cut from the face side of the panel to avoid damaging the finish paper as you push the blade through. The saw cuts on the forward stroke, but take care not to rip the face paper as you pull the saw

CUTTING DRYWALL: THE SCORE AND SNAP METHOD

To cut drywall, all you really need is a utility knife and a straightedge, but a drywaller's T-square makes the work even easier. You simply score one side of the drywall, snap the panel along the cutline, and then cut the panel loose.

1. Score one side
Use a sharp utility knife to score the paper along the edge of a T-square. The cut doesn't need to be deep–just through the paper and into the gypsum core.

2. Snap the panel
For a clean cut, always snap the panel away from the scored side.

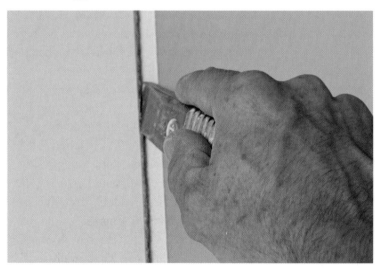

3. Cut it loose
If the first cut was made from the finished side of the panel, simply cut through to the back paper. Because it is the back paper, the slightly torn edge will never be seen.

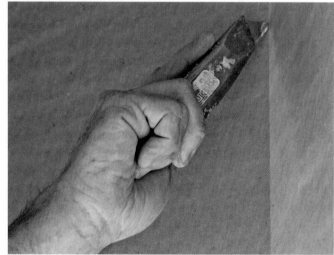

4. Or score again
If the first cut was made through the back paper, score the finished face along the creased edge, and then snap the board in the opposite direction.

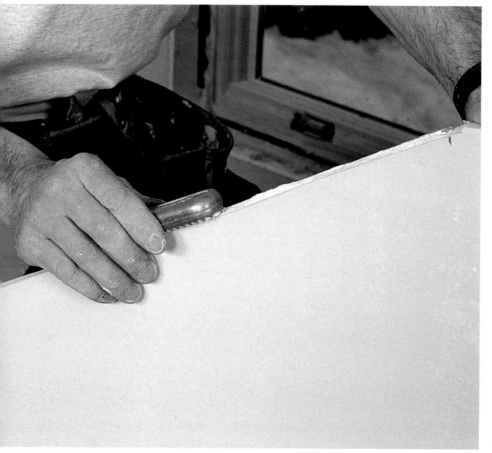

Clean up the mess No matter what method you use for cutting drywall, ragged edges can be cleaned up with a rasp. Here, a utility knife with a rasping edge leaves a smooth surface.

THINK AHEAD

For precise and easier cuts around the tops of windows and doors, score the height of the opening on the back of the panel before attaching it.

the face side of the panel and cut it out with a drywall saw. The top of the window opening can also be cut with a saw, but it's easier to use a utility knife to score the height of the window opening on the back of the panel before attaching it. Scoring the back first allows you to snap the waste piece forward and cut along the face side after the panel is hung and the sides are cut (see the facing page).

If you want to do a fast job and don't mind the dust it generates, use a drywall router to cut the opening. Just attach the panel and run the router in a counterclockwise direction along the inside of the opening. If you're careful, you can rout out large openings even after the window jambs and interior doors are installed.

Cutting holes for small openings

Cutting out holes for electrical outlet boxes, switches, and other small openings is trickier than making continuous straight cuts. However, with a little practice and some careful measuring, it's really not that hard to master. There are a few ways to mark and cut the openings, but the main distinction is whether you make the cuts before or after you hang the panel.

To cut an opening before hanging a panel, measure the box's coordinates and transfer them to the panel. It sounds simple, but the problem with this method is that the box never seems to line up perfectly with the cut opening (see the bottom photo on p. 64). This misalignment is usually because the wall, floor, or attached panel isn't perfectly square or level or has gaps. But even if everything is square, it's still pretty easy to make a mistake. Some outlet covers and fixtures barely cover a 1/4-in. area around the box, so absolute precision is important or you'll need to patch later (see p. 164). To improve your chances

back. (The saw teeth will damage the back paper slightly on the forward stroke, but this is not a cause for concern.)

Cutting holes for large openings

If the door and window jambs are not yet installed (which is best from the drywall contractors viewpoint) you can hang the drywall right over the openings before cutting them out. With the panel installed, cut along each side of the opening with a drywall saw. Score along the top of the opening on the back of the panel with a utility knife, snap the panel forward, and cut off the waste with a utility knife.

If the interior door and window jambs have already been installed, it is safest to measure and cut out the opening before hanging the drywall. Mark the opening on

TWO WAYS TO CUT OUT WINDOWS

When faced with windows or other large openings, drywall right over them and then cut out the opening. The waste piece can be removed using various tools or combinations of methods, but I usually use a combination of sawing and scoring to remove the waste. And though it's noisy and creates a great deal of dust, using a router to remove the waste is often the quickest option.

1. Score, saw, and snap

If door and window jambs are not yet installed, it's easy to score the back face of the panel along the top. After cutting the sides with a drywall saw, simply snap the panel and break the waste free. You can also score the back of the panel at window-header height before installing drywall over the opening.

To remove the waste piece, score the front side with a utility knife.

Here, the author has already cut along the side of the opening and is snapping the pre-scored section forward.

2. Rout it out

To cut out a window opening with a router, simply guide the bit along the inside of the framing around the window opening.

When removing the waste piece with a router, be sure to move the router in a counterclock-wise direction.

TRANSFER BEFORE YOU HANG

When cutting out the openings for electrical boxes prior to hanging the panels, begin by transferring the box locations onto the backside of the drywall. It's fast and easy work to mark the edges of the box with chalk or a marker, and then transfer the markings to the drywall by setting the panel in place temporarily.

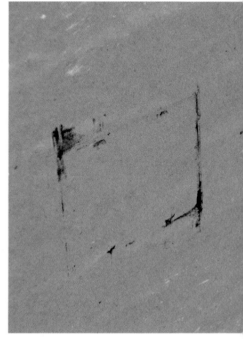

1. Mark it out
Chalk or a marker run around the edge of the electrical box will rub off when you set the panel in place.

2. Follow the outline
After positioning the panel and tapping around the outlet area, the exact location of the electrical box transfers to the back of the drywall panel.

What to avoid Marking and cutting openings before attaching the drywall often results in miscuts, which means gaps or busted out edges that have to be patched.

of the cutout lining up, rub the face of the outlet box with chalk or a marker, and then press the panel against it. The chalk leaves an outline of the box on the back of the panel.

Because of the potential for error with the "cut first" method, I prefer to cut out boxes after the drywall is tacked in place, which is faster and more accurate. Notice that I said "tacked in place." Use only enough fasteners to keep the panel from falling, and don't nail or screw to the stud or joist to which the box is attached. Fastening too close to the

Sight down the panel
When sawing or routing the opening after hanging the panel, sight down the panel to find the center of the opening before tacking the drywall in place. Once the panel is tacked to the studs, begin cutting the panel from the center mark.

box will put pressure against it, causing the drywall to break apart as you finish the cut.

The fastest way to locate the box is to do so before tacking the drywall in place: Simply set it in position and sight down to locate the center of the box with a saw cut as seen in the photo above. Another method for locating an outlet is to use a framing square or a drywall T-square to locate the box before hanging the drywall. You can transfer the measurements to the drywall once it's tacked in place (see the photos on p. 66). Round boxes on walls and ceilings can be cut out just as easily, though the method of marking the location is a little different (see "Cutting Round Openings" on p. 67).

An alternative to cutting out electrical boxes with a utility saw is to use an electric drywall router (see the photos on p. 68). Before routing an outlet box, however, first make sure the power is off and the electrical wires are pushed far enough into the box so that the router bit will not reach them. The router bit should stick out of the router only about 1/4 in. more than the thickness of the drywall. To locate the box on the drywall, you can use one of the methods discussed earlier, or use locators that protect the wires and punch out the center of the electrical box on the drywall. Then simply rout around the outlet in a counterclockwise direction. You can also use the router for cutting out larger

WORK SAFE

Before using an electric drywall router to cut a hole for an electrical outlet box, make sure the power is off and the electrical wires are pushed well back into the box.

MARK, TRANSFER, AND SAW

Measure the location of outlets before attaching the drywall. After tacking the panel in place, transfer the measurements to the drywall using the square, and then carefully cut out the opening with a utility saw. Bear in mind that you need to cut around the outside of the box.

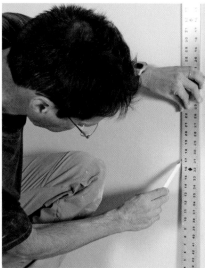

1. Record the location
Use a T-square to locate the outlet, and mark the exact location of the opening on the floor. Remember to write down both sides of the box as well the height of the top and bottom.

2. Transfer the measurements
With the panel tacked in place, mark the location of the box on the drywall. When tacking the panel, don't fasten it alongside the stud near the outlet—doing so can cause the panel to bust out when you cut.

3. Saw around the box
Use a utility saw to cut along the outside edge of the electrical box.

4. Fasten the panel
Gently push the panel in to check for accuracy and then finish fastening.

CUTTING ROUND OPENINGS

An accurate way to cut out an opening for a round fixture box is to measure the box's coordinates, tack the drywall panel in place, transfer the measurements to the panel, and then make the cut.

3. Draw a circle By connecting the lines, square the opening off. Then locate the center and use a compass to mark out the round opening.

1. Measure the location Record measurements to locate the top, bottom, and sides of the outlet.

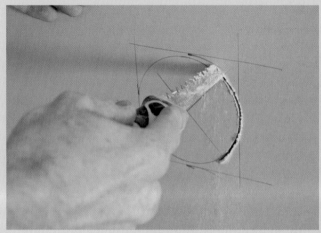

4. Saw to the line Use a utility saw to carefully cut around the outside edge of the box.

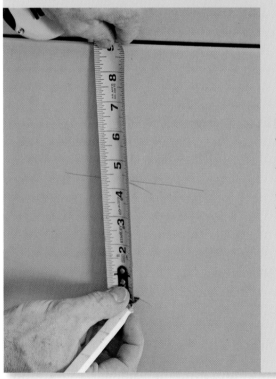

2. Transfer the marks Tack the panel in place and then transfer the measurements to the face of the panel.

5. Fits like a glove After sawing the opening, the panel fits snugly around the box.

USE LOCATORS AND A ROUTER

If you're routing out for electrical boxes after tacking the panels in place, using locators is an easy way to find the center of the boxes. They snap into place over the wires in the outlet. Then, once the drywall is tacked in place, they punch through to mark the center of the box.

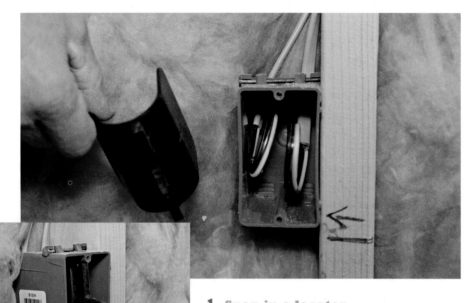

1. Snap in a locator
Insert a locator into the box to protect the wires and mark the location of the box.

2. Find the center
Tack the panel in place and push in near the box. The point of the locator will break through the drywall to locate the center of the box.

3. Rout around the box
Push the running bit through the panel and move it until you hit the side of the box. Pull the bit out, hop it over to the outside of the box, and rout in a counterclockwise direction.

openings, such as those for heat ducts and vents. The tool takes a little getting used to, but it makes a nice clean cut, and it's fast.

GENERAL GUIDELINES FOR HANGING DRYWALL

A properly planned drywalling job is a team effort, and within the team each person should have specific responsibilities. When drywalling an entire house, my crew and I start by hanging all the large ceilings first. With a crew of three, two people can measure, cut, and lift the panels into position, and the third can screw the panels down and cut out any electrical boxes. Once the ceilings are attached, we usually follow the same procedure for the walls, hanging all the larger panels as a team first and then splitting up to fit and hang all the smaller pieces individually.

It is difficult for one person working alone to hang anything longer than an 8-ft. piece of drywall on a ceiling or even on the upper part of a wall. Having enough help is important, especially because it's preferable to hang longer lengths of drywall. Whenever possible, use panels that span the entire length of a wall or ceiling.

If one panel doesn't cover the length, still use long panels to avoid having too many butted seams. A butted seam is when the ends—not the tapered edges—of two panels are butted together. There are two potential problems here. One is that both ends are attached to the same 1½-in. framing member. If one panel is cut a little long, there won't be much space to attach the other panel. The result is a toenailed panel that will more than likely be damaged. The other problem is that a butted seam is a weak joint. Any expansion or contraction in the framing or drywall will result in a cracked or ridged seam. So take care when measuring and attaching butted seams, and always stagger butted seams away from each other and away from the center of a wall or ceiling. (See p. 144 for a few alternatives to butted seams.)

FASTENER SPACING

FRAMING TYPE	FRAMING SPACING	MAXIMUM FASTENER SPACING
Ceiling joists	16 in. o.c., 24 in. o.c.	12 in., 10 in.
Wall Studs	16 in. o.c., 24 in. o.c.	16 in. 16 in.

WORK SMART
For a tight fit across the framing, fasten panels at one edge and then work your way across to the other edge.

Sometimes, however, butted seams are unavoidable. I prefer to place butted seams above or below a window and above a door opening. I use drywall adhesive if possible to avoid screwing into the wide dimension of the framing in the headers for the top seams. I like to backblock the short seams below a window if possible.

FASTENING DRYWALL

The preferred method for attaching drywall to wood or metal framing is to use drywall screws. Screws are inserted with a drywall screw gun so that the screw head sits just below the surface of the panel without breaking the face paper (see the bottom photo below). With the screw gun set to the correct depth, the screw pulls the panel tight against the framing; when the screw stops turning, the clutch disengages. The screw head spins the paper as it sinks in, leaving a slight dimple and a clean smooth edge around it.

Make sure you hold the screw gun firmly, as shown in photo in the top photo on p. 70, and insert the screw straight (a screw that's even slightly tilted will not set deep enough on one side and may tear the face paper on the other). Space the screws evenly on each framing member according to the specifications in the chart above. Place screws at least 3/8 in. in from the perimeter of the panel to avoid damaging the edge.

If you use nails instead of drywall screws, make sure you use ring-shank nails specified for attaching drywall to wood framing. As with screws, set the nails at least 3/8 in. in from the edges and follow the same spacing schedule across the face. When the ends of the panels butt against each other, fasten nails every 8 in. along both sides of the joint.

When using nails instead of screws, all nails "in the field" (across the face of the panel) should be double-nailed. Begin nailing at one edge and work toward the opposite edge. To help keep the drywall tight against the framing, apply hand pressure on the panel next to the nail as you drive it in. Set one nail lightly and then set another nail 1½ in. to 2 in. away. Gently hit each nail until the last blow of the drywall hammer firmly sets each one in shallow, uniform dimples. Do not break the paper, and keep damage to the gypsum core in the dimpled area to a minimum.

Don't set screws too deep
The screw on the left has been installed incorrectly. It is too deep and the head is tearing the face around it. The screw on the right, which just dimples the face paper, is set correctly.

Use a soft touch Nails, like screws, should be set in a shallow dimple (left), not hammered so deep that they break the paper and damage the gypsum core (right).

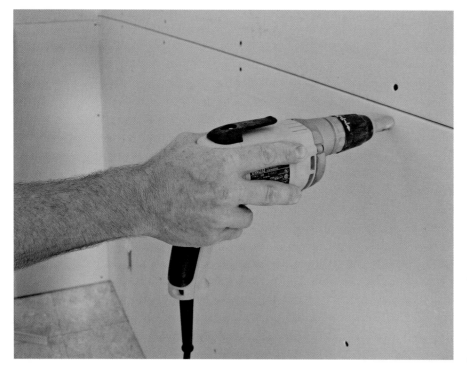

ABOVE: Hold the screw gun firmly as you drive a screw so that your entire hand and fore-arm absorb most of the stress.

RIGHT: Using a collated screw gun, it is faster and easier. This one is also a cordless model which makes the process even easier.

WORK SMART

When nailing or screwing along the bottom of a panel or along the edge of a doorway or window, place fasteners as close as possible to the panel edge (but no closer than ³/₈ in.). The trim will cover these fasteners, which means a few less screws or nails to tape.

If you use nails, I recommend that you do so only along the edges of the panel, and then fill in the rest with drywall screws in the field. I used to use nails to tack the panels in place, but I find now that screws do a better job. The object is to get the panel tacked up as quickly as possible to lessen the physical strain—and the new screw guns are faster than ever. Once the panel is tacked in place, I cut out all the openings and then screw the centers and any spots that I missed along the edges. I prefer to use screws rather than nails along butted seams for a more stable joint.

As discussed in Chapter 2, fastener length is important. The problems with using fasteners that are too short are obvious, but using fasteners that are too long can also present difficulties. Overlong screws are likely to tip or go in crooked, damaging the drywall. Also, the longer the screw or nail, the more likely it is to pop as the framing shrinks.

Whether you use screws or nails, it takes a lot of fasteners to attach all the panels to a ceiling or wall. One way to cut down on

the number of fasteners needed (and to help eliminate the problem of fastener pops and loose panels) is to use the "floating corners" technique, as explained in the sidebar on p. 79. Another fastener-saving method is to secure the drywall with adhesive. For more on this process, see sidebar on p. 74.

HANGING CEILINGS

In a room that will have drywall attached to the ceiling as well as to the walls, always attach the ceiling panels first. By hanging the ceiling first, the panels can be cut a little short so that they slip easily into place. The wall panels, installed later, will fit against the ceiling to help support the edges.

Hanging a ceiling—at least without a mechanical panel lift—is a two-person job. And a third set of hands never hurts. I usually use adjustable step-up benches to hang ceilings that are 9 ft. high or less. For more on lifting and attaching panels without a mechanical lift, see the photos on p. 72. I know a few drywall hangers who use stilts

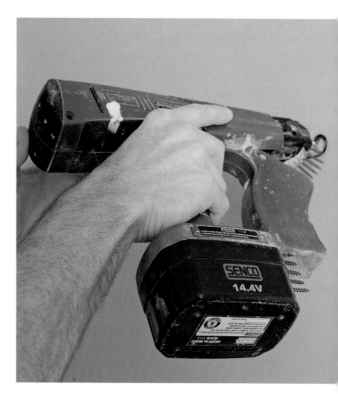

GRAIN ORIENTATION IN DRYWALL

In Chapter 1, I listed the maximum o.c. framing spacing for the various types and thicknesses of drywall. In many instances, however, the framing must be closer if the ceiling panels are hung parallel to the joists. I've known this to be true since I started drywalling, but I never really gave too much thought as to why. After reading an article about grain orientation in drywall in *Fine Homebuilding* magazine (#98), I now understand the reason.

Arden Van Norman performed a simple test to prove that drywall is stronger with grain than across it. He cut one 1-ft. by 4-ft. piece from the end of a panel and one from the side, as shown in the drawing at right. Stacking bricks in the middle of each piece quickly shows that the end piece is much weaker than the side one. Drywall is approximately three times stronger in the long direction. Accordingly, drywall hung perpendicular to the framing members is stronger than drywall hung parallel, so it is less likely to sag.

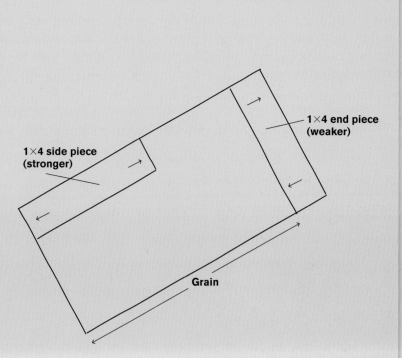

1×4 end piece (weaker)

1×4 side piece (stronger)

Grain

A simple test proves that drywall is stronger with the grain than across it.

RAISING A PANEL

Though the first few boards can be awkward, two people can do efficient work hanging ceilings without a lift. Start with two step-up benches centered under the section to be hung, and be sure to carry fasteners on your belt.

PREVENT SAGGING CEILINGS

- **Fur out the ceiling if on-center spacing is not adequate.**

- **Use a type of drywall more resistant to sagging.**

- **Control humidity in the structure before the work begins, while it is being done, and after the installation is complete.**

- **Prime before texturing. And always let the primer dry thoroughly before texturing.**

- **Hang the drywall perpendicular to framing.**

- **Avoid attaching drywall over sagging insulation.**

1. Get into position
Keep one end of the panel low while you position the other.

2. It's a balancing act
Support the panel with gentle head pressure as you screw it in place. Alternatively, you can use a T-support to hold the panel in place (see the photo on p. 35).

when attaching drywall. One crew member on the floor does the cutting and hands the panel to two other crew members on stilts. They in turn lift the panel into place on the ceiling and attach it, cut openings for any electrical boxes, and take the next measurement. Under ideal conditions, working on stilts is the fastest way to hang drywall on ceilings, but I don't usually use them. The two members on stilts can't cut and carry panels, which means a lot of work for the person on the floor. In addition, the work area must be kept clean and uncluttered to minimize the risk of falls.

My favorite way to hang high ceilings, especially cathedral ceilings up to 15 ft. high, is to use a mechanical panel lift (see the photo on the facing page). This tool does the heavy lifting while I position the panel. And once I've aligned the panel, the lift holds it in place while I attach it. It makes your work a little easier, and lifts can be rented from many drywall suppliers and home centers.

Save your back When using a lift to install a cathedral ceiling, it's easiest to hang the first panel at the peak and work your way down to the sidewalls.

Ceiling panels can be hung perpendicular to the joists or parallel to the joists. I prefer to attach the ceiling panels perpendicular to the joists for a number of reasons:

- Ceiling panels are less likely to sag when hung in this direction (see the sidebar at "Grain Orientation in Drywall" on p. 71).

- It allows the butted seams to be attached to a solid nailer for the length of the seam or floated between the joists, as described on pp. 144–145.

- It is easier to see the joists when fastening the panels.

- It gives the structure greater strength.

- It won't matter that much (and may not even be noticed) if the on-center spacing of a ceiling joist is off.

- It allows the drywall to float over slightly un-even joists, making them less conspicuous.

The only time I hang drywall parallel to the joists is when doing so avoids creating butted seams on the ceiling, or when the method of application affects the fire rating or structural design. Before opting for this method, though, check the spacing of the joists carefully—they must be spaced so that the edge of each panel falls on the center of a joist. If the tapered edges don't hit on center, you may have to cut the long edge of the panel, which will create a long butted seam.

WORK SMART

If you're hanging a cathedral ceiling without a lift, it's easier to attach the lower panel first and then work you way up to the top. By starting at the bottom, you'll have an edge for the next panel to rest on while you hang it. This is easier than trying to lift a panel up to fit against the bottom edge of the panel below it.

ADHESIVE CUTS DOWN ON FASTENERS

Using adhesive has any number of advantages to using mechanical fasteners alone:

- It reduces the number of fasteners required by up to 75 percent.

- It creates a stronger bond than that of nails and screws.

- It is not affected by moisture or by changes in temperature.

- It results in fewer loose panels caused by improper fastening.

- It can bridge minor irregularities in the framing.

Use an adhesive that is approved for wood-to-drywall applications. Apply a ³⁄₈-in.-wide bead along the entire length of each framing member. Wherever the panels butt together, apply a bead of adhesive to each edge of the framing member. Install fasteners along the perimeter of each panel immediately after it is hung.

On panels attached horizontally to walls, no face nailing or screwing is necessary, except on butted seams—and then only enough to pull the panels flush (every 10 in. to 12 in.). If panels are attached vertically, the face should be screwed into each stud on 24-in. centers. For ceilings, install one screw every 24 in. To cut down on the number of screws, you can remove the face screws after 24 hours.

When using adhesive, it's helpful to pre-bow the panels before you hang them. Stack the panels face side up, with the ends supported on 2X4s (see the drawing below), and leave them overnight. When a pre-bowed panel is fastened around the perimeter, the center is forced tight against the adhesive on the framing, thereby eliminating the need for temporary fasteners.

Allow the adhesive to dry for at least 48 hours before starting the taping process. (Note that the adhesive method does not work over a plastic vapor barrier or insulation where the kraft paper overlaps the framing.)

Let gravity do the work When using adhesive, pre-bowing the drywall helps pull the panels closer to the framing members.

Skip the screws Applying a bead of drywall adhesive along each framing member reduces screw pop and the number of fasteners you need to use.

Pre-bowing drywall panels prior to adhesive application ensures a tight bond.

Face side up

Support the ends of panels on 2×4s.

And take care not to create a seam on a joist that is either crowned up or sagged down, as it will be difficult to hide when taping. Also check to make sure the type of drywall you are using is approved for hanging parallel to the joist with the on-center spacing.

No matter the direction in which the panels are hung, if you cannot avoid butted seams, stagger them and keep them as far away as possible from the center of the ceiling. Discontinuous butted seams are easier to conceal and less likely to crack. (For more on butted seams, see Chapter 6.)

Before hanging drywall, some ceilings are first furred with 1×3s perpendicular to the joists. A ceiling may be furred for a number of reasons: to help straighten out a wavy ceiling, to decrease the distance between the nailers (ceiling joists), or to provide solid nailing over rigid insulation. The $2^{1}/2$-in.-wide strips make an excellent target when fastening the drywall. The strips should be treated just like ceiling joists, and the drywall should be hung following the same procedures.

HANGING WALLS

Once you've attached all the ceilings, it's time to start working on the walls. It is usually a lot easier to hang walls than ceilings. You'll probably have to make more cuts for electrical boxes and other openings, but at least you're not working over your head. Before hanging walls, it's a good idea to mark the location of the wall studs on the ceiling and floor to make them easier to locate once they are covered. Also, mark the location of electrical boxes and other openings that will be cut out after the drywall is attached (see p. 62).

As with ceilings, you can hang wall panels in one of two ways—horizontally or vertically. In commercial work, walls are often higher than 9 ft., so it sometimes makes sense to hang drywall vertically to reduce seams. On walls

that are longer than 16 ft., hanging drywall vertically helps eliminate butted seams. However, for walls that are 8 ft. high or less (or 9 ft. high if I'm using 54-in. panels), I usually prefer to hang drywall horizontally. Here's why:

- It decreases the linear footage of seams that need taping by up to 25 percent (see the drawing on p. 19).

- It provides extra bracing strength, because more studs are tied together.

- It makes the seams easier to hide, because light usually shines along finished seams, which makes them less obvious. When the seams are perpendicular to the studs, they simply flow over any studs that may not be perfectly straight, helping hide imperfections.

- It makes the seams easier to tape, because they are at a convenient working height.

To hang drywall horizontally, hang the top panel first, fitting it tightly against the ceiling. If the wall has a window, cut the panel to length, carry it over, and then use a utility knife to score the back side of the drywall at the top of the window opening (see p. 63). To save time, stand the panel on the floor exactly below where it will be attached, leaning it against the studs. Start nails about 1 in. down, lining them up with each stud. Lift the panel up against the ceiling and drive the nails home.

After the top of the panel is tacked in place, cut out any openings, including door and widow openings. Then fasten the rest of the panel to the framing. Next, cut the bottom panel to fit against the top panel. This panel should be about $1/2$ in. shorter in height so that it doesn't fit tightly against the floor and break apart when it is fastened into place. Cutting the panel a little short also

WORK SMART

Before lifting the top panel into place, lean it against the wall and tack in nails at the stud locations. Lift and position the panel and drive the nails home. If using screws you can mark the location of every study with a pencil at trim time.

Position the fasteners When hanging panels high on the wall, start nails or screws along the top edge of the top panel before lifting the sheet into place.

Attach the panel Lift the panel up against the ceiling and tap the nails into the framing members.

USING A PANEL LIFTER

Slide the lift under the bottom edge of the panel.

Bear down on the back end of the lift to raise the panel.

leaves room for you to slide a panel lifter or a prybar underneath to help lift the drywall into place (see the drawing at left).

Most electrical outlets are located near the floor, so tack only the top of the panel in place, and then cut out the electrical boxes as explained on pp. 64–65. Remember not to put too much pressure on the panel, which could cause the face to break apart around the box.

As with ceilings, butted seams should be staggered and placed away from the center of a wall. Butted seams can also be located above doors and above or below windows to create a shorter seam. Try to keep the seam at least

8 in. in from the edge of an opening, because the wall is more stable there. Also, the slight crown that forms during taping could affect the trim miter joint if the seam is located at the corner.

When hanging panels on an outside corner, run the panels long and trim them after they're attached (you can use the same technique on a bottom panel that adjoins a door opening). Running the panel long means taking one less measurement, and it also allows for a little more flexibility. If the framing isn't square or plumb at the outside corner, the panel can be cut to fit the exact angle so that there won't be wide gaps under the corner bead.

Keep it off the floor A panel lifter slides under a sheet of drywall and, as its name suggests, lifts the panel into place so that you can focus on attaching it.

1. Leave it long A panel can be attached full length and trimmed afterwards along an outside corner wall. Here, the author is scoring the backside of the panel along the stud with a utility knife.

2. Cut off the excess Snap the panel forward and cut along the creased edge with a utility knife to free the waste.

ATTACHING DRYWALL TO METAL FRAMING

Drywall can be hung on metal framing in much the same way as it is on wood framing, but there are a couple of things to note. Metal studs and joists are made out of a thin piece of steel bent into a C-shaped stud. Before attaching drywall to the metal studs, check to see which direction the open side of the stud faces (they should all be installed in the same direction). On a long wall that will have butted seams or when hung vertically, the drywall should be attached from the end that the open side of the stud faces (see drawing below).

For the seams to end up flat, the drywall must be attached in the proper sequence. Fasten the edge of the first panel to the unsupported open edge of the stud. Screw on the entire length of the panel before attaching the abutting panel. If the panel were first attached to the solid side and then to the unsupported side, the screw may deflect the open end and force the panel edges outward. When screwing on the rest of the panel, keep the screws closer to the solid edge of the stud. (Note that you should always use screws, not nails, when fastening drywall to metal framing).

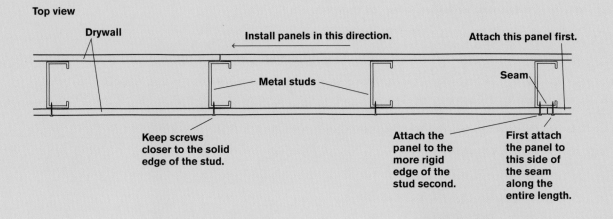

Top view

Drywall

Install panels in this direction.

Attach this panel first.

Metal studs

Seam

Keep screws closer to the solid edge of the stud.

Attach the panel to the more rigid edge of the stud second.

First attach the panel to this side of the seam along the entire length.

TRIM ACCESSORIES

After the drywall has been attached, all outside corners, uncased openings, beams, and soffits should be protected with corner bead. Corner bead resists impact and forms a straight raised edge for taping. Whenever possible, it should be installed in one piece. For standup beads on walls, cut the bead with snips approximately 1/2 in. short of the ceiling height, but push it tight against the ceiling. The baseboard will cover the gap along the floor. The gap at the floor reduces the risk of the bead binding and coming loose or cracking should the wall settle. If more than one piece is required, butt the beads together —don't overlap them. Make sure that the

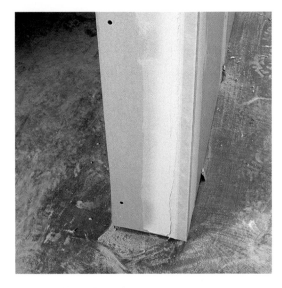

Protect the edges Corner bead resists impact and provides a straight edge for taping.

FLOATING CORNERS TECHNIQUE

The inside corners where wall meets wall or ceiling meets wall are prone to cracking and fastener pops caused by stress at the intersection. One way to reduce fastener problems is to eliminate fasteners at one or both edges in the corners. I call this the "floating corners" technique.

On ceilings, place the first screw 7 in. to 12 in. in from the edge along the perimeter of the ceiling. When the top panel of the wall is pushed up against the ceiling, it will support the edges of the ceiling panels. Screw in the upper edge of the top wall panel, about 8 in. to 12 in. down from the ceiling.

For the vertical corners on the wall panels, omit fasteners on the first panel installed in the corner (see the drawing at right). When you fasten the abutting panel, it helps support the first one. Follow this method for the entire height of the wall corner. Screw or nail the remaining ceiling and wall areas using standard fastening procedures. By eliminating the fasteners in the corners, the drywall is still held firmly in place, but if the corner framing flexes or settles a little, the corners will most likely be unaffected. (Corners that are not fastened still need to have standard wood framing behind them.)

Another version of the floating corner technique uses drywall clips to hold the panels in place. Once attached to the edge of a panel, drywall clips have a nailing foot that is perpendicular to the face of the panel. This allows you to attach both sides of an inside corner to the same stud, eliminating the need for a third stud on an inside corner and backup framing along ceiling edges. When using a drywall clip on a ceiling, keep the first screw back 7 in. to 12 in. from the edge.

A clip for any occasion On the left is a drywall clip that attaches to the drywall before hanging. On the right is a nailer that attaches to the framing before the drywall is attached.

A handy accessory When there's no nailer on one edge of an inside corner, a simple product such as this drywall nailer will hold the panel in place.

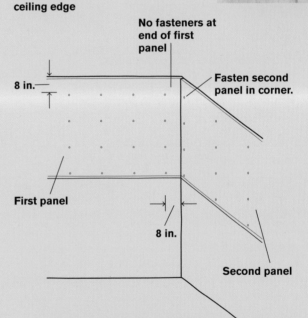

No fasteners at ceiling edge

No fasteners at end of first panel

8 in.

Fasten second panel in corner.

First panel

8 in.

Second panel

SUMMARY FOR HANGING DRYWALL

- Always hang ceilings first.

- Don't cut panels so that they fit too tightly, and never force panels into place.

- Place tapered edges together whenever possible.

- Try to hang panels perpendicular to the framing.

- Try to span the length of a wall or ceiling with one panel.

- Stagger butted seams away from each other and away from the center of a wall or ceiling.

- When hanging a cathedral ceiling, start at the bottom edge of the ceiling. If using a lift, start at the top edge.

- Cut out electrical boxes and other small openings after the panels are tacked in place.

- Use screws rather than nails.

- Use screws and adhesive for best results.

- Fasten drywall close to the edges of doorways and windows and along the floor to avoid having to tape those fasteners.

- Attach corner bead to all outside corners, uncased openings, beams, and soffits.

HANGING A GARAGE

Garages, which are typically large rooms with high ceilings, require a somewhat different hanging strategy than most rooms within a house. Garage ceilings are usually too large to cover without butted seams, so I almost always hang the drywall perpendicular to the joists. If the ceiling is over 9 ft. high, I often hang the garage walls parallel to the studs—that is, vertically rather than horizontally. By standing the panels on end, I avoid having any butted seams on the walls. If you hang wall panels vertically, just make sure that the studs are reasonably straight and that the seams will fall on the studs.

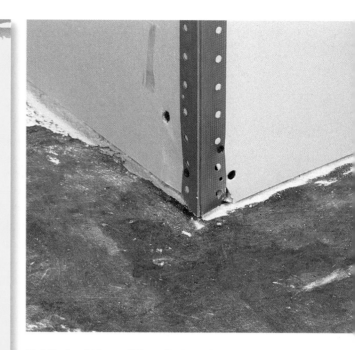

Cut it short For wall installations, keep the bead off the floor about ½ in. to avoid potential problems should the building move or settle.

butted ends are even with each other and that they lie straight.

As mentioned in Chapter 2, there are a number of corner and trim beads available. The following is a brief explanation of how they are attached.

Metal beads

When attached to drywall hung over wood framing, galvanized metal bead is usually nailed in place. When attaching it to drywall hung over metal framing, I like to use a corner crimper and ⁹⁄₁₆-in. staples that go through the drywall and into the framing. When using screws, nails, or staples, attach the bead every 8 in., placing pairs of fasteners opposite each other on either side of the corner.

There is also a metal bead with barbed edges that hold the bead in place, requiring a minimal number of fasteners. Use hand pressure or a rubber mallet to push the bead into the drywall. A fastener at each end or at the center may be necessary to help align this type of bead.

HANGING GABLE WALLS

For the gable ends of a room with a cathedral or sloped ceiling, I usually hang the bottom panel first (see the drawing below). The floor is a good flat surface from which to measure, and the bottom panel usually has a square end for at least part of the height. For longer runs it is a good idea to snap a line on the wall and install the drywall to the line, so that an uneven floor doesn't create unnecessary gaps in the drywall seams. And remember to shim panels off the floor to allow for settling and to prevent potential moisture from wicking up into the drywall. Setting the panels on top of each other makes it easier to hold them in place, especially when the ceiling is high. Note that you should not locate or fasten a butted seam on the center support of the gable end. The building may move or settle at that point, causing stress to the drywall. Don't forget to think about where the seams will fall as you stack the panels up, you may need to start out with a panel ripped in height to avoid having a seam fall on a transition point or a header on the wall.

From the ground up When hanging a gable wall, begin at the bottom of the wall and work your way up to the angled ceiling.

Measure the angles Use a drywaller's T-square to lay out measurements for an angled cut.

Give the drywall a job Setting the second panel on top of the first helps to hold it in place as you fasten drywall to the framing.

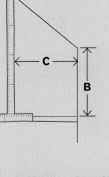

1. Attach the bottom panel.

2. To measure the second panel, rest a 4-ft. T-square on the top edge of the bottom panel and slide it toward the edge until the square hits the ceiling.

3. Measure length A.
4. Measure height B.
5. Length C is the distance from the end of the wall to where the 4-ft.-high panel hits the ceiling.
6. Transfer the measurements to the second panel and use a chalkline or a straightedge to mark the angle cuts.

RIGHT: Nail on metal bead
Attach corner bead before taping. When installing metal bead, place nails on both sides of the bead and space the pairs about 8 in. apart.

BELOW: Or use a crimper A corner crimper provides an alternative to nailing. Crimp the bead every 4 in. to 6 in.

Roll it on A 90-degree roller tool helps embed the bead in the compound and pulls it tighter against the drywall.

Coat the corner bead Tape-on corner beads can be run through a tool that leaves compound on the back side of the bead. The compound works as an adhesive to hold the bead in place.

VINYL BEADS

Vinyl bead is more durable than metal bead, especially if it is fastened with adhesive and then stapled.

1. Spray it down
To attach vinyl bead to the drywall, spray an even coat of adhesive along the corner.

2. Lay on the bead
The adhesive holds the bead in place over the seam in the corner.

3. Secure it in place
Stapling the bead ensures that it will stand up to the inevitable bumps against the corner.

PVC beads

Corner bead made of PVC is both durable and easy to install. Joint compound is used to hold the bead in place. I prefer to use a tool that applies the compound to the back of the bead and then use a roller tool to press the bead into place on the corner. These beads and the ones I explain on the following pages are all easily attached to drywall, whether it has been installed over wood or metal framing. And all of them greatly reduce the cracking at the corners that is common with regular metal bead.

Vinyl beads

There are a many different vinyl beads on the market, and all of them can be installed using any one of three methods. First, dry-fit the bead for length and check the fit. From there, you have three options. The first is to attach both legs of the bead every 6 in. to 10 in. with 1/2-in.-long staples. The second is to spray

PAPER-FACED BEADS

Paper-faced metal and plastic beads are quite durable. To install, apply compound to the wall, align the bead, and then use a roller to embed it properly. Remove excess compound with a taping knife. These beads can also be run through a hopper similar to the one on p. 82 which applies compound to the bead.

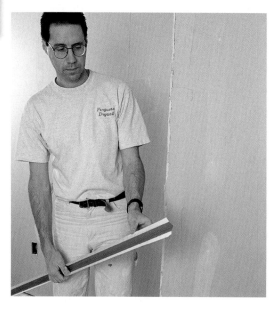

1. Prepare the corner bead
Start by trimming the corner bead to length, making sure to cut it ½ in. or so shy of the floor.

2. Coat the wall
Apply an even coat of joint compound to the wall.

3. Roll it on
Use a 90-degree roller tool to embed the corner bead into the joint compound.

4. Smooth the corners
Use a taping knife to remove excess joint compound.

vinyl adhesive on the drywall and then on the bead, and then immediately attach the bead to the corner, pressing the legs into place (see the photos on p. 83). You can also use staples in addition to adhesive to create an even stronger corner. The third option is to set the bead in joint compound and then press the bead into place until the compound exudes through the holes. Then press and smooth the legs into place using a taping knife.

Paper-faced beads

Both the paper-faced metal and the paper-faced plastic beads that I have used are installed with joint compound. Because edge seams often intersect corner beads, paper-faced beads are installed after the seams have been taped and coated with the first layer of joint compound. The compound fills the tape between panels and provides a more level surface for the corner bead. You can use either a taping knife or a corner roller to set the bead in the compound. Each brand and type (square or bullnose) has its own specially designed roller tool. Whichever method you use, press the bead into place and embed the paper flanges flat against the wall (see the photos on the facing page).

SHAPED BEADS AND THEIR ACCESSORIES

Bullnose corner beads have been around for a while now but they've recently become quite popular. And they do add a refined look to the drywall job. On one of the first jobs I ever used the bullnose style all I had done was attach the bead and I was already getting compliments. They are available in diameter sizes ranging from ⅜ in. to 1½ in. There are many accessories that go along with the styles: to make the transition from bullnose to straight, and for inside or outside corners. There is even a chamfer-style bead that is a good alternative for customers who want to keep straight lines but still like a little flair.

An array of options Numerous trim accessories make work easier for the bead installer, finisher, and trim carpenter.

CHAPTER

4

Taping

For me, taping over freshly hung drywall is the most enjoyable part of a drywalling job. It's fast-paced work that's not too physically demanding and it's pretty much dust-free, which is a nice break after the hanging stage. Taping is also the part of the drywalling process that requires the most skill and the most patience. As you'll see, there's more to taping than just concealing the joints between panels. A properly taped joint should be as strong and as durable as the drywall panel itself.

When this book was originally published in 1996, I said that I preferred hand taping to using mechanical taping tools. Times change and so have the tools and my opinions on using them. Now I'm really hooked on mechanical taping tools because they speed up the work and produce a quality application with a consistency that hand taping cannot match.

The taping sequence is the same for both hand taping and taping with mechanical tools. In this chapter, I'll take you step by step through the hand taping sequence followed by a brief description of the mechanical tools, with pros and cons of each method. In addition, I'll describe some common taping problems and ways to avoid and correct them.

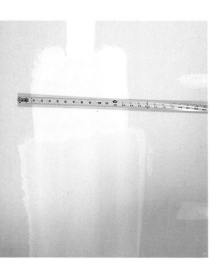

TAPING BASICS

Drywall is typically finished, or "taped," with three coats of joint compound, and then lightly sanded to produce a smooth surface suitable for decorating with most types of paints, textures, and wall coverings.

Three coats of joint compound are necessary to conceal the joints, corners, and fasteners. In some cases (when applying a setting-type compound and some lightweight compounds, for example), you can get acceptable results with just two coats, but three coats helps ensure a more professional-looking job.

- The first coat, which is commonly called the tape-embedding coat or the rough coat, does not have to be perfect. It just has to be neat and of consistent width and thickness.

- The second coat is the filler coat; this is the time when you hide the joint tape and feather the edges of the joint compound.

- The third coat, often referred to as the finish coat, is a thin layer of compound applied lightly over the second coat to smooth out any remaining rough areas.

Each coat is applied a little wider than the previous coat, and the edges are feathered to leave a smooth surface. Sometimes a thin skim coat is applied to the entire surface after the third coat is dry. This results in the highest-quality finish.

What should be taped

Joint compound alone has little strength: If a joint between panels were filled only with compound, the joint would inevitably crack. To strengthen the joint, paper or fiberglass-mesh tape must be used with the compound. The compound acts like an adhesive, but it's the tape that actually joins the two panels together. With the tape centered on the joint and embedded in the joint compound, the face paper of the two panels essentially becomes one solid surface. The layers of compound that cover the tape are used to conceal the joint.

The same principle applies to cracks, holes, and hammer marks that tear the surface of the drywall: They all need to be covered with paper or mesh tape to strengthen the surface.

Inside corners on walls and ceilings are also joints that need to be strengthened as well as concealed. Paper tape is embedded in the corner and, after it dries, covered with two or more coats of joint compound. Fasteners, dents, and slight imperfections can be concealed with joint compound alone. Because the surface is unbroken, the area is still strong, so tape is unnecessary.

What to expect when taping

Taping requires patience as well as skill. If I'm using drying-type compounds and apply the first coat of tape and compound on Monday, I wait until Tuesday, when the first coat

ABOVE: Achieving smooth joints Joints between drywall panels are covered with paper or fiberglass-mesh tape and coated with three layers of joint compound.

BELOW: Cover every seam All fasteners, joints between panels, and inside and outside corners require taping.

is fully dry, to go over everything again with the second coat. On Wednesday, I apply the third coat. As each coat of joint compound is applied, I must become more particular, smoothing out the compound to blend in with the surface of the drywall.

The time it takes to finish taping a certain square footage of drywall is affected by many different circumstances, including the height of the ceiling, the number of joints and corners, the quality of the hanging job, and the temperature and humidity at the job site. I usually plan to take the same amount of time for each coat: If it takes 8 hours to apply the first coat, it will take about 8 hours for the second coat and another 8 hours for the third.

Taping can be a messy job, and it is very difficult to avoid getting joint compound on your hands, your clothes, and the floor. I keep an old taping knife and an empty pail handy so I can scoop up dropped joint compound before it gets walked on.

Before you begin

Before you start taping, you need to double-check a few things around the room:

- Make sure that all the drywall panels are firmly attached.

- That all the electrical outlet boxes and other openings have been cut out.

- That the corner bead has been installed where necessary (some types of corner bead are attached after the tape has been embedded).

- The temperature of the air, joint compound, and drywall surface should be consistent—at least 55°F if you're using drying types of joint compound and 45°F if using setting types. Ideally, the temperature should be 65°F to 70°F.

PROTECT THE WORKSITE

Whether you're working for clients or making small repairs around your house, the taping process makes a mess—dust is inevitable and misplaced compound is likely. Before beginning, protect the work environment.

1. Cover finished floors
Stairs and other finished surfaces should be covered to prevent damage during the drywall process. Just be sure stairways remain safe to walk up and down.

3. Protect delicate surfaces
Fiberglass shower or tub units are very sensitive to scratching. This unit will get a lot of traffic while taping, so protection is a must.

2. Seal off the HVAC
Special covers protect duct work from filling with dust and debris.

REPAIR DAMAGED DRYWALL

Drywall is sometimes damaged during transport or hanging. Oversized gaps should be prefilled with joint compound. Damaged areas on flat sections of panels can be cut out, filled with compound, and covered with tape.

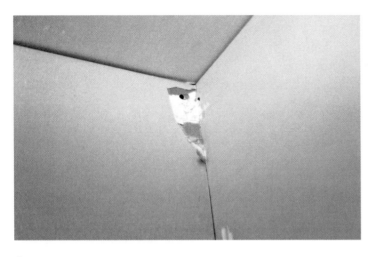

1. Look for trouble
Damaged areas at inside corners (and anywhere else) should be filled with compound before you apply the first coat.

2. Prefill the gaps
A taping or setting-type compound is ideal for prefilling gaps before taping.

THINK AHEAD

Before you begin, make sure the work area is clean and un-cluttered so that walls and ceilings can be finished along their entire length without worrying about trip-ping or falling over drywall scraps or tools. This is especially im-portant if you're work-ing on stilts.

- Good ventilation and low humidity also help the joint compound dry and set up properly.

- If there are any damaged areas of drywall, such as busted-out inside corners or outlet-box openings, cut away the loose drywall and fill the holes with a coat of joint compound.

- Also fill any gaps between panels that are more than 1/8 in. wide. Allow these areas to dry before applying the first coat. If time is of the essence, use setting-type compound as filler (see p. 52).

Mixing joint compound

As explained in Chapter 2, joint compounds are available in powdered and ready-mixed forms. I mix powdered compounds (either setting types or drying types) with water in a 5-gal. joint-compound pail, using a heavy-duty 1/2-in. electric drill with a mixing paddle or a special mixing tool (see the photos on the facing page).

Setting-type compound If you're mixing a setting-type compound, it's especially important to make sure that the pail and mix-ing paddle are clean, because even a thin film of setting compound on either one can cause the new mix of compound to set up prema-turely. The hardened compound can also come loose and get mixed in, leaving chunks in the fresh compound.

Follow the directions on the label concerning the proportions of water and compound. Pour the specified amount of cool (not cold or hot), clean water into the pail, and then add the compound. Mix until the compound reaches the desired consistency. It should be stiff enough to hold its form on the trowel (see the photos below), but not so stiff that it is difficult to smooth. Be careful not to overmix, because too much mixing can shorten the hardening time. It's also important not to mix more compound than you can use within the specified time. Once that time has expired, the compound hardens chemically. Don't try to remix any setting-type compound that has started to set up—it's unusable.

Drying-type compound To mix "powdered drying-type compound," add the compound to the specified amount of water and mix well until the powder is completely damp. Let the mixture stand for 15 minutes and then remix. This type of compound does not set up—it has to air dry—so it can be kept for extended periods of time as long as it's covered. It can be remixed, if necessary.

Ready-mixed compound The most common type of drying compound is called "ready-mixed compound." If a ready-mixed compound is fresh, just a little stirring is necessary. If it has been sitting around for a

MIXING POWDERED COMPOUNDS

Using setting- or drying-type compounds in their powdered form allows you to mix only the amount you need for the job at hand.

1. Add the powder and water
Powdered compounds can be mixed in large or small amounts—just be sure to combine powder and water in the proportions recommended by the manufacturer.

2. Mix the compound
Use a mixing paddle attached to a heavy duty drill to mix the powdered compound with cool water.

3. Know when to stop
Mix the compound until it is stiff enough to hold onto the trowel without sliding off. Drying-type compounds should be left to stand for 15 mintues, then remixed.

ABOVE: Mixing small batches
Use water and a taping knife to mix small batches of powdered compound in your pan.

RIGHT: Using ready-mixed compound **When loosening ready-mixed joint compound, using a masher-type mixer helps avoid adding too much air to the compound.**

THINK AHEAD

If possible, go through the work area the day before you begin taping to fill any gaps larger than ⅛ in. with joint compound. You must fill the gaps anyway, and this way the compound will dry before you begin taping.

while, you may need to loosen it by adding a little water. Even if you don't need to add water, it's a good idea to mix the compound so it has the same consistency throughout the pail. I prefer to use a masher-type mixer rather than a powered mixing paddle for this light stirring.

Ready-mixed compounds are generally used at the consistency in which they come, but they can be thinned for taping. I often thin the compound for the third coat. Add a little water at a time to avoid overthinning (if the mixture becomes too thin, add more compound to attain the correct consistency). If the compound freezes, allow it to thaw at room temperature and mix it without adding water. If the compound has sat too long and separated so that a clear liquid forms on top, it can usually be remixed. If it smells sour or looks moldy, the compound has gone bad and should not be used.

An efficient taping system

When I start a room, I apply a coat of joint compound to all fasteners in the field on a wall, then embed tape on the seams, and then embed tape in the corners. If there is an outside corner, I finish the section by applying a coat of joint compound over the corner bead before progressing to the next wall. This is an efficient way of taping rather than first taping all fasteners, then walking around the job again and taping only seams, and so on. In the interest of clarity, however, I'll present all the information on taping fasteners, taping seams, taping inside corners, and taping outside corners in separate sections.

TAPING FASTENER HEADS

I like to tape fastener (screw and nail) heads first, so that I don't accidentally mess up a seam that I've already taped. You need only a thin layer of joint compound to conceal the fasteners, and it's easiest to tape a row of two or three fasteners in a single strip rather than

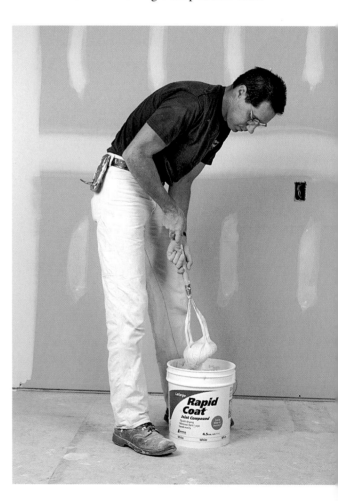

individually. Using a 5-in. or 6-in. taping knife, apply just enough pressure to fill the indentation and leave the face of the drywall panel covered with a thin film of compound. Don't be tempted to fill the indentation with one thick coat; applying three thin coats of compound and tapering the edges brings the indentations level with the panel surface and requires only minimal sanding. If necessary, apply the second and third coats to fasteners as you apply the second and third coats on the seams.

TAPING SEAMS

There are two types of drywall seams: tapered-edge seams between panels, formed when two long edges of the panels come together, and butted seams, which are created when nontapered panel ends are joined together.

First coat

The seams between drywall panel edges take considerably longer to first-coat than do fastener heads, because the tape has to be embedded in the joint compound. There are two ways to tape these seams: with fiberglass-mesh tape or with paper tape.

Mesh-tape method I often use self-adhesive fiberglass-mesh tape on the tapered-edge seams between panels. Mesh tape is fast and easy to use, and you don't have to worry about loose tape and air bubbles under the tape, which can be problems with paper tape.

On the downside, most mesh tape is not as strong as paper tape, so it's important to use the right type of joint compound. You can embed mesh tape in any type of setting-type compound, but if you're working with drying-type compounds, make sure you use a taping compound, not a topping or an all-purpose compound (see p. 50). I prefer to use

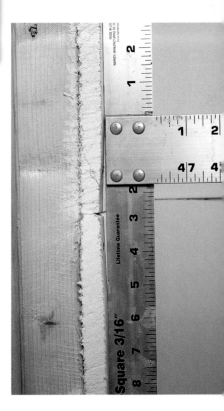

Panels designed with tape in mind To allow room for tape and compound, the taper along the long edge of drywall panels creates a recessed joint where panels butt together.

COVER THE FASTENERS

Before taping any of the seams, make sure that nails or screws in the middle of panels are covered and smoothed with joint compound. Fasteners along seams and corners will be coated when the tape is embedded, so there's no need to cover them with compound first.

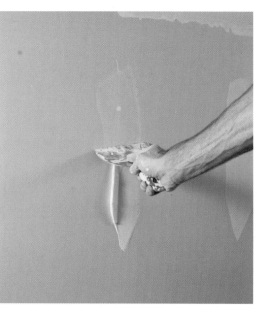

1. Lay on the compound
Apply compound to a strip of fasteners in one smooth motion –in this case I worked my way up the wall.

2. Remove the excess
Remove the compound by pulling the knife in the opposite direction.

3. Leave a smooth surface
When correctly removed, only the dimpled area is filled with compound.

Score the roll "Ringers," strands of mesh tape that unravel when the tape is unrolled, are common. To prevent them, score the edges of the roll with a utility knife.

a setting-type compound, which is stronger and shrinks and cracks very little when drying.

When using self-adhesive mesh tape, it's easiest to tape all the joints in the room before applying the compound. Press the tape firmly over the joint so that it lies flat with no wrinkles, and cut it to length with a sharp taping knife or a utility knife. Using a hawk or a large (4-in. by 14-in.) beveled trowel as a palette, apply joint compound to the entire length of the joint with a 5-in. or 6-in. taping knife. A thin, even layer of ¼-in.-thick compound is all that you need. Don't worry about the compound being smooth at this point.

MESH TAPE FOR TAPERED SEAMS

Though not as strong as paper tape, fiberglass-mesh tape offers plenty of strength along tapered seams. You need only a roll of tape, joint compound, a 4 in. by 14 in. beveled trowel, and a 5-in. or 6-in. taping knife.

1. Tape the seams
Lay tape over the seam so that it is centered, smooth, and free of wrinkles.

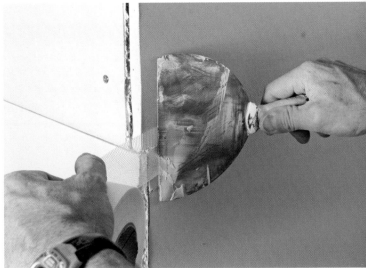

2. Cut the tape
There's no need to make it difficult—mesh tape can be torn along the blade of a taping knife.

3. Cover it with compound
Put a small amount of compound on the taping knife and press the compound onto the center of the joint for the width of the trowel.

4. Smooth the compound
Use a beveled trowel to smooth the compound. Hold the trowel almost flat against the wall so that only the back edge is used to pull the compound.

PAPER TAPE ON TAPERED SEAMS

Unlike mesh tape, paper tape is held in place by a thin layer of joint compound that is applied before the tape goes on. On either tapered or butted seams, paper tape can be set in and covered with any type of tape-embedding compound.

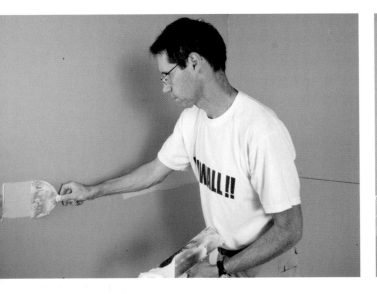

1. Apply the compound first
Begin by spreading a thin layer of joint compound along the seam using a 5-in. or 6-in. taping knife.

2. Set the tape in place
Paper tape is then pulled tight along the seam and lightly pressed into the compound.

3. Cut the tape
When you reach the end of a seam, paper tape can be torn by hand or along the edge of a taping knife.

4. Embed the tape
Use a taping knife to embed the tape tight against the seam. Make sure the tape is flat, wrinkle-free, and embedded in the recess of the tapered seam.

Now switch to the 4-in. by 14-in. beveled trowel to smooth the compound. With the trowel centered on the seam and held almost flat against the panels, pull the trowel along the joint, smoothing the compound with the back edge. Leave a layer of compound that just covers the tape and fills the recessed areas of the tapered seam. The edges should be fairly smooth and feathered. If a lot of compound builds up in front of the trowel and pushes out around the sides as you smooth the seam, either you have put too much joint compound on the seam or you're taking too much off. When you've finished the seam, the joint compound should be about 3/16 in. thick in the center and 6 in. or less wide from one tapered edge to the other. Remember: The first coat doesn't have to be perfect—just make sure that you don't build up the compound too thickly or leave ridges that will make the application of the second coat more difficult.

Paper-tape method Paper tape forms a strong joint on seams when it is used with any type of tape-embedding joint compound. Paper tape used in conjunction with an all-purpose joint compound is the most common way to tape seams (whether they are tapered-edge or butted).

The procedure for embedding paper tape is somewhat different than for that of mesh tape. Because the paper tape is not self-adhesive, you first have to lay down a ground coat of compound to hold the paper in place. Use a 5-in. or 6-in. taping knife to apply a thin, fairly even layer of joint compound 1/4-in. thick or less along the center of the seam.

Next, center the paper tape on the joint and lightly press it into place. Keep the tape pulled tight and reasonably straight along the joint. Rip the tape to the desired length, making sure that the tape goes far enough into each corner so that the corner tape overlaps the joint tape.

Butted seams A butted seam is created when the nontapered ends of two panels are joined together. Here, the second piece is being slid into place.

Use paper tape on butted seams Butted seams attached to wall studs or ceiling joists are weak joints subject to cracking. Using paper tape gives the seam a little extra strength.

Minimize the effect Butted seams can be properly placed above a doorway. To minimize the bump created by taping, be sure the tape is embedded well.

TAPING AT CEILING HEIGHT

For best results, I prefer to tape the entire length of a seam or inside corner in one pass. That's no problem when you're working on a horizontal wall seam 4 ft. from the floor, but ceilings and the tops of inside or outside corners present more of a challenge.

For ceilings 9 ft. high or less, I find that a pair of adjustable stilts allows me the greatest maneuverability for taping joints and fasteners. If stilts are not practical for you (or if you're not allowed to use them for drywalling where you live), set up a plank long enough to work the length of a seam at an appropriate height. For ceilings over 9 ft. high, you'll have to set up some kind of scaffolding, as discussed on pp. 36–37.

In most rooms, all you need to reach the top of an inside or outside corner is an overturned, empty joint-compound pail. I find it easiest to work from the top down.

Walking tall Working on stilts allows you to tape seams and corners in one pass without using staging.

Quick scaffolding Setting a plank on two joint-compound pails below a seam provides a simple way to reach the ceiling.

A convenient stool The top of most inside corners can be reached by standing on an empty joint-compound pail.

With the paper tape in position, pull the taping knife along the center of the tape. I usually start at the center of a seam and pull toward each end. (If the joint butts into an inside corner, be careful not to leave too much compound under the tape as you approach the corner to avoid raising a bump.) Keep enough pressure on the knife to properly embed the tape as you go. The pressure on the knife should push the extra compound out from the edges, leaving a layer ⅛ in. thick or less under the tape. Make sure the tape is tight against the panel at the edges. Clean excess compound from along the edges of the joint with the taping knife.

If the paper tape wrinkles or bunches up as you embed it with the taping knife, it's probably because the initial layer of compound was too thick or was not pulled tight when set in place. If you must use two pieces of tape—on a joint over 16 ft. long, for instance—still start at the center of the tape and work both ways.

Second coat

The second coat of joint compound, also known as the filler coat, is the step when the largest amount of joint compound is applied and the seams are filled and widened. An all-purpose, topping, or setting-type compound can be used for the second coat. Before you begin, check the surface and knock off any noticeable ridges or chunks of hardened compound with the edge of the taping knife. Smooth areas and blend them together as necessary, but keep in mind that there's still one more coat of compound to apply, so everything doesn't have to be perfect.

Tapered-edge seams The second coat of joint compound is usually applied to seams after the inside corners are second-coated (see p. 105). Use a 6-in. or wider taping knife to apply the compound about 8 in. wide, with the seam in the center. The coat should be about 3⁄16 in. thick and fairly even. Whenever

possible, apply the compound to the entire length of the seam before you start smoothing it with a 4½-in. by 14-in. beveled trowel. Keep the trowel turned almost flat to the drywall and apply pressure to one edge, feathering the edges of the compound as you pull the trowel. Some compound will be removed as the edge is feathered. Then do the same for the other edge of the compound.

Next, center the trowel and glide it along the joint, applying constant, even pressure to both edges of the seam. Hold the trowel almost flat against the seam with the back edge doing the work. If all goes well, the edges of the seam will remain feathered and the center will be smoothed to an inconspicuous crown. Repeat this method until most of the air bubbles in the joint compound have been removed. The second-coated seam should be about 10 in. to 12 in. wide, and the tape should not be visible. Try not to remove too much joint compound. If you find that you're pulling off too much, you're probably holding the trowel at too steep of an angle. Apply more compound to the seam and try again, this time holding the trowel flatter to the surface.

Butted-end seams Because the butted ends of drywall panels that are attached to studs and ceiling joists are not recessed, as tapered edges are, you create a slight bump at the joint when you apply tape and the first coat of compound. To conceal the bump, you need to apply a wider band of compound than you do with tapered-edge seams (you may also need to apply four coats of compound to blend the bump into the drywall surface).

Before applying the second coat to butted seams, I usually run my hand across the joint or hold a straightedge against it to it to determine how wide I need to spread the compound to blend in the seam. The center is the high area, so you need to cover the tape lightly and build up the joint compound

WORK SMART

Try to tape the entire length of a joint with one continuous length of tape—it is faster and won't leave you with loose ends of tape exposed. For longer runs, say over 16 ft. long, use two pieces of tape to avoid wrinkles and the possibility of leaving too much compound behind the tape.

WORK SMART

For best results on inside corners, use a flexible 6-in. taping knife for the second coat.

APPLY THE SECOND COAT

Known as the filler coat, the second application of joint compound goes on wider and covers many of the imperfections left as the tape was embedded. The filler coat should go on smooth, but don't expect a perfect surface at this stage of finishing.

1. Lay on the compound
A 6-inch taping knife is used to apply compound over the taped seams. Before spreading, the second coat should be about 8 in. wide and ³/₁₆ in. thick.

2. Feather the edges
Pull a beveled trowel held almost flat against the panels, applying light pressure to one edge at a time.

Taping seams correctly The seam on the left is attached to the stud, which creates a bump in the drywall. The compound has to be feathered out 30 in. wide, or more, to help conceal the bump. The seam on the right was back blocked and is recessed, so it can be finished 12 in. wide.

3. Smooth the center
Leave enough compound to conceal the tapered edge of the panels, allowing a little extra for shrinkage and sanding. The finished application should be about 10 in. to 12 in. wide.

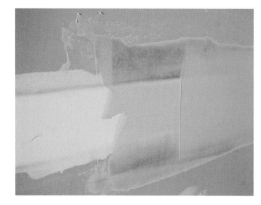

4. What to aim for
In the center of this photo too much compound was removed, which will result in a concave seam. The portion to the right is properly smoothed.

along the sides of the tape. Feather the edges, and then smooth the center. Don't apply too much compound at one time. I usually widen it with a beveled trowel or a 12-in. taping knife to about 10 in. on each side of the tape.

Third coat

If you have been careful with the first and second coats, the third coat should be the easiest and require the least amount of joint compound. Because the third coat is usually the final coat, it is a good idea to do some light sanding before you begin—just knock off chunks of compound and tool marks. Use light pressure to sand every seam and along the inside corners. Use a pole sander with 100-grit or 120-grit sandpaper or a sanding screen (see p. 54). Be careful not to sand down

CHECKING FOR CROWNED SEAMS

Once the second coat is dry, check for potential problem seams with a straightedge or the edge of a long trowel. Hold the straightedge on the center of the seam and check the gap on each side. If it's greater than 1/16 in., feather the compound farther out on both sides to conceal the seam. Starting at the center, apply joint compound the width of two 6-in. taping knives on each side. Build up each side, but not the center, with joint compound, and feather the edges with a beveled trowel.

When this coat is dry, check the seam again with a straightedge; if it is acceptable, lightly sand the seam and apply the final coat in the same way the other seams and outside corners were third-coated.

Spread the compound wider To conceal a crowned seam, as seen on this butted joint, compound should be widened out on each side of the tape. Feather the edges flush to the panel and leave only a thin layer of compound over the crowned seam.

to the tape. The aim is not to sand out every last defect but only to make it easier to get the finish coat of joint compound as smooth as possible. (It helps to think of this step as a light "brushing" rather than sanding.)

There are two ways to apply the finish coat to the seams: with a taping knife (the conventional method) or with a paint roller (the faster method—especially if you're working with a helper).

Taping-knife application Apply the compound over the entire seam using a wide taping knife (I prefer a 12-in.-wide knife) going slightly wider than the second coat. Next, remove most of the joint compound by pulling a 12-in. trowel firmly along the seam. Feather the edges one last time so that there are no thick or rough spots, and then take off any compound left on the center of the seam.

The thin layer of compound left fills in all imperfections, scratches, dents, air bubbles, and so on. The compound dries out a little as it is worked, so you can thin it with water as necessary for easier application.

Tools work for you
The aluminum support strip on wide taping knives can be bowed a little to prevent leaving tool marks in the compound. Most wide knives are designed to bend easily.

APPLYING THE THIRD COAT

Often referred to as the finish coat, the third coat of compound is laid on a few inches wider than the second coat. This final coat of compound can be applied with either a wide taping knife or a paint roller.

Knife on the second coat
One way to apply the third coat of joint compound to a seam is to use a wide taping knife.

Or roll it on
A quicker alternative is to use a paint roller. Dilute the compound slightly to ease application.

Level the surface
Use a wide taping knife to remove and smooth the joint compound on the third coat. Feather the edges first, and then smooth the center.

Paint-roller application Thin the joint compound with a little water and then use a 3/8-in.-nap roller to apply it. Again, lay it on just a little wider than the second coat. Then smooth and remove the compound using a 12-in. trowel in the same manner described for the taping-knife application. I find that rolling works faster than applying the compound by knife, and if you attach a pole to the roller handle, it's easy to reach high seams. (Working with a long-handled paint roller also places less stress on your wrists and arms than applying the compound with a knife or trowel.) One member of the crew can roll the compound on while another finishes the seam. This works especially well on ceilings.

GENERAL GUIDELINES FOR APPLYING THE THIRD COAT

I recommend using a topping or an all-purpose drying-type compound for all third-coat applications. These compounds can be thinned with water and are easy to apply and sand smooth. Taping and setting-type compounds dry out too quickly in such a thin coat, and they are harder to sand.

Start the third coat by applying a thin layer of compound to the fasteners, and then move on to the seams and outside corners. Wherever taped areas intersect, smooth and blend them together, working both seams at the same time. Apply the finish coat to the inside corners after the intersecting joints are finished. When applying the third coat, keep the following points in mind:

• Make the finish coat just a little wider than the second coat.

• Keep all the seams smooth and the edges feathered.

• Fill all scratches and dents to create smooth seams with no trowel marks or air bubbles.

LEFT: Cover previous coats The third coat on a tapered-edge seam should be just a little wider than the second.

BELOW: Using mesh tape If you use mesh tape on inside corners, apply it before the compound. Push the tape tight into the corner so it is centered and free of wrinkles.

TAPING INSIDE CORNERS

Inside corners are a little more difficult to tape than flat seams, because it can be tricky to get one side of the corner smooth without roughing up the other side. I prefer to use paper tape on inside corners. Mesh tape is a little more difficult to work with but it can be used in corners as well. Just remember that mesh tape doesn't hold a crease well and it's easy to cut or sand through.

Generally, the paper tape is embedded in a layer of joint compound and then covered with one or two thin coats. One coat is usually enough, but sometimes two are necessary (industry recommendations call for only one coat over inside corners).

First coat

The method I've used for years is to apply the undiluted compound (all-purpose or taping)

TAPING INSIDE CORNERS

Though taping inside corners is a bit more finicky than taping flat seams, the procedure is largely the same: Lay on a thin layer of compound, set tape over the seam, and embed it in place.

1. Spread the compound
For inside corners, apply the embedding coat of compound to each side with a taping knife. An alternative is to apply slightly diluted compound with a 4 in. corner roller.

2. Apply the tape
Position the folded, precreased paper tape in the corner. Pull it tight and press it into the compound every foot or so. Tear the end of the tape to a slight point that fits the corner.

3. Embed the tape
Use a drywall knife to embed the tape into the corner one edge at a time. Remove the wrinkles and feather the edges.

right from the bucket with a 4-in. or 5-in. taping knife. Spread a layer about 4 in. wide and ⅛ in. thick or less into each edge of the corners. Make sure the entire inside corner is covered with compound, with no dry areas or unfilled gaps between the panels.

An alternative is to apply the compound with a 4-in. corner roller. You'll need to thin the compound with a little water, but in one swipe the roller gives you an even layer of compound on both sides of the corner. This method is quite a bit faster than using a taping knife and works well with the mechanical corner roller and finishers mentioned on p. 114.

Fold the tape along its crease and lightly press it into the corner every 12 in. or so, keeping the tape pulled tight as you go. Now embed the tape into the compound with a 4-in. or 5-in. taping knife, working on one side of the corner at a time.

It takes some practice to embed the tape on each side of the corner without accidentally pulling it loose, wrinkling it, or leaving too much joint compound underneath. Start with light trowel pressure to embed the tape, and then go over it a few more times with increased pressure to force out the excess joint compound. When you're finished, the first coat on the inside corners should be free of wrinkles and the edges of the compound should be feathered.

Second coat

The best method for hand taping inside corners is to tape one side at a time, allowing the first side to dry before taping the other. Each side must be carefully smoothed and feathered. With this method, one side is taped as the job is second-coated and the other side is taped during the third coat. In other words, the completed corner ends up with only one coat of compound over the tape on each side, which means you need to apply the compound a little thicker than you do on flat

FILLING LARGE GAPS

Drywall isn't always hung perfectly. A problem you sometimes run into when taping inside corners, especially in older homes, is large gaps in the corners between panels. Gaps are typically caused by out-of-square or off-level walls or ceilings or by errors made during measuring.

Sometimes a gap can simply be filled with compound, but if it's wider than ½ in. or so, the compound will fall out. The best remedy for this problem is to first put a layer or two of self-adhesive mesh tape into the corner. When you apply the joint compound, the mesh holds it in place. The paper tape can then be positioned in the corner in the normal way.

Allow a little extra time for the corner to dry before applying the next coat of compound, because the extra thick layer of joint compound can crack if it is second coated too soon.

1. Pretape over large gaps Larger gaps in corners may not hold compound when prefilling. It helps to cover the gap with mesh tape first.

2. Cover the mesh Force compound through the tape so the gap is filled and the compound stays in place. When the compound is set or dried you can install precreased paper tape.

INSIDE CORNERS: THE SECOND COAT

Don't try to apply compound to both sides of an inside corner at the same time. Cover one side of the corner when you second coat flat seams on the walls. Then allow that coat to dry and work the adjacent corner when you apply the third coat to the walls.

1. One wall at a time
When second coating inside corners coat only one side of a corner at a time. Let it dry before you coat the other side.

2. Smooth the corner
The opposite, uncoated edge stays cleaner if you square the taping knife to the corner.

WORK SMART

When taping an inside corner on a wall, work from top to bottom. When taping a long inside corner where the wall meets the ceiling, work from the center toward the ends.

seams. Because it's difficult to get one coat as smooth as two, a little extra sanding and light touch-up work may be necessary later. This method is faster than double-coating each side, and it provides excellent results.

Before applying compound to the second edge, let the first edge dry and scrape or sand off any chunks of dried compound. Be careful when sanding over exposed tape because it may peel off or you may sand right through it. When applying compound to the second side of an inside corner, use the same techniques used for taping the first edge.

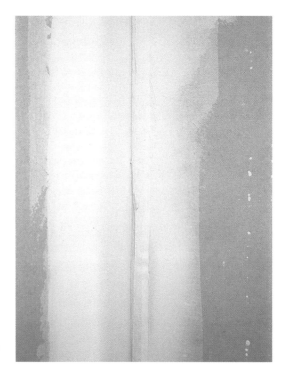

A clean start When you finish an inside corner one edge at a time, sand or scrape off any excess chunks of compound before applying the final coat to the opposite edge.

TAPING OUTSIDE CORNERS

For me, outside corners are a lot easier to tape than inside corners. There is no need to put any tape on the corner bead (though you can tape the edge of metal corner bead to reduce corner cracking). In addition, there are usually no seams or gaps along the corner bead edge (if there are gaps, use joint tape). This advice also applies to the newer tape-on or glue-on beads, which I prefer over nail-on metal beads.

First coat

Apply the first coat of joint compound to the corner bead as you go through taping seams and inside corners throughout the room. Just blend in the areas where seams or corners intersect the corner bead. Using a 5-in. or 6-in. taping knife, cover the bead with joint compound and then press the compound into place with the edge of a beveled trowel or taping knife. Using the raised outside edge of the corner bead as a screed, pull the trowel along the corner, smoothing out the com-

TAPING OUTSIDE CORNERS

After the corner bead has been installed, the first coat of compound conceals it from sight. The first coat doesn't have to be perfect, just be sure the belved edge is clean. Applying the second coat allows you to smooth out any rough spots and blend it into intersecting joints.

1. Apply the first coat
When applying the first coat to corner bead on an outside corner, spread the compound about 6 in. wide, keeping the raised bead clean and using it as a screed for a curved trowel or taping knife.

2. Work out the rough spots
When applying a wider fill coat over corner bead use the raised outer edge of the bead as a screed while you smooth the sides and feather theedges. This coat is typically 8 in. to 10 in. wide.

3. Blend intersecting seams
Taped areas must be blended together where they intersect. Here, a trowel and knife are used to blend a horizontal seam and an outside corner.

pound and feathering the edge along the drywall surface. Some of the newer beads—particularly the tape-on beads—are tight-fitting and require only one fill coat and a third (finish) coat. In this case, apply a wider first (fill) coat and pay more attention to getting it smooth.

Second coat

Outside corners are easy to second coat, because the raised outer edge of the corner bead acts as a screed for smoothing the compound. Apply the joint compound about 10 in. wide. Using a wide taping knife or a beveled trowel, apply pressure on the outside edge of the joint compound and on the edge of the corner bead, holding the trowel almost flat against the compound. When you've finished the second coat, the outer raised edge should still be visible, the center should be smooth, and the edges should be feathered into the surface of the panel.

If a seam or an inside corner intersects an outside corner, both areas can be taped at the same time. Blend the areas together, filling and smoothing as necessary with a

FIRE TAPING

Garages, utility rooms, and furnace rooms are often hung with fire-resistant drywall. In these nonliving areas, there's clearly no need to do three coats of taping, but you do have to apply one coat of joint tape and compound to achieve the desired fire rating. This single coat is commonly referred to as fire taping. Apply tape and one coat of compound to all seams and inside corners in the normal way; you don't have to tape the fastener heads. Outside corners require metal corner bead, which can be attached after you've finished taping, but the bead doesn't have to be taped. All gaps wider than $1/16$ in. around pipes, overhead door brackets, and other protrusions should also be taped.

There is a self-adhesive fire-rated tape available that doesn't require a coat of joint compound to maintain its fire rating. It is an excellent choice for fire taping gable ends and attics.

A quick job Only the tape-embedding coat is necessary when fire taping garages and other nonliving areas.

Use the right tape Fire tape is a self-adhesive drywall tape that does not require joint compound to achieve its fire rating.

6-in. or 12-in. taping knife. You need a very light touch at the intersection—just skim the surface with the edge of the knife to avoid marking up the other seam. Blending the two seams together when they are both wet can be tricky, so an alternative is to apply the second coat on the corner and allow it to dry before second coating the intersecting seam.

Third coat

Apply the final coat of joint compound to the outside corners in the same way you final-coated the seams—with a 12-in. taping knife or a roller (see p. 102). For the final coat, use either an all-purpose compound or a topping compound (my preference).

Apply a thin layer over the entire taped area, going 1 in. or so wider than the last coat. Feather the joint compound with a 12-in. taping knife. Remove most of the compound, leaving only enough to smooth the bead and feather the edge into the drywall surface.

A final check

After you've applied the final coat and before you start sanding, walk through each room to check that the taping job is satisfactory. Look over the seams and corners, checking for indentations, scratches, and areas where the tape shows through. Touch up any imperfections with a thin application of joint compound before going on to the finish-sanding process (see Chapter 5). If anything requires special attention, such as a crack, a crowned seam, or an overcut outlet box, correct them before you begin sanding.

Skim Coating

If you follow the detailed instructions given up to this point for applying the first, second, and third coats, you'll achieve what the industry calls a level 4 finish (see the appendix on p. 212). To take the job to a level 5 finish, you need to apply a skim coat of compound over the entire drywall surface.

Skim coating is recommended if the surface will be highlighted by bright lights or if you plan to decorate the walls with paint that has a glossy (or even eggshell) finish or a thin wallcovering. If you tape only the joints and fasteners, the porosity of the untaped paper surfaces will differ from that of the taped surfaces. In addition, the texture will be different; the taped surfaces will be smooth and fine, the paper surface will be a little rougher. In areas that have been sanded lightly, the paper fibers will be raised. These differences are magnified by certain paint and lighting.

Remodeling is another instance where you might consider skim coating drywall; for example, if you're trying to blend new drywall panels with an existing painted surface. A skim coat helps minimize the textural differences between the surfaces as well as variances in absorption.

To apply a skim coat, thin down a topping compound. The compound should not be runny, but it should be thin enough to trowel or roll on easily. For larger areas, I like to use a paint roller. Work a 30-sq.-ft to 40-sq.-ft. area at a time, so that the compound doesn't dry out before you smooth it. Once you have the area covered with a thin coat, use a 12-in. taping knife to smooth the surface and remove some of the compound. The end result should be a smooth surface that is free of tool marks and ridges.

As you can imagine, skim coating to create a level 5 finish is time-consuming work. To do a good job, you need good lighting and a finisher who really understands the process. Otherwise, it can create and uneven surface covered with tool marks and even air bubbles. Because of the time and skill required, level 5 finishes are not frequently applied.

Thank goodness a number of drywall and related companies have come up with an alternative to skim coating. Spray on finishes can be applied over a sanded level 4 finish to

THINK AHEAD
As you apply the third coat, note any areas that require additional feathering or filling. You must take care of them before you sand.

ONE-DAY TAPING

The taping method described in this chapter can take anywhere from 48 to 72 hours to complete (from the application of the first coat to the thorough drying of the third coat). That's fine when you're working through an entire house, but there are times when it's desirable to do all the taping in one day. Fortunately, fast-drying setting-type compounds allow you to do just that.

Setting-type joint compounds harden chemically in anywhere from 20 minutes or 30 minutes to 4 hours or 5 hours, depending on the type used. The compounds with the shortest setting times are ideal for one-day finishing. All three coats can be applied in the same day; if the taper is skilled enough, only two coats are necessary (the compound can be applied more heavily, because there is very little shrinkage as it sets up). Proper temperature, humidity, and airflow help complete the taping process in one day. The sequence of steps for one-day taping is as follows:

1. Embed the tape on seams and in corners, and cover any corner bead.

2. Apply the first coat to the fasteners.

3. Apply the second coat to all taped areas as soon as the first coat has set up.

Steps 1 through 3 should be complete by the middle of the working day. Use a compound that sets up in 2 hours or less, or mix the joint compound before you need it, to shorten the setting time after it is applied. (If that isn't fast enough for you, there are liquid and powder accelerants that speed up the setting time. They can turn a 90-minute compound into a 20-minute compound.)

4. After the second coat has hardened, apply the third coat. Use an all-purpose ready-mixed compound or a topping compound for this thin, final coat. These compounds are easier to work with and sand when the third coat is dry.

achieve a level 5. Now, a high-quality finish can be achieved by simply spraying on one of these products. Most of the spray-on coatings that I have seen or used are applied quite heavy (between 15 and 20 mils wet). For that reason, it can't be backrolled (sprayed and then rolled out while still wet). But all of these products equalize the differences in porosity and texture just like a skim coat of joint compound. Another advantage is that most also prime the surface for painting at the same time.

Roll out a skim coat A skim coat provides the highest level of drywall finish, referred to as a level 5 finish. Here, the author is using a roller to apply the skim coat. The compound will be removed with a wide taping knife.

Cut the drying time Accelerants can be added to setting-type compounds to make them set up faster, changing a 90-minute compound to a 20-minute product.

Or knife it on You can also apply the skim coat with a large taping knife.

Leave a thin film Smooth the compound with a taping knife. As you work, the knife removes excess compound, leaving only a thin film. The finish should be perfectly smooth with few tool marks.

LEVELS OF DRYWALL FINISHING

If you're a professional, it's important to be as specific as possible when drawing up a contract for a drywalling job. I've seen contracts where the finished taping job is referred to in such vague terms as "taped to industry standards" or "taped to a workman-like finish."

This type of language can lead to problems. I know a taper who never received his final payment, because the owner wasn't satisfied with the finished taping job. It seems the owner did his final inspection with the help of a 500-watt halogen light, and he found a lot of little problems that he wanted fixed (never mind that the surface would never be exposed to that type of lighting again).

In an effort to prevent these types of misunderstandings, four major trade associations developed Recommended Levels of Gypsum Board Finish, a document that does a great job of explaining the levels of finishing and where specific finishes are best suited. (The relevant sections of this document are reproduced in the appendix on p. 212.)

To summarize, there are a number of factors to consider before you begin a taping job. These include the following:

- The degree of decorative treatment desired.
- The type and angle of surface lighting.
- The choice of paint and the method of application.
- The finish of the wall-covering material.

Factors that require a high level of finishing include the following:

- Critical lighting conditions.
- Any paint with a glossy (or even eggshell) sheen as a final finish.
- Thin wall coverings as a final finish.

Factors that require a lower level of finishing include the following:

- Textured surface as a final finish.
- Heavy-grade wall coverings as a final finish.

MECHANICAL TAPING

In Chapter 2, I gave a quick overview of the mechanical taping tools available. In this section, I'll briefly describe how each tool is used. If you want more information, many manufacturers offer classes on how to use their products. In some cases, you can rent the tools to get the feel for them and to see if you like them.

Don't expect these tools to turn you into a master taper overnight. They are quite heavy, and it will take some time to get used to them. In most cases, the taper must push the tool along the seam and use manual pressure to force the compound through the tool.

The basic tool is the automatic taper, which applies the tape and the proper amount

Spray it on A level 5 finish can be spray applied over a finished level 4.

WORK SMART

When applying a skim coat, remember that the inside corners have already been coated, so there is no need to cover those areas again.

MECHANICAL VS. HAND TAPING

The pros and cons of each taping method are listed here.

MECHANICAL TAPING

- Produces consistent uniform results.

- Once mastered (usually only a day or two), is faster than hand taping, especially on larger jobs.

- Often requires a class to learn proper use.

- Requires only some of the tools. For example, you can use only boxes for finishing seams.

- Requires tools that are quite expensive to rent or purchase; need to use them on a regular basis to offset the cost.

- Requires less sanding than hand-taped jobs.

- Doesn't require an entire set of tools for each person. Two or three people can stay busy with only one set.

HAND TAPING

- Is always necessary for difficult sections and areas that need special attention, such as crowned seams.

- Takes quite a while to master.

- Doesn't require a large investment to obtain a complete set of tools.

of joint compound simultaneously as the tool head is rolled along the seam or inside corner. After the tape and compound are applied, a corner roller is used to embed the tape in the inside corners. A 3-in. adjustable corner finisher is used to clean and feather the compound after the corner roller embeds the tape. The corner finisher can also apply and smooth the finish coat on the inside corners; to do this, joint compound must flow into the finisher and then onto the corner.

An angle applicator is essentially a box attached to the corner finisher and filled with joint compound. The joint compound is forced out of the box and through the corner finisher, which in turn smoothes and feathers the joint compound.

Flat boxes, also known as mud boxes, are used to apply and smooth joint compound over taped joints during the second and third coats. What I like most about them is the uniform results they produce. Flat boxes come in three widths—7 in., 10 in., and 12 in. I use a combination of 10-in. and 12-in. boxes. The box width determines the seam width, but you can adjust the blade trowel edge to achieve a precise crown on the compound.

Joint-compound loading pumps (or mud pumps) are designed for the many tools that need to be filled with joint compound. The pump comes with different attachments that fill the automatic taper and the mud boxes. The drywall pump that I use is lightweight, stable, and easy to clean, and it has a reversible handle for left- or right-handed pumping.

For those people who like the idea of automatic tools but don't want to spend so much money, or simply can't justify buying an automatic taper because it isn't always the best choice of tools, there are less expensive, more basic tools available. With these, a long tube is filled with thinned compound and then a special mud shoe (they come in various styles for different jobs) is attached

to the end. As the compound is forced out of the tube through the mud shoe the proper amount of compound is applied to the seam or inside corner. The tape is then applied and embedded by hand.

TAPING PROBLEMS

As is probably obvious if you've read this far, the joints between panels can be a potential problem area. Some problems become apparent during taping, whereas others may not be noticeable until after the surface has been painted. In this section, I'll describe the most common problems, explain how to correct them, and suggest ways to avoid them in the first place.

Photographing

Photographing can occur when a wall or ceiling is coated with glossy paint (including high-gloss, semigloss, and satin finishes).

MECHANICAL TAPING TOOLS

The basis of mechanical taping tools is the mud pump, which has a variety of nozzles for fitting different taping tools: from an automatic taper, which applies both the tape and the proper amount of compound in a single pass, to flat boxes and angle boxes.

1. Tape and mud in one pass
An automatic taper simultaneously applies tape and joint compound to a joint.

2. Embed the tape
After the tape and compound are applied to an inside corner with an automatic taper, a corner roller is used to embed the tape.

3. Smooth the walls
A flat box applies joint compound over taped seams: 7-in., 10-in., and 12-in. boxes are available.

4. Clean up the corners
A corner finisher is designed to follow a corner roller. It smooths excess compound left during the embedding process.

5. Finish the corners
An angle box has a corner finisher attachment that is used to apply the final coat to an inside corner.

Under direct natural light, the seams and strips of taped fasteners may still show through, even though they were taped and sanded correctly. This is because the panel surface and the taped joints have different porosities and textures. This condition can be prevented by skim coating the entire surface before painting or by applying a good-quality primer-sealer or a flat latex paint before applying the finish coat of paint (see Chapter 8). If you notice photographing after the drywall has been painted, lightly sand the surface using 150-grit sandpaper, and then paint it with a good-quality flat latex paint before recoating it with the finish paint.

Crowned and concave seams

Crowned seams occur when taping compound is applied too heavily and the center of the seam is left higher than the surface of the panels. When light shines across the seams, they become quite obvious. If the seams have not been painted, the crowned areas can be sanded down with 120-grit or 150-grit paper. If they have already been painted, it is difficult to sand these areas, which is why it's important to look for crowned seams during

Painting reveals flaws Even after painting, seams and taped fasteners may be visible in certain light. This condition is called photographing.

HAND-POWERED COMPOUND TUBES

More economical than mud pumps are simple automatic tools that use hand pressure to force compound out of a tube and through a mud shoe attachment. When using these tools, tape is usually still applied and embedded the old fashioned way—by hand. But there are tools available to apply and embed the tape.

1. Lay on the compound
Compound is applied to an inside corner for the final coat using hand pressure to force compound out of a tube.

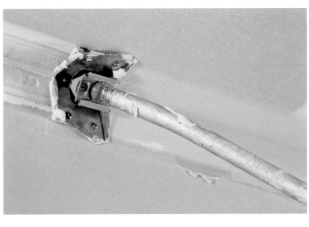

2. Finish the taping
The compound is then smoothed out with a corner finishing head.

the final check. You can conceal the seams by widening the band of compound on each side of the crowned area. Feather the joint compound on each side, being careful not to raise the crowned area any higher. Check the joint with a straightedge when the compound is dry. If the crown has been corrected, apply a finish coat of compound before sanding.

Concave seams are the exact opposite of crowned seams. These defects, which appear

THINK AHEAD

Using a tape-on or glue-on corner bead greatly reduces problems with edge cracking in the first place.

Settling can cause trouble There are three butted seams on this 10-ft. high wall. Care must be taken when taping to reduce the bumps created. If the seams rise as the building dries out or settles, the joint will have to be feathered out again.

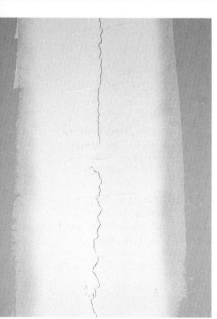

TOP: Pitting is caused when small air bubbles remain in the joint compound.

ABOVE: If it dries too fast Cracked seams can occur when the taping compound dries too quickly or is applied too thickly.

as slight depressions along the taped seams when light shines across the joints, are usually the result of not applying the joint compound heavily enough during the second coat. Oversanding also causes concave seams. To correct the problem, reapply the second and third coats of joint compound.

Pitting

Pitting looks like a series of small pits or craters on the taped finish surface. The pits are small air bubbles that were not properly filled or that were exposed during sanding. Air bubbles result from overmixing or undermixing the joint compound. Small air bubbles may also appear on a wet surface if insufficient pressure is applied when smoothing the joint compound.

If a large number of air bubbles appear as you tape, keep going over the joints with the trowel, applying more pressure until most of the bubbles are gone. Going the opposite direction with the trowel also helps reduce bubbles. If you don't notice the bubbles until the surface has been painted, apply a thin finish coat over the problem areas. Then sand and prime the areas before repainting.

Cracked and shrinking seams

If seams crack during the taping process, it's usually because the joint compound dried too quickly—often as a result of direct high heat or sunlight. As long as the tape and the joint compound are still solid, you can retape the cracked area. Make sure that the seam is thoroughly dry and use enough pressure to force the compound into the crack. If the tape is cracked or the compound is loose, you'll have to remove the affected areas. Cracked seams can be avoided by lowering the heat to increase the drying time. If the outside temperature is warm (above 80°F), close the windows so the airflow won't dry the compound too quickly.

Although it may sound contradictory, cracked seams may also result from joint compound drying too slowly. If a second coat is applied over a first coat that is still damp, the compound may shrink excessively. As the compound dries, cracks form where the compound is thickest. Any loose areas should be removed and filled with joint compound before retaping and finishing. To avoid this problem, make sure the building is heated more efficiently (to at least 60°F to 65°F) and keep the humidity low by opening or closing windows, running fans, raising the temperature, and using a dehumidifier. In addition, make sure the previous coat of joint compound is thoroughly dry before applying the next coat.

Shrinkage that appears along the center of taped seams after sanding is a related problem that is also caused by taping over joint compound that has not thoroughly dried. Remember that joint compound usually dries on the outside edges first, so a seam that appears dry may still be wet underneath. To correct the slightly recessed area caused by shrinkage, apply a layer of compound to fill the area, and then sand it lightly.

Bubbled tape

Bubbled or loose paper tape is caused by a poor bond between the tape and the joint compound. If the tape is not properly embedded in the compound, it can come loose and raise a bubble. The bubble may be a round spot only 1/2 in. in diameter, or it may run the entire length of a seam. Small bubbles can be cut out with a utility knife and retaped. For larger, loose areas, remove the entire section of tape and embed new tape, then apply a second and a third coat of joint compound. To avoid bubbled or loose tape, make sure that you apply a thick enough layer of joint compound before you embed the tape and apply enough pressure with the taping knife to embed it properly.

Popped nails and screws

Nail and screw pops don't usually show up until several months or years after the original taping job, but they do occasionally become apparent before painting. When sanding fasteners, a pole sander applies quite a bit of pressure against the panel. If a screw or nail has not pulled the panel tight against the framing, the pressure of the pole sander can push the panel tight and pop the fasteners,

raising a pronounced bump on the surface or exposing the fastener head.

If fastener pops appear before you paint, refasten the panel while applying hand pressure next to the fastener to ensure that the panel is tight against the framing. The loose screws or nails should be reset or removed. Retape the fasteners with three thin coats of joint compound. If the drywall surface is damaged around the fastener, first place a piece of mesh tape over the damaged area. (For more on repairing fastener pops, see Chapter 7.)

Cracked or loose corner bead

Sometimes you'll find a crack that looks as if someone has drawn a line with a pencil about 1 in. or so in from the corner along the length of the bead. Or the corner will appear wrinkled, with some compound missing here and there. The corner bead can also be ridged out, creating an indentation where it meets the wall. These problems are more common with nail- or crimp-on metal beads and are usually the result of structural movement or settling.

To repair the crack, remove loose material, nail again where necessary, and apply a layer or two of joint compound to refinish the bead. Make sure that there is a 1/2-in. gap between the bead and the floor.

ABOVE: As the building ages This crack along the edge of a metal corner is the result of structural settling.

BELOW: Paper tape reduces cracks One way to help reduce cracking along the edge of a metal bead is to reinforce the border with paper tape.

CHAPTER

5

Sanding

If taping is my favorite part of a drywalling job, I'd have to say that sanding is my least favorite. The dust makes the job unpleasant, and it is tedious, time-consuming, and fairly difficult work. It takes me almost as much time to sand and clean up as it does to apply one coat of joint compound (just under an hour for a typical 12-ft. by 12-ft. room). However, sanding is the final step in the drywalling process. And, in my opinion, it's also the most important. It's your last chance before painting to turn a so-so taping job into a quality finished job.

Some tapers claim to be so skillful at taping that they don't need to sand at all. In my experience as a drywall contractor, however, I believe that a beautiful finished job requires at least some sanding after the final coat. (Depending on your taping ability, you may need to sand between coats as well, as discussed on p. 100.) Nevertheless, there are times when I have not sanded ceilings prior to texturing. In most light, those ceilings look just fine. Most customers, however, aren't satisfied with a finished job that looks good in most light. They want a job that looks good all the time and in any light.

Aim for a uniform surface The goal of sanding is to smooth out the joint compound and to blend the edges into the drywall face paper so that you're left with a flat, uniform surface.

Make sure the mask fits snugly. When you breathe, air should not enter around the edges. If air does get in, you'll notice white dust on your face around the edges of the mask when you take it off after sanding. Change the filter or mask when breathing becomes difficult. It's also a good idea to wear a hat and a pair of safety goggles for protection against fine dust, especially when you're sanding overhead.

Attaching a sander to a shop vac can keep up to 95 percent of the sanding dust from becoming airborne. This greatly reduces the worker's exposure to dust and helps keep the area cleaner. Pole sanders also reduce your exposure to dust, because you stand farther away from the work surface.

The goal of sanding is to remove excess joint compound, smooth out tool and lap marks, flatten crowned areas, and feather the edges of compound to blend into untaped surfaces. Because you have to sand all taped seams, corners, and fastener heads, you end up going over a large percentage of the drywall surface. For that reason, give yourself plenty of time to sand. A rushed sanding job can compromise even the best hanging and taping job. But if you take your time and have the right attitude (just keep in mind that once you're done you can start painting), the results are rewarding.

GETTING READY TO SAND

Protect yourself

Sanding drywall joint compound generates a lot of dust. Many of the ingredients in joint compound, such as talc, calcite, mica, gypsum, silica, and clay, can irritate your eyes, nose, throat, and respiratory tract. Protect yourself by ventilating the room and wearing a dust mask that is approved for protection against nontoxic dust and mist.

Protect the workplace

You not only need to protect yourself while sanding, but also the room you're working in. Most likely, a lot of the protection has already been put in place. When it comes time to sand, however, you may need to tighten things up a bit (unless, of course, you're drywalling in new construction). On a remodeling job, remove all furnishings or cover them with drop cloths and plastic before drywalling. The fine dust generated during sanding can infiltrate the tiniest of cracks, so make sure you seal under all doors (including kitchen cabinets) to keep the dust from spreading. Seal the edges of the plastic with masking tape.

Try to contain the dust within the work area. And resist the temptation to open all the windows—it can create a draft that may actually push dust into other parts of the building. Instead, install a fan in a window to blow air out of the work area and get the dust moving in the right direction. In addition, hang plastic over doorways to isolate the rooms where you are working from other areas.

THINK AHEAD

To keep out dust, cover the front of kitchen cabinets and built-ins with plastic sheeting. Seal the entire perimeter of the sheeting with masking or painter's tape.

MANAGING DUST

The fine dust particles created during sanding are, at the very least, a nuisance. The dust is inevitable, but also manageable—collect or expel as much of the resulting dust as possible. Always protect your eyes and wear a dust mask approved for protection against nontoxic dust and mist. The mask should fit comfortably and form a tight seal around the edges.

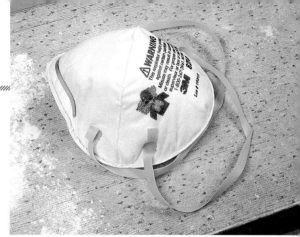

Create less dust
Certain types of compound cut down on the amount of dust that lingers in the air as you sand. Dust still falls to the floor, but using the right compound helps create a more comfortable workplace.

Blow the dust outside
To pull dust out of a room, install a portable fan in a window and close off other openings. Closing off other openings helps create a vacuum to prevent dust from entering other rooms.

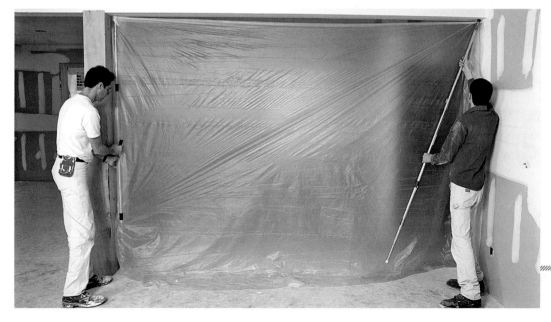

Seal off living space
To protect areas from dust and debris, create a temporary wall with light plastic. The telescopic poles shown here hold the plastic against the ceiling and the floor.

ROUGH SAND WITH A POLE SANDER

A pole sander outfitted with 150-grit or finer paper makes quick work of rough sanding the fastners, seams, and corners. Done correctly, rough sanding eliminates the worst spots of a sanding job.

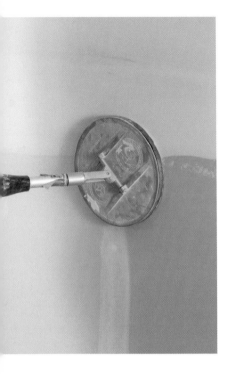

1. Sand fasteners first
By sanding strips of fasteners prior to sanding seams, you reduce the likelihood of scuffing up the seams.

2. Finish off the walls
Using a 4-ft.-long or longer handle allows for plenty of leverage and it keeps you at least an arms length away from falling dust.

3. Get close to your work
Working on stilts makes it easier to sand ceilings and high areas. Wear goggles or glasses to protect your eyes from dust.

THE SANDING PROCESS

I have a variety of sanders that hook up to a vacuum. Some have rotating and vibrating heads and some work just like regular pole sanders, which require physical movement to sand. If I'm concerned about dust control, these are the sanders I choose.

If electric sanding tools aren't specifically made for sanding joint compound, I'd stay away from them. I do most of my sanding with hand tools (primarily a pole sander). Following the right steps, the work moves swiftly.

Sanding is a two-step process. I first use a pole sander to remove excess joint compound, such as marks left by taping tools, crowned areas where too much compound was applied, and intersecting joints that need blending. I call this the rough sanding stage. To finish up, I do a final sanding using one or more hand tools.

A pole sander fitted with a 150-grit sanding screen or paper does an excellent job of smoothing out 95 percent of the taped surfaces. If you're sanding a nice, smooth taping job, you can use an even finer grit. On areas where an ultrasmooth finish is a must I go over the sanded surface with 180- or 220-grit to eliminate any scratches in the compound and to smooth out roughed-up paper. When sanding, try to avoid scuffing up the drywall face paper by staying close to taped areas. The finer grits work better with lightweight joint compounds or with topping compounds, which are slightly softer than all-purpose compound and scratch more easily with the coarser grits of sandpaper.

Start by sanding the screw or nail heads lightly in the direction of the strip of joint compound. Check the edges to make sure they are smooth. When sanding screws, you'll be putting pressure on the drywall around the screw head. If the screw has not properly pulled the drywall panel tight against the framing, it may pop loose under the pressure. The joint compound may come off the screw head, or you may see the drywall move in and out around the screw. To correct the problem, use a Phillips screwdriver and turn the screw until it is tight again. If it goes in too deep or does not tighten up, place another screw

about 1 1/2 in. away and then retape the area with three coats of joint compound.

After sanding the fasteners, use gentle, even pressure to push the pole sander along the seams and outside corners. Always work in the direction of the seam or corner. Keep the edges smooth and sand down any high spots or chunks of joint compound on the seams. Run the pole sander over the entire taped area. Be especially careful when sanding inside corners, because there is only a thin layer of joint compound covering the paper tape. Blend in the edges smoothly, and go along the inside edge only lightly with the pole sander. The inside edge will be finish sanded later with a hand sander, dry sanding sponge, or a folded piece of sandpaper.

Even though you can reach most ceilings with a pole sander, I prefer to work on stilts. Using stilts gets me closer to the ceiling, where I can better see the area I'm sanding. Most of the dust then settles away from my face instead of on it. The work is also less strenuous. (Wear safety goggles or glasses to help keep the dust out of your eyes.)

Note troublespots This is your last chance to correct problem areas. If you do any repairs that will need sanding, make a note on the compound next to the area.

CHECKING FOR PROBLEM SEAMS

Hold the straight edge of a wide trowel across the seam to check for crowns and recesses.

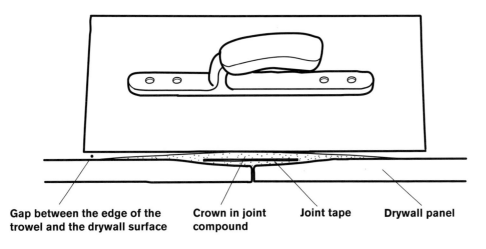

Gap between the edge of the trowel and the drywall surface **Crown in joint compound** **Joint tape** **Drywall panel**

OVERSANDING

If you sand too much (a common problem with beginners) and expose the joint tape or damage the drywall face paper, you may have to reapply the third coat of joint compound. In more serious cases, you may need to reapply the second as well as the third coat.

If your sandpaper is too coarse, you may scratch the compound or drywall face paper. If you do, lightly sand the surface with a finer sandpaper or with a sanding screen (200 grit usually works well). If the scratches still show, apply a thin finish coat of compound and lightly sand it again when dry.

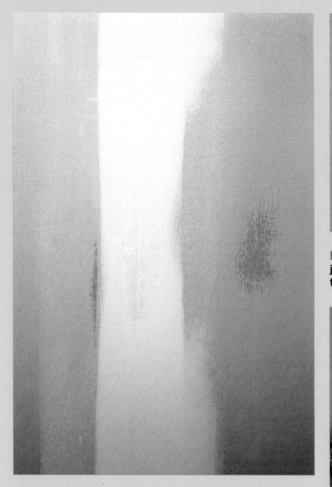

Sand only the compound Oversanding can damage face paper and seams. This area will need another coat of joint compound.

Don't ask for too much Some scratches and dents in the joint compound are too deep to remove without oversanding the entire area.

Fill the flow Rather than trying to sand out the scratch, fill the area with a thin layer of joint compound and then sand it again after the compound has dried.

FINISH SAND BY HAND

Final sanding is best done up close and by hand. Various techniques and sanding tools ease the process.

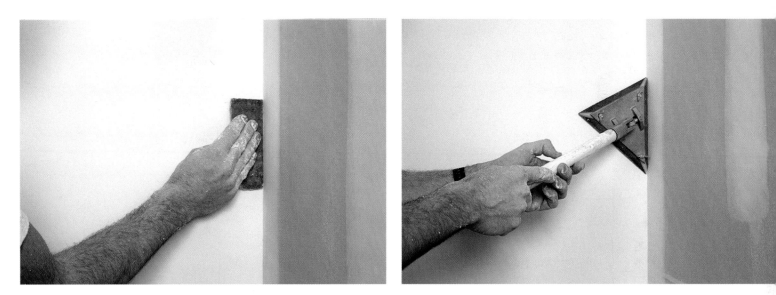

Folded sandpaper for tight spots
Folding a piece of sandpaper is a low-tech but effective method for sanding in tight spots.

Triangular sanders for corners
A triangular sander is an excellent tool for producing inside corners that are clean and straight.

Sponges fit any job
An angled, fine-grid sanding sponge also works well to touch up inside corners. Sanding sponges come in an array of sizes and pro-files to make sanding easier.

WORK SMART

Use a triangle-shaped sander to get into tight spots. The thin edges clean up inside corners and the points get right into intersections.

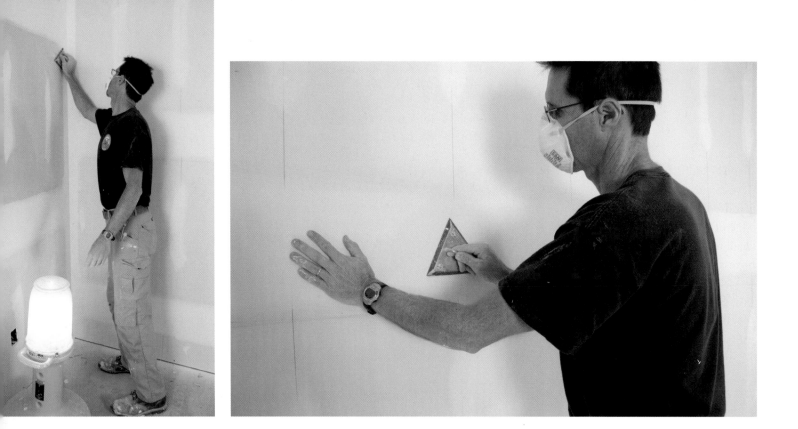

ABOVE: Cast light on the subject Shinning a bright light helps highlight problem areas during final sanding.

ABOVE RIGHT: Feel your way through As you go over taped areas with a hand sander, look and feel for defects that need to be sanded out or patched.

Don't try to remove every last defect with the pole sander—you may sand out the scratch or dent but in the process oversand the entire area. Some defects may need to be filled with joint compound and then sanded again later, so it's a good idea to keep a trowel with a small amount of joint compound handy. So they won't be overlooked, fill in the defects as you go along. But keep in mind, this is your last chance to correct any problems. If you do any repairs that will need sanding, make a note on the compound next to the area.

If you notice a seam that is indented or slightly crowned, you may need to apply a third coat of joint compound, or in a worse case, a second and a third coat. A good way to check whether a seam is crowned too much is to hold the edge of a wide trowel across it (see the drawing on p. 123). If the trowel rocks more than 1/16 in. on either side of the center of the seam, try sanding out the crown, if this does not correct them you may want to widen the seam by feathering out the joint compound on each side, being careful

not to add any to the crowned center. If the trowel indicates a recess of more than 1/16 in., fill in the seam with joint compound and then reapply a third coat.

Finish sanding

After all the taped surfaces have been sanded with a pole sander, I switch to a hand sander for the finish sanding. I also use a dry sanding sponge or a folded piece of sandpaper or sanding screen for the finish work. Before you get started, make sure you have adequate lighting. A bright light shining along a wall or a ceiling helps highlight defects or problems you may not see with poor lighting or with natural lighting alone (see the photo above left).

Use a hand sander fitted with 150-grit or finer sandpaper or sanding screen and go over all the seams, corners, and fasteners. Look and feel for any defects. Lightly sand problem areas and any edges that are not feathered properly. Once again, remember not to oversand. If a defect is deep or if you sand through to the tape, repair the area with a thin coat of joint compound. Mark those areas with a pencil (a pen or marker bleeds through most paints) and resand them, if necessary.

Use a dry sanding sponge, a triangle-shaped sander, or a folded piece of sandpaper to smooth small defects. I prefer to use a fine-grit dry sanding sponge to smooth the inside edge of an inside corner and for most of the small touch ups. Be careful around electrical boxes, because drywall face paper tears easily where it has been cut. I use a folded piece of sandpaper or a sanding screen to get into spots where other sanders can't reach and to prevent damaging the area around a defect.

Make sure you remove or sand hardened chunks of joint compound from taped seams and corners wherever they butt up against the floor, a window, or a door. These areas must be smooth so the trim or casing can lie flat against the wall. Use the corner of a taping knife to clean out hardened compound from electrical boxes (be careful not to cut the wires!). A dry sanding sponge is still a sponge—though it cuts down on ridges, it may smooth areas rather than flatten them. In these cases, a slight bump will show after painting. Also use caution when you're sanding bullnose corner beads with a sanding sponge—they can easily expose the raised edge along the bead.

Sanding a level 5 finish

When a thin film of compound has been applied over the entire surface to achieve a level 5 finish, there is usually very little sanding to do. Look the area over while shining a bright light on the surface. Where necessary, sand with an extra fine grit sandpaper. Don't forget the reason a level 5 finish was applied in the first place—to equalize all he different textures and porosities created during the taping and sanding process. Even if you aren't applying a level 5 finish, take great care to minimize all the slight differences, because

you never really know what the final decoration will be or what kind of lighting might be installed in the future.

WET SANDING

Occasionally, you may be working on a job where no dust at all is acceptable—for example, in an office building that contains sensitive computer equipment or in a home where a family member is allergic to dust particles. Even with careful covering and sealing of the work area, the fine dust that sanding creates is still going to get into unwanted areas.

Consider wet sanding, or sponging, for such cases. Because joint compound is water-soluble, you can blend the edges of taped areas and small defects with a wet sponge. When only a small touchup is required, an all-purpose household sponge or a smooth, soft cloth works effectively. For a larger wet sanding job, use a high-density polyurethane sponge made specifically for this purpose. The drywall sponge has small cells that retain water without excessive dripping.

To wet sand, dip the sponge in clean, cool water that is free of soap or additives. Wring out just enough water to eliminate dripping. Clean the sponge frequently as you work. As

TOP: Work down to the floor Out-of-the-way areas like the bottoms of inside and outside corners must be smooth and clean so that trim work will fit tight to the wall.

ABOVE: Corners can be delicate When sanding bullnose cornerbeads, it's easy to oversand and expose the beaded edge. A more rigid sander reduces this problem.

Wet sanding reduces dust
When wet sanding, use a wet (not dripping) sponge to smooth out taped areas. Rub the sponge back and forth in the direction of the seam, corner, or strip of fasteners.

you would when dry sanding, rub the sponge in the direction of the seam or corner. Avoid rubbing across a seam or into a corner too much, because this may cause rippling in the finish. Use as few strokes as possible, and be careful not to soak the joint compound. If the sponge is too wet, water may run down the walls, leaving visible streaks when dry. In addition, avoid excessively wetting the drywall paper, because it can rip easily when wet.

Although wet sanding is effective for blending the edges of taped seams and small defects, it doesn't work so well on ridges and larger chunks. Unlike sandpaper, which cuts down excess compound, a sponge only blends or rounds over an area. If you plan to wet sand, make sure you do an excellent taping job. After the third coat of joint compound is dry, examine the surface carefully, using a bright light to help highlight any problem areas. Apply a thin coat of joint compound to defective areas and allow it to dry before wet sanding.

As you work, don't forget these final cautions and reminders:

• Take your time.

• Wear appropriate protection.

• Use appropriate sanders and grits for the situation.

• Be aware that different compounds sand differently.

• Always have good lighting that you move along with you as you sand.

DRY SANDING VS. WET SANDING

DRY SANDING

ADVANTAGES	DISADVANTAGES
Cuts down high spots easily	Very dusty
Most crowns and edges can be sanded out	Easy to oversand
Faster than wet sanding	Need to wear a dust mask
A pole sander can be used to reach high areas without a bench or scaffold	
Excellent results after three coats of joint compound	

WET SANDING

ADVANTAGES	DISADVANTAGES
Not dusty	Requires a better taping job
Requires fewer tools	Will not correct large defects
Easier cleanup of work areas	Just blends the area
No need to wear a dust mask	Slower than dry sanding

- Try to find out what the final decoration will be for each critical area. You may need to bring the finish up to another level even at this late stage.

- Make sure you show respect for the trades that will follow.

GENERAL CLEANUP

After you've finished sanding, you can begin cleaning up. I use a wet/dry vacuum cleaner for this task, making sure to vacuum (or brush) out all the electrical boxes and remove dust from around window and door frames and along floor edges against walls. It's a real pain to have your brush or roller pick up dust or chunks of compound while painting, so do a thorough job.

In new construction, I recommend scraping hardened chunks of compound off the floor and then sweeping up the mess. A vacuum or a wet mop will pick up most of the remaining dust. If you've used drop cloths and plastic, carefully roll them up and shake them off outside. You'll probably still need to vacuum the floor or carpet, especially around the edges.

DUST-FREE SANDERS

For sanding jobs where you really need to keep dust to a minimum, try using a dust-free sander. This tool is a pole or hand sander with an attachment that fits onto a wet/dry vacuum. It is used in exactly the same way as a regular pole or hand sander. The only difference is that most of the dust ends up in the vacuum cleaner, not on the floor. The model I often use is designed as a pole sander, but you can remove the handle, reattach the hose, and use it as a hand sander as well.

Keep the dust wet This version of a dust-free sander further reduces dust by sucking it into a bucket of water.

ABOVE: Prevent scratches The sanding head on this tool rotates to cut down on the number of visible scratches seen in the finished job. It makes dust-free sanding fast and easy.

LEFT: You pick the sander This dust free sander is outfitted with a vibrating sanding head to make work easier on your arms.

6

Special Installations

If all walls were straight and square with no butted seams and all corners were 90 degrees, drywalling would be a rather mechanical and predictable job. But, as those who are trying their hand at drywalling will soon find out, problem areas, unusual seams, and off-angle corners present themselves sooner or later. Solutions to these situations may be as simple as having to install extra fasteners to meet fire-code regulations or as complicated as having to bend drywall panels around a curved wall with a very tight radius.

In this chapter, I'll explain how to tape off-angle corners, archways, and curved walls; how to handle butt joints; how to hang drywall next to a tub or shower; and how to install multiple layers of drywall. In addition, I'll walk through the process of using resilient steel channel, working with cement board, and using drywall as decoration.

Most of these special installations really aren't much harder than hanging drywall on a straight wall or ceiling, as long as you understand how to approach them and use the right techniques and materials.

OFF-ANGLE CORNERS

When a sloped ceiling meets a flat ceiling or a wall, the inside corner formed, which is usually much greater than 90 degrees, is known as an off-angle corner. It is important that these corners look straight. Giving these corners a beautiful straight center line shouldn't be difficult or time consuming to achieve. In addition to these types of corners being visible, they are also subject to cracking due to structural movement or settling.

Fortunately, there are a number of tapes and beads tailor-made for these situations. One of my favorite beads is a vinyl product that adjusts to different angles and has a flexible center to accommodate normal structural movement or settling. It takes a little extra work to install and finish, but the end result makes it well worth the work (see the photos on the facing page).

The center (creased area) of this bead should not receive a coat of joint compound. In fact, the very center should be completely clean after installation. Because there is no filling to make corrections later it is important to install the tapes as straight as possible. Begin by floating out any dips in the drywall with joint compound. After the compound dries, use a scrap piece of the bead to mark along the tape's legs at both ends of the run and snap a chalkline between the sets of marks. Apply an approved spray adhesive to the drywall (I spray on two quick coats). Press the tape into position immediately, using the chalkline as a guide.

This type of bead can also be embedded in joint compound. Apply the compound to the drywall and roll the bead into place, centering it as you go. Sight along the inside edge and make adjustments, if necessary. Then press down on the legs with a taping knife. The legs will be concealed with joint compound and blended into the drywall, but the flexible center must remain free of compound.

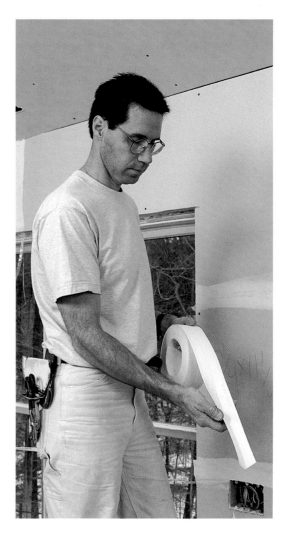

There are similar products that are adjustable to different angles but don't have a flexible center that stretches (they're simply hinged). If they are vinyl, apply them using the methods just mentioned. If they are not vinyl, embed them in compound. Use these beads only on angles that are less likely to crack due to structural movement.

Some of these tapes can be used on both inside and outside off-angle corners. For inside corners, install them by applying joint compound to the drywall and pressing the bead into place with a taping knife. When applying finish coats of compound, there is no need to apply compound to the center of the tape—just feather the edges. When used as an outside corner the tape is folded to

OFF-ANGLE INSIDE CORNERS

Vinyl corner bead can be glued to off-angle corners and then covered in compound. When finished correctly, the result is a nice, straight crease that provides excellent expansion control.

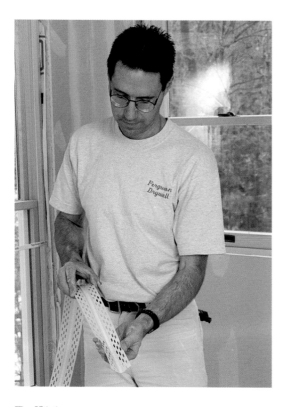

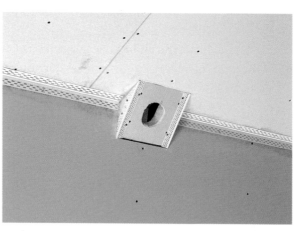

1. Glue it in place
The bead can be attached with spray-on contact cement and staples.

2. Or embed the tape
Corner bead can also be embedded in joint compound using a taping knife. Once the bead is set in place, sight down its length and adjust as needed.

Built to move
This inside corner bead has a rubber center that flexes to fit odd angles and stretches to accommodate settling.

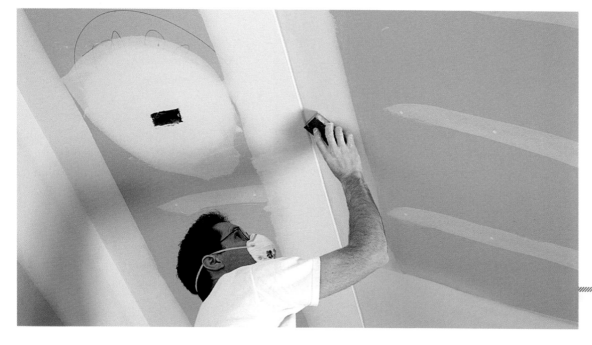

3. Keep creases clean
When properly taped and sanded, the sides of the joint are feathered into the drywall surface, but the center crease is free of compound.

WHY DO ANGLES CRACK?

COMMON REASONS FOR CRACKING

- Structural movement
- Snow load
- Materials dry out after construction
- Building spreads

WAYS TO PREVENT PROBLEMS

- Use a flexible inside tape or a wider stronger tape
- Control heat and humidity
- Use a stronger compound
- Use specially designed framing materials like X-crack®

Movement is inevitable Off-angle inside corners are subject to movement. It doesn't take much structural movement for most corner tapes to crack and come loose.

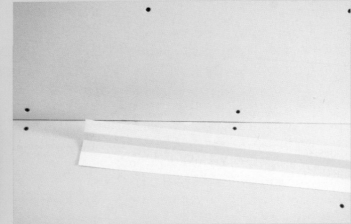

Use wide tape Wide, off-angle inside corner tapes, like this 4-in.-wide tape-on bead, prevent cracking because they're more forgiving as buildings settle and move.

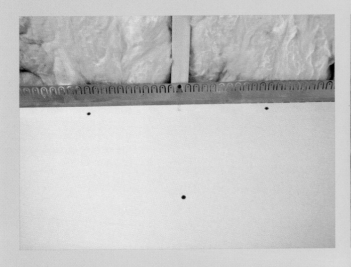

Straighten uneven framing X-crack is an adjustable hinged product that is attached to the corners of framing before drywall is set in place. It helps straighten uneven framing and reduces cracking.

Provide consistent heat The drywall environment needs consistent heat throughout. This heater actually causes more cracks than it prevents because it leaves some areas hot and others cold.

become a corner bead with a slightly beaded edge. These beads should be finished like any other outside corner (see Chapter 4). These products come in rolls, can be cut to length, and adjust to accommodate a wide range of angles.

Bullnose beads are also available for off-angle inside and outside corners. They come in standard lengths in metal, vinyl, or paper-covered metal or plastic. Bullnose beads are attached and finished in the same way as 90-degree corners (see Chapter 3). Keep the rounded edges as clean as possible during taping and sand any remaining compound off when dry.

Rounded corners technique

Before all of these new tapes and beads became available the options were pretty limited. To avoid crooked corners, I used regular paper tape embedded in compound. This method is not terribly strong and it is difficult to create straight finished lines . . . but it can work.

I have had a lot of success rounding these off-angle, inside corners. It is a good technique that I still use occasionally on unusually crooked corners where the new beads just won't work. I also use this technique if I am working in an older home and trying to match existing corners. For more on this process, see the drawing below and the photos on p. 136.

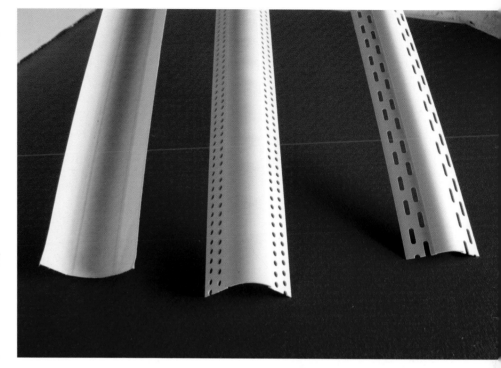

Options for corner bead
On the left is a bullnose inside corner bead. At center is a 90-degree bullnose bead and on the right is a ¾-in. bullnose off-angle outside corner bead.

ROUNDING AN INSIDE CORNER

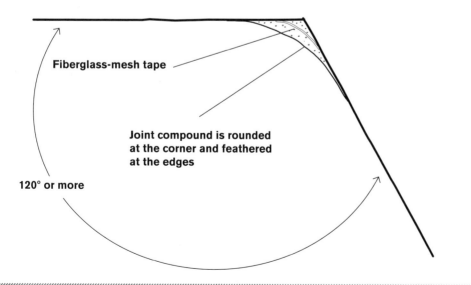

Fiberglass-mesh tape

Joint compound is rounded at the corner and feathered at the edges

120° or more

ROUNDING CORNERS TECHNIQUE

Rather than using beads to manage off-angle corners, tape can also be used. This technique comes in handy when you're trying to match existing joints in older homes, or if the corner is very crooked.

1. Tape the joint
When rounding an off-angle corner, begin by covering the angle with mesh tape.

2. Choose a setting-type compound
Use a 6-in. taping knife to apply a thin layer of setting-type joint compound about 4 in. or 5 in. wide on each side of the joint.

3. Begin rounding the corner
Pull the knife lightly across the corner in one direction for the length of the joint, and then pull the knife back across the corner in the opposite direction. The center of the joint should be filled and slightly rounded and the edges should be feathered.

4. Apply the second coat
Use a 12-in. knife to round the corners after applying the second coat in a manner similar to the first coat. This is still a relatively thick coat, so I advise using a setting compound.

5. Lay on the third coat
After sanding lightly, a paint roller works well to apply the third coat of joint compound. A regular drying-type compound can be used.

6. Finish the joint
Smooth the compound with a 12-in. knife, removing the bulk of the compound as you work.

Rounding makes the corner appear straight, even though it is slightly off, because there is no obvious interior angle. As with regular inside corners, rounded corners can be finished with three coats of joint compound. I recommend using fiberglass-mesh tape combined with a setting-type joint compound for the first coat. First, cover the corner with the mesh tape. If there are large gaps between panels or damaged sections, apply an additional piece of mesh tape to cover those areas. Next, use a 6-in. taping knife to apply a thin coat of joint compound to each side of the corner. At this stage, it's not necessary to cover the tape completely; a layer about 1/8 in. thick and 4 in. or 5 in. wide is sufficient.

Once you've applied the compound, pull the taping knife across the corner at a 90-degree angle. After you've gone across the corner in one direction, there will still be gaps and rough edges in the compound; to correct those areas, pull the knife across the corner in the opposite direction. Take your time, and don't apply too much pressure (very little joint compound should be removed if you're doing it right). As you pull the knife gently across the corner, feather the edges of the compound and slightly round the center. By now the tape should be completely covered and there should not be any large gaps or high ridges left by the knife.

For the second coat on a rounded corner, use a setting-type compound, an all-purpose compound, or a ready-mixed taping compound. I prefer to use a setting-type compound for this coat, because a pretty heavy layer of compound is left in the rounded area of the corner, which can result in excessive shrinkage if you use a drying type. Shrinkage can cause deep cracks that require taped reinforcement to correct.

Using a 6-in. knife, apply about the same amount of compound to each side of the corner as you did during the first coat. On this coat, use a 12-in. straight-handled knife to round the compound (see the bottom left photo on the facing page). Pull the trowel across the corner in one direction and then in the opposite direction, just as you did for the first coat. Once again, very little compound should be removed as the corner is rounded and the edges are feathered.

Before applying the third coat, lightly sand any high trowel marks and feather the edges with a pole sander and 120-grit sandpaper or sanding screen (be careful not to oversand or dig up the center areas). For the third coat, use a topping or an all-purpose ready-mixed compound. You can apply joint compound with a 6-in. or 12-in. knife, but I find that a roller works best, because it easily follows the curve of the rounded corner (see the bottom center photo on the facing page). Cover the entire taped area with a thin layer of joint compound, widening each edge. Then use a 12-in. trowel to remove the compound, in much the same way that the third coat on a regular seam is finished (see p. 102). All trowel marks and indentations should be filled, and only a thin film of compound should remain on the rest of the corner.

CURVED WALLS AND BARREL CEILINGS

Drywall can be formed to fit almost any curved surface, whether convex or concave. Depending on the radius of the curve, it can be applied wet or dry. The first curved surface I ever tried to drywall was a convex wall with a very short radius. At that time, the only advice I'd been given was to wet a regular 1/2-in. drywall panel and allow it to sit for a while before hanging it. Given my lack of experience, it's not surprising that I didn't have much luck with this job. I ended up having to cut the drywall, which I had wet on both sides, into narrow strips in order to get it to bend around the studs. After the narrow

WORK SMART

There is a heavy buildup of compound on a rounded corner. To resist cracking, be sure to use a setting-type compound for the first two coats.

than 15 in. Hanging these radii would be very difficult even with wet ¼-in. flexible drywall.

- Use ¼-in. flexible drywall on short-radius curves for both inside (concave) and outside (convex) curves. The drywall can be attached either parallel or perpendicular to the framing. Place the screws a maximum of 12 in. o.c. Two layers of 1/4-in. drywall are usually necessary for strength and to blend in with the 1/2-in. drywall used on straight sections of the wall. Apply one layer at a time, staggering the joints. If possible, avoid end joints butted on the curved surface of the wall.

- For curves with a tight radius (less than 32 in.), dampen the drywall so it can conform to the tight curve without breaking.

ABOVE: Bend it slowly
When fastening drywall to a concave surface, gently and slowing push it into place. Begin fastening at the center and work toward each edge. For tighter bends, you may have to fasten starting at the edge to prevent cracking.

RIGHT: Convex or concave surfaces ¼-in. drywall is flexible enough to bend around both concave and convex surfaces.

strips dried, I had to tape each seam and then skim-coat the entire surface.

Looking back, I realize what I did wrong. First, the wall was much too tightly curved to bend a 1/2-in. drywall panel around it. Second, I should not have wet both sides of the panel. Third, the studs were spaced too far apart for such a tight curve. If you are planning to attach drywall to a curved surface, here are a few important points to bear in mind:

- To avoid creating flat areas between studs, the framing should be closer together on curved walls than on straight walls. Maximum stud spacing is 9 in. o.c. for most curves; for really short radii, a maximum of 6 in. o.c. is recommended (see the chart on p. 141). Hopefully the builder has not built an inside curve that has a radius less than 20 in. or an outside curve with one less

Two ways to hang When attached to a tight curve, drywall can be positioned either horizontally or vertically. I prefer vertically as in this example.

Use two thin layers When attaching drywall to a barrel ceiling, stagger the joints between layers. Here, multiple layers of ¼-in. drywall are being attached with the curve to avoid butted seams.

Moisture helps it bend For tight curves, dampen the side of the panel that will be compressed.

WORK SMART

Drywall is more flexible along its length. However, it's a good idea to hang it perpendicular to the framing, because it is easier to conceal the joints when taping with the curve.

RIGHT: Sandwich the panels
Place the wet sides of two drywall panels together and let them sit for about an hour before attaching them. Tightly covering the assembly with plastic prevents the edges from drying out.

BELOW TOP: A clean finish
The very visible upper portion of this curved wall was skim coated (given a level 5 finish).

BELOW: Ease the transition
To create a transition between the bottom of the barrel ceiling and the walls, the author attached an additional, 3-in.-wide layer of drywall at the top of the wall.

Using a garden sprayer, a sponge, or a paint roller (see the bottom photo on p. 139), apply water to the side that will be compressed around the curve (i.e., the back of the panel on convex curves). For a 1/4-in., 4x8 panel, use about 30 oz. of water (35 oz. for a 3/8-in. panel, 45 oz. for a 1/2-in. panel). Stack the panels with the wet surfaces facing each other and let them sit for at least one hour before you attach them. Covering the panels with plastic prevents the edges from drying out. When the panels dry, they will return to their original hardness.

- When attaching drywall to the outside of a curved wall, start at one end of the curve and fasten it to the studs as it forms around the bend (see the bottom photo on p. 138). When drywalling the inside of a curved wall I was always told to start by attaching the panel at the center of the curve, but sometimes this will cause the panel to crack. I have had better luck working it over from an edge.

- If the drywall is wet, allow enough time for it to dry thoroughly before taping.

BENDING DRYWALL

DRY-BENDING REGULAR DRYWALL

THICKNESS	MINIMUM BENDING RADII
1/4 in.	3 ft.
3/8 in.	6 ft.
1/2 in.	12 ft.
5/8 in.	18 ft.

WET-BENDING REGULAR DRYWALL

THICKNESS	MINIMUM BENDING RADII	MAXIMUM STUD SPACING
1/4 in.	2 ft.	6 in.
3/8 in.	3 ft.	8 in.
1/2 in.	4 ft.	12 in.

> **WORK SMART**
>
> Even if the radius of a curve is large enough to apply flexible drywall without wetting it, pre-bow the panels for easier installation. Follow the directions on p. 74.

- When taping a curved wall you may want to finish to a level 5, because it is a very visible area.

ARCHWAYS

Drywalling a curved archway is a process similar to that of drywalling a curved wall. As with curved walls, 1/4-in. flexible drywall works best for short-radius archways (on gentler arches, use regular 1/4-in. or 1/2-in. drywall). Cut the drywall to the desired width

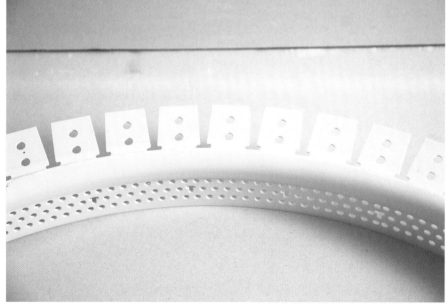

and approximate length. You can either start at the center and work toward the edges, or start at the spring line.

If you don't want to buy a whole sheet of 1/4-in. flexible drywall just to do one archway, you can use 1/2-in. regular drywall instead. In this case, score the back paper of the drywall strip at 1-in. intervals (or closer, if the curve is tight). As the strip is fastened into place around the arch, the back will separate at the

ABOVE: No notching necessary This bullnose archway bead is designed so that it is not necessary to notch the edge, which allows for easy finishing.

LEFT: Working with flexible drywall A piece of 1/4-inch flexible drywall works well for covering the bottom of an arch. Build up two layers of drywall before attaching beads.

THE SCORE AND BEND METHOD

Instead of using flexible drywall, regular drywall will bend to fit archways if the back paper is scored prior to application.

1. Score first
Half-inch drywall will conform to an archway if the back paper is scored at regular intervals across its width. The tighter the curve, the closer the cuts.

2. Set it in place
As the scored drywall conforms to the curve of the arch, screw it into place.

cuts, allowing the drywall to conform to the shape of the curve (see the photos at left). After the drywall has been attached to all sides of the archway, fasten corner bead to the outside edges.

There are a number of beads made specifically for arches. Most beads are available in square-edge and bullnose configurations. There is even an archway bead that comes in a 100-ft. roll; some are vinyl, others are made of a flexible pvc product, and others are paper-coated vinyl. All of these archway beads have one thing in common: They are precut at 1-in. intervals along one side, so that they can flex to fit the outside curve of the arch. Start at one end of the archway, fastening the bead as you go and keeping it snug against the wall and curved surface.

Once the corner bead has been fastened to the archway, attach a rigid, matching corner bead to the vertical sides of the opening. Make sure the surfaces are flush and fit together evenly where the two corner beads butt together. Apply joint compound to the corner bead on the archway in the same manner as that for any corner bead. For an arch that looks nice and even, make sure the spring lines are the same height.

BUTTED SEAMS

Throughout this book, I have stressed the importance of trying to avoid butted seams between the untapered ends of panels. If, however, you have to have butted joints, make sure to keep them away from the center of the wall or ceiling and take time to feather the taped joints carefully. No matter how careful a job you do, however, the joints may still be visible after the room is painted. I'm embarrassed to say that I found this out when I returned to a job to take some photos for this book. What had looked like a perfect job on the day I finished had developed slight ridges at the center of the butted joints.

ARCHES: WHY CHOOSE ONE SHAPE OVER ANOTHER?

Any arch can look good in the right setting–just remember, the shape you choose will greatly affect the spring lines.

An **Elliptical Arch** can have the same spring line, rise, and finished opening height no matter how wide the finished opening. These consistent measurements, no matter the width, guarantee a consistent and attractive-looking opening.

Because **Round Top Arches** are made from a single radius measurement, the rise varies as the finished opening width varies. It is not possible to have the same spring lines and finished opening heights with round top arches of different widths.

Segment Arch Just like ellipses, segment arches can have the same spring line and rise no matter what their width. Segments are good to use when a wide finished opening is desired, but the ceiling is too low for an elliptical or a round top.

WORK SMART

If you're using ¼-in. drywall on the inside of an archway, you may need two layers to blend in the sides and provide added strength.

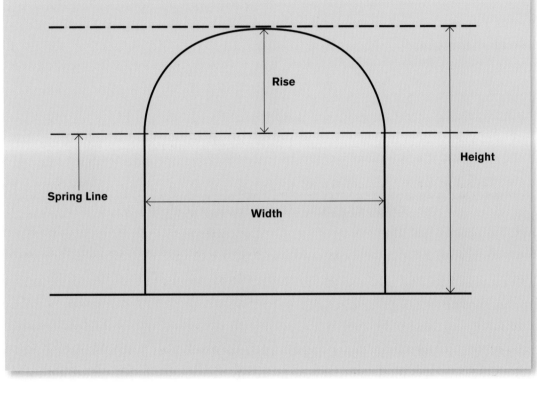

The deformation, known in the trade as "ridging," was only visible in certain lighting, but it was enough to bother me.

Ridging

Building materials expand and contract as the temperature and humidity inside a building change. As the building materials move, tension builds up against the drywall panels. The tension is relieved as the panels bend outward, usually at a joint.

Ridging can occur in regular tapered-edge seams, but it is much more common in butted end joints. After the ridging has stopped, typically in six months to a year, the ridged joint can be blended into the surrounding area by applying joint compound to both sides of the ridge and feathering it into the panel surface (see the discussion of crowned seams on p. 101). There is, however, a way to minimize ridging in the first place: by back-blocking the butted seam.

THE BENEFITS OF BACK-BLOCKING

- Finishes the butt seams flat and smooth, simplifying the installation of counters, trim, and cabinets.

- Produces finished seams that are the same width as beveled-edge seams.

- Takes less time and materials to finish them than typical butted seams.

- Allows the joint to float between the framing, virtually eliminating cracking and ridging.

- Eliminates callbacks.

Finishing butted seams
The butted seam on the left is finished wide to hide the bump created when the drywall is attached to a stud or joist. The seam on the right is back-blocked and much easier to finish.

Back-blocking

Back-blocking is designed to minimize ridging by placing butt joints between framing members. The drywall is hung perpendicular to the framing members, so that the butt ends can be reinforced along the back of each panel, behind the joint. The panel seams can be reinforced by installing a drywall panel behind the seam (see the drawing below). But commercial products designed for back-blocking are much easier to use. For more on this process, see the photos on the facing page.

BACK-BLOCK WITH DRYWALL

This method of back-blocking, from the USG handbook, has been used successfully for years, but it is time consuming to do and to my knowledge it has never really caught on.

Remove the temporary drywall brace and the wood strips when the compound between the drywall panels and the back piece of drywall has set up. A slightly recessed joint is left, which can be concealed during taping.

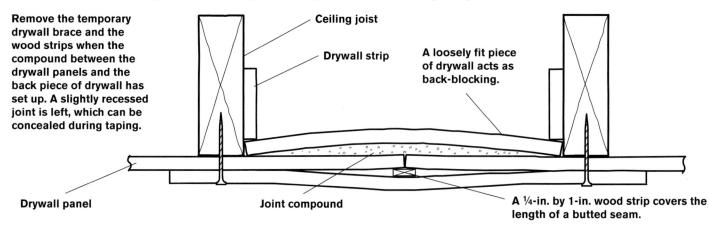

Ceiling joist

Drywall strip

A loosely fit piece of drywall acts as back-blocking.

Drywall panel

Joint compound

A ¼-in. by 1-in. wood strip covers the length of a butted seam.

BACK-BLOCKING THE EASY WAY

When butted seams on nontapered ends are inevitable, position them between framing and use a back-blocking device to recess the joint automatically.

1. Attach the back-blocking
After installing the first panel so that it ends between the studs, attach a back-blocking device (in this case, a product called RockSplicer) behind the seam you're creating.

2. Seams recess automatically
Here you can see the screw is set back from the edge to reduce damage to the drywall core. The raised edge of the RockSplicer helps recess the seam.

3. Attach the second panel
The butted edge of the second panel is screwed through the drywall into the back-blocker. And because it falls between framing members, it's unlikely to crack or ridge.

4. A durable seam
The design of the back-blocker pulls the seam in, creating a recess and making it easier to conceal at the taping and finishing stage.

Tape if you must Gaps between drywall and other surfaces, like tubs or showers, can be taped with either mesh or paper. Still, it's likely to crack over time. For better results, use an L-bead.

BUTTING DRYWALL TO A DIFFERENT SURFACE

When drywall is butted up against a tub/shower unit, trim work, or a wooden beam, it can be very time consuming to fit each panel perfectly and leave no gaps or broken edges. I used to flat tape up to these surfaces and can get excellent looking results. But whenever you butt different surfaces cracking can occur because of different levels of expansion and contraction or because of structural movement. Whenever possible, I use L-beads instead.

Applying L-Beads

I prefer to use L-Beads between the drywall edge and the abutting surface for a number of reasons. The L-beads provide a tight fit, but also resist the edge cracking flat taping is

INSTALLING L-BEADS

L-beads are a great way to achieve a clean edge where drywall abuts any surface other than drywall. The bead pictured here has a tear-away strip of material that shields the abutting surface from joint compound and potential scratches.

Remove the protective strip
During sanding, the tear-away edge is removed and the result is a clean, straight edge.

Install the bead
One edge of the L-bead slides into a gap left between the drywall and the butted surface.

prone to. If the drywall edge is in an area that can get wet—like against a shower—L-bead protects the edge and prevents moisture from wicking into the drywall.

L-beads are installed after the drywall is hung—just leave a slight gap for the edge to slip into. They are covered with compound, unlike most J-beads, so you get a smooth finished look. Some L-beads have a removable edge that protects the abutting surface from compound when coating over the bead.

I like the vinyl L-bead with a tear-away strip that acts as a shield to protect the abutting surface (see the photos on the facing page). Before you install the bead, attach the drywall about ⅛ in. short so that you can slip the leg of the bead between the drywall and the abutting surface. Secure the bead in place—the vinyl product I use is simply stapled tight against the drywall surface—and apply two or three coats of compound to hide the bead. After sanding, remove the protective strip to reveal a nice clean surface.

A lot of L-beads are tape-on beads, meaning that compound holds the bead in place. They are available in stick form or in rolls. To protect surfaces from compound use low-stick masking tape. You can also get flat beads with the tear-away strip, which are handy to have when no gap was left and when you are working around a drywall return against an arched window.

MULTILAYER APPLICATIONS

Double or multiple layers of drywall are sometimes required for increased fire resistance or for reduced sound penetration. You can secure all layers with fasteners in the standard manner, but a good alternative is to use adhesive to attach the outermost, or "face," layer. Using adhesive increases the strength of the structure and reduces the number of fasteners needed. For firecode, you may still need all the required fasteners.

WRAPPING DOORWAYS AND WINDOW BUILDOUTS

Sometimes, windows and doors are recessed. Rather than install extension jambs or even trim, you can drywall these areas and install corner bead. Attach drywall to the recessed surfaces, making sure you use a sufficient number of fasteners, especially if you will be using a mud or glue-on bead. If you cut the drywall straight enough and smooth the edge, you won't need to tape against the window frame. If the gap is narrow enough, flexible caulk may be all that is necessary. Usually, however, an L-bead is installed.

Encasing openings The jambs on windows and doors can be drywalled and beaded, eliminating the need for wooden extension jambs and casing.

ABOVE: Glue on the last layer When attaching the face layer of drywall in a multilayer application, apply a bead of adhesive at the location of the framing members.

RIGHT: Compound acts as adhesive Joint compound can also be used as an adhesive when attaching the face layer of drywall. This method also works well for attaching drywall directly to above-grade concrete walls.

WORK SMART

In multilayer application, taping seams and corners before applying the second layer helps protect against fire and reduce sound travel.

Using drywall adhesives with single-layer applications was explained in Chapter 3; the procedure is the same when applying the face layer of drywall in multilayer applications. Apply a 3/8-in. bead of adhesive over the location of each framing member and then use screws to fasten the panel around the perimeter and every 2 ft. in the center of the panel.

You can also use joint compound as an adhesive to attach the face layer. Apply a strip of joint compound approximately 1/2 in. thick and 5 in. wide every 16 in. or 24 in. (depending on the framing spacing). Then use a notched trowel to groove the compound and leave beads of compound 3/8 in. wide by 1/2 in. high and spaced 1 in. apart. When using this method for wall applications, pre-bow the panels (with the bow facing in against the wall) and fasten only the edges. For ceilings, you'll also need a fastener in the center of the panel on each framing member.

If you use screws or nails to attach double or multiple layers of drywall, it's important to attach each layer with the correct number of fasteners. Never just tack the first layer or

layers and fasten only the last layer correctly. Each layer is heavy and must be attached properly to prevent sags, loose panels, and popped nails or screws. In addition, make sure that the screws for each layer penetrate the framing at least the minimum depth of 5/8 in. for wood framing, 3/8 in. for metal framing (see the chart on p. 39).

There are a couple of ways to layout the multiple layers. Just remember that for both fire protection and sound control it is best to avoid overlapping seams. One method is to attach the first layer parallel to the framing and the second layer perpendicular to the framing. This layout provides a simple answer to preventing seam overlap

Many people, however, find it easier to attach each layer perpendicular to the framing, especially if the o.c. spacing of the framing is off. Just be careful to keep seams on the face layer away from seams on the underlying layer; the panels should be staggered so that the seams are at least 10 in. apart. On a ceiling, for example, start the first layer with a 24-in.-wide panel and the second layer with a 48-in.-wide panel. Use the longest lengths possible and make sure that any butted seams do not line up with butted seams on the first layer.

FASTENING FOR FIRE CODE

For single-layer applications of fire-resistant drywall to meet fire-code specifications, the panels must be correctly attached to the framing. Fasteners should be spaced no more than 8 in. apart along each framing member. Under normal conditions, the panels will stay in place with fasteners spaced 12 in. or 16 in. apart, but under the extreme conditions of a fire, the panels may come loose prematurely, thereby greatly reducing the fire rating of the application. (For more on fire-resistant drywall, see p. 11.)

CEMENT BOARD

Drywall, even moisture- or mold-resistant drywall, should not be used in areas that are potentially wet areas. There are just too many products available today that are much better suited for these areas.

Cement board, which is used in wet areas such as tiled showers, (see p. 14), is cut with the score-and-snap method in much the same manner as drywall. Use a utility knife and a T-square or straightedge to cut through the glass mesh on one side. To break the panel at the cut, tap the back with a hammer as you apply pressure away from the cut. Then cut the back with a utility knife and snap the panel forward again.

ABOVE TOP: Screws designed for the job These screws, called Drywall-to-Drywall screws, are used in conjunction with adhesive to attach one layer of drywall to another.

ABOVE: Stagger the seams When hanging drywall in two layers, the seams should not line up. Here we are attaching a second layer of drywall perpendicular to the first.

LEFT: Straight cuts in cement board are made using the score-and-snap technique.

You can use joint com-
pound as an adhe-
sive to attach drywall
directly to concrete
walls—as long as the
concrete is clean,
smooth, and dry.

Fastening concrete board
Galvanized-metal roofing nails
can be used to attach cement
board. The author prefers using
special screws such as these
to attach cement board. It is
a good idea to use adhesive
as well.

Cement board dulls a utility knife very
quickly, so change the blade often to ensure
smooth and easy cuts. A carbide-tipped knife
keeps a sharp edge a lot longer. You can also
make square and round cutouts in cement
board with a utility knife and a hammer (see
"Cutting Round Openings" on the facing page).

Cement board should be attached with
special galvanized nails (not drywall nails) or
with screws designed for attaching cement
board to either wood or steel framing.
Galvanized nails used for metal roofing also
work quite well (see the photo above). They
have a large, flat head and are ringed for
added holding strength.

Before attaching cement board, it's a
good idea to apply construction adhesive to
the studs. The adhesive adds strength to the
structure, which is particularly important
when tile is being applied over the cement
board. The board is smooth on one side for
adhesive applications and rough on the other
side for thin-set mortar applications.

CONTROL JOINTS

There aren't a lot of control (expansion)
joints used in residential and light commercial drywall jobs, but occasionally they are
required. I, however, think they should be

CUTTING ROUND OPENINGS IN CEMENT BOARD

To cut a round opening in cement board, mark the location of the opening on one side of the board. Drive a nail through the panel to help locate the opening on the back. Cut through the fiberglass mesh with a utility knife, and then gently tap the opening on the finish side with a hammer until the cutout falls away. Chip away any irregular edges with the blade side of a drywall hammer.

1. Mark the opening Mark the opening on both sides of the panel. Use a nail to locate the center of the opening on the back.

2. Cut both sides Use a utility knife to cut through the fiberglass mesh on both sides of the cement board.

3. Remove the cutout Tap around the edges of the opening with a hammer until the cutout breaks apart and falls out.

used more often. The Gypsum Association recommends installing control joints wherever partition walls or ceilings transverse construction joints. An example of this is a stairway in a two-story house. If the drywall joint is anywhere near the transition from the first to the second floor, the seam will ridge out. And because these areas usually have an overhead light shining down along a wall, the seam is often difficult to conceal.

You could hang a panel to span the transition point, but ridging is still possible. That's why I like to use a control joint in those areas. The joint accommodates changes at the weakest point—in this case, the drywall seam. Leave a gap between panels, embed the control joint in compound or glue or staple it in place. Be sure to leave the center of the control joint clean so it can expand and contract as needed.

WORKING WITH MOISTURE-RESISTANT DRYWALL

Moisture-resistant drywall is different from regular drywall and has some specialized uses and attachment requirements.

- Do not use moisture-resistant drywall for areas subjected to constant moisture, direct exposure to water, or continuous high humidity. Cement board or gypsum-core tile backer is recommended for those applications.

- Space framing 16 in. o.c. for walls and 12 in. o.c. for ceilings.

- Attach panels perpendicular to the framing.

- Space fasteners 12 in. o.c.; if you are installing heavy tiles, space fasteners 8 in. o.c.

- Coat all cut edges with a water-resistant tile adhesive or a waterproof caulking before applying joint compound. Place the drywall ¼ in. above a tub or shower lip. Be sure to coat the cut ends as described.

- Do not install moisture-resistant drywall over a vapor retarder if the wall will be finished with tile or some other impervious wall finish.

- Use a setting-type compound to tape the seams. You can also use water-resistant tile mastic to skim coat the drywall.

- Use a nonabsorbent grout and sealant when finishing with tile.

- Maintain the system by periodically sealing the tile; maintain the caulk around the edges and other openings as well.

TOP: Installing a control joint
The center of the control joint expands and contracts as the structure moves. This joint has a tear-off strip, which keeps the center clean during installation.

ABOVE: Room to move
When finished, the center of a control joint remains free of joint compound.

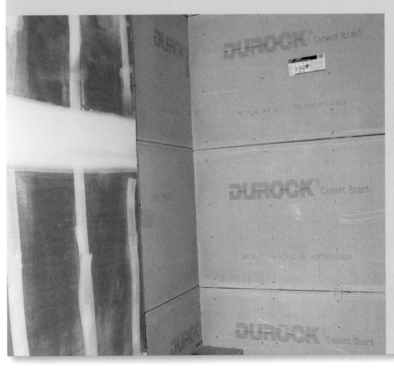

For humid rooms
Moisture-resistant drywall is often used in a bathroom in combination with cement board. Moisture-resistant drywall is not for areas that actually get wet. Cement board is.

MOLD-RESISTANT DRYWALL

Mold has become an issue because it is more prevalent in structures built during the last 25 years. Homes are more airtight, more complex, and built under more accelerated building schedules than ever before. Here in upstate New York construction at the beginning stages of winter really didn't exist when my father started his excavating business many years ago. Now my brother owns the business and he works deep into the winter, digging and pouring foundations.

It is impossible to eliminate all molds and mold spores, but controlling moisture can control indoor mold growth. Mold-resistant products play an important role in minimizing mold growth. Mold-resistant drywall has a specially treated core and paper surface. Some is faced with fiberglass mat instead of paper. Like moisture resistant drywall, it shouldn't be used in wet areas, but I have started to install mold-resistant drywall in most kitchens and baths where I once used moisture-resistant products. It is installed and attached in the same manner as regular drywall, but should be finished with fiberglass tape instead of paper (because fiberglass is an inorganic material).

That said, if mold-resistant products of any kind are installed improperly, they offer little protection from mold growth. Mold can grow on anything. A good example is some mold resistant drywall that I was about to use on a job. Apparently the two sheets delivered to me were on the top of the pile in the warehouse: the back of the top sheet was covered with a heavy layer of dust and it also looked like someone had spilled coffee on it. Now this specially treated drywall was covered with a food source. For mold to grow, all it needed was a little moisture.

WATER + OXYGEN + NUTRIENTS = MOLD
Moisture Control = Mold Control

Good building practices help control mold:

- Good building design.
- Using quality building products.
- Keeping building products dry before and during construction.
- Deliver sensitive products only when they are ready to be used.
- Keep building materials clean and dry by covering them with a waterproof tarp.
- Lumber should read below 16 percent on a moisture meter.
- Install building products in proper order to insure protection from the elements.
- Insulate properly.
- Install a continuous weather-resistant barrier on exterior walls.
- Cover crawl spaces to control moisture.
- Use exhaust fans.
- Follow proper maintenance procedures.
- Relative humidity should remain below 60 percent for mold not to grow.

ABOVE: Keep it clean and dry Dirt and water are a bad combination. Here, you have both and the result is mold.
Photo provided by Bob Rudd, CIE

RIGHT: Soap is a food source Mold can even grow on the face of this porcelain tile because the soap itself became a food source.
Photo provided by Bob Rudd, CIE

Multiple layers with crown
Multiple layers of drywall combined with vinyl crown all get beaded and finished with compound for an elegant look.

DECORATING WITH DRYWALL

Finished drywall is usually thought of as a smooth or textured wall or ceiling. But over the past few years a number of products—including many of the beads discussed earlier—have helped make drywall work a larger part of the decorating process. With L-beads, arched and flexible L-beads, bull-nose, and chamfer stops, drywall can be layered and trimmed to achieve an endless array of designs. There is even drywall available with an embossed surface that looks like wainscoting or a raised panel when finished.

To layer drywall, begin by hanging the walls and ceilings in the conventional manor. Attach subsequent layers of drywall using screws and drywall adhesive. Because the outer edges of the layers will be covered with L-bead, each layer has to be tight against the underlying layer. In some cases temporary screws may be needed until the adhesive sets up. You can use either a vinyl or a tape-on bead. The vinyl is available in a wider variety of styles and adhesive and staples make for easy attachment. For a professional-looking job, it's important that you install the drywall layers and bead to a snapped line. With a little savvy and a few simple techniques, there's almost no limit to the looks you can achieve with drywall.

CREATING LAYERED CEILINGS

Drywall can be cut to various sizes and shapes, then attached over the first layer of drywall to create an endless combination of styles.

Lay on the layers
Drywall can be applied in multiple layers to whatever pattern you choose. Edges should be covered in L-bead.

The finished ceiling
When painted with slightly different shades of paint color, the layers are brought to life.

MAKE YOUR OWN WAINSCOTING

With regular drywall, L-bead, and some finishing work, you can create a raised-panel look for more formal rooms.

1. Lay out the design
Begin by layering strips of drywall in the pattern of raised panel wainscoting.

2. Trim the edges
The edges are covered with an L-bead. In this case a chamfer-style edge bead was used.

3. Finish it out
A solid wood top cap creates an elegant finished look.

ABOVE: Buy wainscoting premade
This unique type of drywall has an embossed pattern. When installed, it creates a raised-panel design on walls and ceilings.

LEFT: A dramatic effect Soffets needed to conceal duct work and plumbing were covered with layers of drywall and capped with chamfer bead to create a unique ceiling.

7

Repairs

No matter how well you hang and tape drywall, there will inevitably come a time when you need to make some repairs. Drywall adds little structural strength to a building, and it is not a rock-hard surface that can withstand repeated abuse. Some repairs are simply necessitated by the demands of daily life in a busy household, where doorknobs may strike against walls, pets may scratch surfaces, and children may playfully bang toys against anything in their path. Other repairs may be necessary if the drywall develops cracks or ridges as the building settles, or when water damage occurs. Finally, remodeling often involves moving electrical outlets or light fixtures or closing off a window or a doorway.

Drywall repairs, when done properly, become a permanent and inconspicuous part of the wall or ceiling. Some repairs are simple and can be done with one or two thin coats of joint compound; others require additional framing and at least three coats of compound. The tools and taping techniques used for repair work are the same as those used for standard taping jobs.

POPPED NAILS AND SCREWS

Popped nails and screws are one of the most common drywall problems. Fortunately, they're also among the easiest to repair. The problem occurs when the drywall is not fastened tightly against the framing, when the framing lumber shrinks or twists, or when an object strikes the wall. With time or abuse, joint compound comes loose from the fastener and pops off, exposing the fastener head or pushing out the joint tape. Fastener pops may appear soon after the wall or ceiling is finished, or they may become visible several years later.

Whatever the cause, the best remedy is to place another drywall screw about 1 1/2 in. away from the popped nail or screw, and then remove or reset the popped fastener. Apply

hand pressure to the panel next to the area as you set the new screw. After the new screw or screws have been set, check the popped fastener and reset it again, if necessary (or simply remove it).

If the paper surface of the drywall has not been damaged, the fasteners can be finished with three coats of joint compound and sanded lightly. If the paper surface has been torn or the core of the drywall has been damaged, remove the loose material, fill the gap with joint compound, and then apply a small piece of mesh tape to the damaged area. Cover the repair with three thin coats of joint compound. Keep the compound thin over the patched area and feather it out as wide as necessary so that it blends into the wall.

REPAIRING POPPED FASTENERS

As buildings move over time, or when nails and screws aren't fastened tight against the framing in the first place, fasteners have a tendency to pop out proud of the drywall surface. Either way, there's a quick fix.

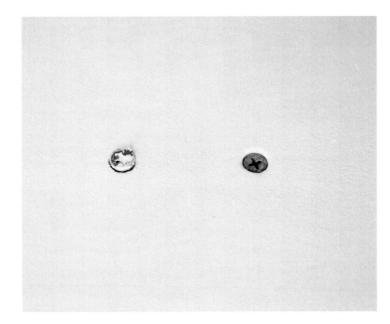

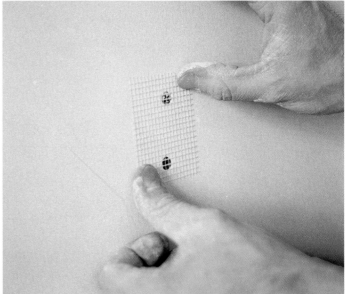

Secure the drywall
To repair a popped screw, place another screw 1½ in. away, and then remove or reset the popped fastener.

Cover it with compound
Most depressions left from removing fasteners can be filled with compound alone, but if there is damage to the drywall surface, cover the heads with mesh tape before applying the compound.

CONCEALING FASTENER DEPRESSIONS

When hanging drywall, it's easy to overdrive screws or tap nails in a little too deep. To repair the resulting depression, use joint compound and, in some cases, mesh tape.

Fasteners poorly set
Both the nail and the screw shown here are set improperly, creating the potential for a depressed area around the fastener, even after applying three coats of compound.

Tape and mud
To repair a fastener depression, drive a drywall screw 1½ in. away, remove loose material, and then reset the original fastener. Pre-filling and using mesh tape may be necessary if damage is extensive.

Fastener depressions

Areas around fastener heads where the joint compound is recessed below the surface of the panel are called fastener depressions. Depressions usually occur for one of two reasons: Either too little joint compound was applied during taping or the fastener was driven too deeply into the panel surface, damaging and weakening the panel's face paper and interior gypsum core. When sanded, the compound is removed from the indentation because the drywall pushes in as you sand over the loose fastener. A fastener depression often isn't visible until after it has been painted.

To diagnose the problem, push firmly against the drywall panel alongside the depression. If the panel is secure, you simply need to apply another coat or two of joint compound and then lightly re-sand the area to even out the depression. If the drywall moves in and out even a slight amount, the panel is damaged. To correct the problem, place a screw 1½ in. away from the original

Keep the toolbox stocked
The author likes to keep drywall repair kits handy. Shown here are precut patches for small holes, metal clips for larger areas, and pre-cut patch kits for electrical outlets.

WORK SMART

If the face paper is torn, apply mesh tape to reinforce the repair.

fastener, and then press against the panel again to check for movement. If the panel is now tight, use a taping knife to remove loose material from around the original fastener, and then reset the nail or screw. Cut a piece of fiberglass-mesh tape to cover the fasteners, re-tape the area, apply three coats of joint compound, and lightly sand it once it's dry.

REPAIRING HOLES IN DRYWALL

Holes in the drywall surface that result from long-term wear and tear range from small nail punctures to large gouges. The extent of the repair depends on the size of the hole. Nail holes, nicks, and small dents can simply be covered with compound; small holes require paper or mesh for reinforcement; and larger holes may require the use of furring strips to support a drywall patch.

Repairing small holes

A small nail hole (such as that left when a picture hung on a wall is repositioned) can usually be filled with just one or two coats of compound. Remove any loose material first and depress the area around the hole slightly with the handle of a utility knife.

Small holes or dents created when a blunt object, such as a doorknob, hits a wall can usually be repaired without major work. Completely cover the damaged area with mesh tape, crossing the tape over the hole (see "Repairing Small Holes," on the facing page). Depending on the size of the hole, you may be able to fill it with joint compound before applying the tape. Next, apply joint compound over the tape with just enough trowel pressure to force compound through the tape. Feather the edges of the compound

REPAIRING SMALL HOLES

Small holes—whether from doorknobs, removed nails, or moving accidents—can be patched with a store-bought patch or using mesh tape.

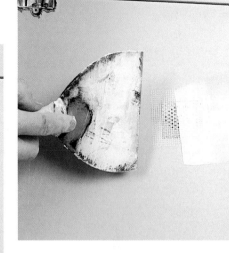

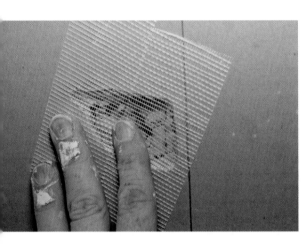

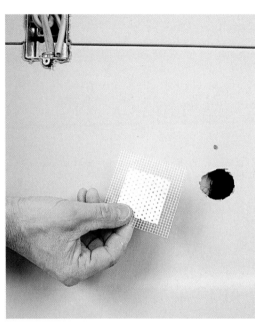

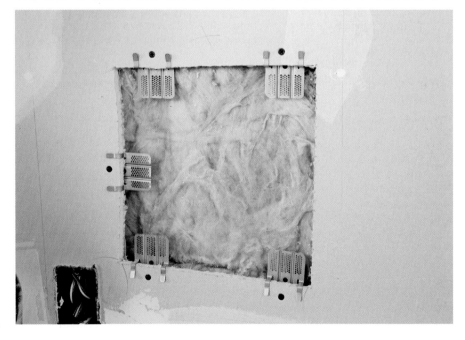

Patch the hole
To repair a small hole (under 2 in. or so in diameter), cover it with a self-repair patch or crisscross the hole with layers of mesh tape. Mesh tape should be pressed in slightly to create an indentation.

Cover it with compound
Apply joint compound to the patch. If using mesh tape, use a taping knife to force some of the compound through the mesh and into the hole. Finish with two additional coats of compound.

and do not build up the center too much; otherwise, you'll create a bump that will be visible in certain lighting. Apply the second and third coats, feathering the area further and keeping the center even.

Repairing large holes
If an area is badly damaged, cut it back until you reach solid drywall. To make the repair, cut a drywall patch and use it as a template to form the damaged area into a square, rectangle, or circle (see "Repairing Large Openings," on p. 162). Once the damaged area is removed, the opening will probably be too large to repair with mesh tape and compound alone. An actual piece of drywall will be used and it has to be attached in some way. To provide a fastening surface for the patch, use a furring strip (or strips) cut about 6 in. longer

Store-bought drywall clips For repairing large holes where another piece of drywall must be fitted into place, you can use special clips in place of wood furring.

REPAIRING LARGE OPENINGS

Large holes—anything larger than your hand—should be trimmed back to solid drywall, furred out, and patched.

1. Assess the situation
This looks like a great deal of damage, but if you use the right techniques, repairing a large hole isn't that difficult.

2. Position a drywall patch
Cut a drywall patch a little larger than the opening. Hold the patch over the damaged area and trace its outline on the wall.

3. Keep the edges clean
Use a utility saw to cut out the damaged area.

than the hole. Slide the furring into the hole and secure it in place with drywall screws fastened through the panel and into the furring. Cut and shape the patch to fit the hole, and then screw the patch onto the furring.

Now you're ready to tape the patch. First, fill in any large gaps with joint compound, and then cover the edges with fiberglass-mesh tape. Cover the tape with a thin layer of joint compound. Once again, be sure to feather the edges properly and be careful not to build up the patched area too much. Larger holes require at least three coats of joint compound to be concealed properly. Because the patch is

secured to the panel and is a solid part of the drywall, it is unlikely to crack or come loose. For really large holes, furring strips won't be effective and you'll have to cut the drywall back to the nearest framing member and add cross framing, as when eliminating a door or window (see p. 169).

REMODELING REPAIRS
During remodeling work, electrical outlet boxes, heating ducts, and other fixtures are often moved or eliminated, which means that the original hole must be covered and patched. You can install furring strips to sup-

4. Fur out the opening
Slip furring strips into the squared-up hole and attach them to the drywall with screws.

5. Attach the patch
Position the drywall patch and screw it to the furring.

6. Add compound and tape
Fill gaps around the patch with joint compound, then cover the seams with mesh tape and a coat of joint compound.

7. Smooth it out
Cover the entire patch with a second coat of joint compound, feathering the edges to avoid creating a bump.

port the patch, as described previously, or you can bevel the edges of the opening and the patch. When doors or windows are eliminated during remodeling, you'll need to add framing to the opening before patching it with drywall.

Eliminating an electrical box

When an electrical outlet is eliminated, the box may be removed or left in the wall. If the box is left in place, make sure there are no electrical wires inside (live electrical wires should be covered with a blank cover

plate, not with drywall). To patch the area, start by trimming away any loose paper or drywall around the opening, and then bevel the outside edges with a utility knife. Next, cut a piece of drywall the same size as the opening (see "Patching Unused Outlets: Method One," on p. 165), and bevel the back edges. Adjust the fit of the patch with a utility knife until the patch fits snugly into place without sticking out past the face of the drywall panel.

Apply a generous layer of joint compound to all edges of the patch (or hole), and then press the patch into place, making sure it is

REPAIRING AN OVERCUT ELECTRICAL BOX

Electrical outlet box and switch covers usually don't cover an area much larger than the box itself, so even a minor overcut may require some patching. Before starting the repair, turn off the power to the box. Then apply hand pressure against the drywall panel next to the box. If the panel seems loose, place a screw in the framing member closest to the box. (The patch will be stronger if the drywall is solidly screwed in place around the electrical box.)

Fill large gaps with joint compound first, then cover the hole with mesh or paper tape and embed the tape in the joint compound. When the joint compound is dry, apply a thin second coat that just covers the tape and blend it into the surrounding area. If you're in a rush, use a setting compound to fill the gap—it sets up quickly, allowing you to finish the repair faster. For a small patch, you usually need only two coats before sanding. If, after sanding, you think it still needs another coat, apply a thin layer and re-sand it when dry.

If you can't cover it, patch it
If an outlet cover does not conceal the gap of an overcut electrical outlet box, the area must be patched.

1. Lay on compound Fill around the edges of the cutout with joint compound. Make sure to cover any area that the outlet cover doesn't.

2. Cover it with tape
Cover the gap with a layer of mesh or paper tape.

PATCHING UNUSED OUTLETS: METHOD ONE

Remodeling often means moving outlets. You can patch the holes left from retired outlets easily, using just a scrap of drywall, tape, and a little joint compound.

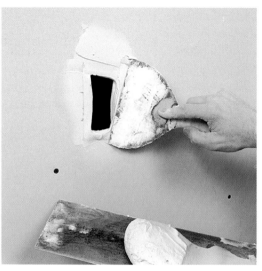

1. Prepare the patch
Bevel the edges of the opening and the patch with a utility knife. The patch should fit snugly and set just a little lower than the face of the drywall.

2. Apply the compound
Spread joint compound around the edges of the beveled hole or patch.

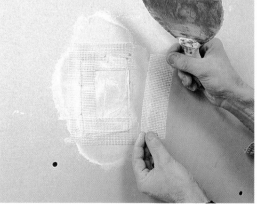

3. Set the patch in place
Push the patch into the compound until it is flush with the wall surface.

4. Tape and mud
Cover the edges with mesh tape and conceal them with two or three coats of compound.

PATCHES WITH FLANGES: METHOD TWO

An easier way to patch an unused electrical box outlet is to create a patch with a built-in paper flange. The patch is easily made from a scrap of drywall.

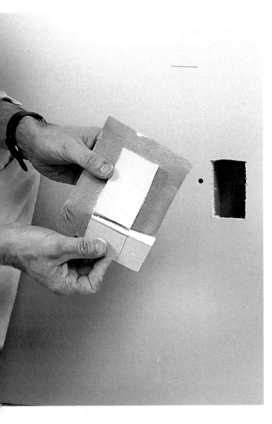

1. Make the patch
To create a plug for the hole and a paper flange to hold it in place, score the patch on the back of the drywall, and then snap and peel off the waste material.

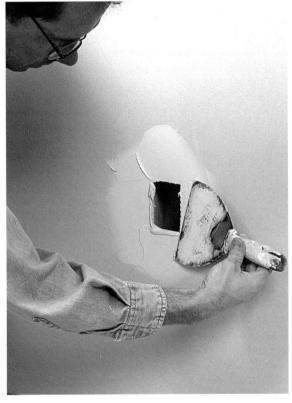

2. Ready the opening
Apply a thin layer of compound around the perimeter of hole.

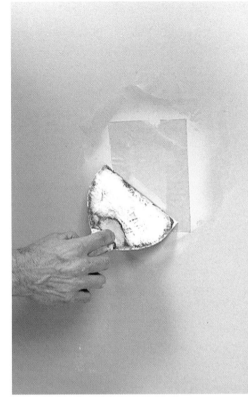

3. Position the patch
Insert the patch into the hole and embed the paper flaps. Apply one or two coats of compound, and the wall is as good as new.

flush with the panel surface. To prevent the patch from cracking along the edges, apply fiberglass-mesh or paper tape to the seams and embed the tape in joint compound. Once the compound is dry, cover the tape with a second coat and feather the edges into the drywall face. After the second coat is dry, lightly sand the area and apply a third coat, if necessary.

One of my favorite ways to cover an electrical outlet opening is to create a paper flange around the edges of a drywall patch (see "Patches with Flanges: Method Two," above). Start by squaring up the hole and cut a drywall patch about 2 in. larger than the hole on all sides. Mark the dimensions on the back of the patch, subtracting about 2 in. on all sides. Make sure the marks are in the center of the patch. Score along the marks and carefully snap one edge at a time, making sure not to break the face paper. Peel the drywall off of the paper, leaving only the actual patch in place. Apply a thin layer of joint compound around the edges of the hole and press the patch into place. Use a taping knife to embed the paper flanges. Apply two more coats of joint compound to conceal the repair.

Making a patch invisible

The trouble with any repair is that we know where it is, so if there is even a slight difference in the texture of the surfaces we are likely to see the patched area. This is especially true if paint with a shine is used and if the painted surface is a little rougher than usual. This is the same principle addressed when I discuss a level 5 finish in Chapter 4. To remedy

the situation, you can apply a skim coat of joint compound to the entire wall (see "Skim Coat for Texture," below). Leave on just enough compound to smooth the surface.

Eliminating large openings

For the best results when eliminating a door or window opening, you should cover the entire wall with a new layer of drywall. This tactic, however, is often impractical, and the more common approach is to patch only the opening. This type of large patch, though, has butted seams on all edges and is very difficult to hide unless you take great care to do the job properly.

SKIM COAT FOR TEXTURE

When patching old outlets or repairing dents and holes, you're often left with two different textures on the wall—one from the existing paint and another from the repair job. To create a uniform sheen on the surface, apply a skim coat of compound on the entire wall.

Surface the whole wall
To equalize the sheen on the wall, skim coat the entire area with a thin film of compound. Once painted, the repair work will blend in seamlessly.

A poor match
After a repair is sanded you are left with a very smooth, porous surface next to the painted surface that is a little rough and not nearly as porous as the compound.

A QUICKIE REPAIR

As you know, taping is a three- or four-stage process that sometimes requires waiting as long as 24 hours between steps. However, if you are making repairs, you usually don't want to wait any longer than necessary to complete the repair and move on to the next job.

One day, I was sanding an addition by myself. It was late in the day and I guess I was in a hurry to get home. I obviously wasn't thinking clearly, because as I disconnected the last cross brace on my pipe scaffold, the two side sections fell over. Both hit the walls. It took me a minute to get over the shock of seeing holes in my just-finished walls. Once I composed myself, I headed to my truck for setting compound, accelerant, and tape.

I cut out the damaged areas and fit in the patches (as outlined on pp. 162–163), but instead of using an all-purpose compound, I used the setting compound and added an accelerant (see "One-Day Taping," on p. 110). Less than half an hour later, I applied a skim coat of drying compound over the repaired area. The quality of the job was intact, and I didn't have to make extra trips back to the job to finish the repair.

Mix what you need For simple repair jobs, you can mix small batches of a setting-type compound in a pan. To help the compound set up quickly, add a little accelerant. A 5 minute patching compound is also available.

Remove water damage This ceiling was damaged by water and a large section was removed. I purposely removed the damaged area so that the long edges were far enough from the ceiling joists so I could back-block. There is also back-blocking between the joists to straighten out any sagged drywall (see p. 145).

The first step is to frame in the opening. Make sure that the framing lumber is straight, and install it about ⅛ in behind the back of the drywall that is already in place. Cut a single piece of drywall to cover the opening. To avoid damaging the edges as you screw the patch in place, make sure the drywall doesn't fit too tightly (leave about ⅛ in. all around). Fasten the drywall in place, and then cut away any high or loose edges with a utility knife or a rasp.

Because all the seams are butted, I recommend using paper tape and a setting-type compound for the first coat to provide additional strength. Apply a broad second coat, feathering the edges. Once the compound is dry, use a straightedge to check for ridges and concave areas. Do this again after the third coat. Four coats of joint compound are usually needed.

COVERING LARGE OPENINGS

When a window or door is moved or eliminated, the opening must be framed in, patched with a section of drywall, and then finished with tape and compound.

1. Frame in the opening
When a window has been removed, frame in the opening with studs. Hold the studs back from the surface of the wall just a little more than the thickness of the drywall.

2. Fill the opening
Fill in the opening with one piece of drywall, leaving approximately ⅛-in. gap all around.

3. Tape the seams
Treat all of the edges as butted seams, using paper tape for added strength.

4. Finish out the wall
Feather the edges as you apply the second, third, and, if necessary, fourth coat of joint compound.

AN OUNCE OF PREVENTION

Roof trusses are often subject to upward arching, or uplift, of anywhere from 1/4 in. to 2 in., with 1/2 in. being about average. Truss uplift is a complicated subject and not all trusses have this problem. But when it happens, the tape on the inside corners of interior partitions can crack, come loose, or pull away, giving the corner a rounded look.

To avoid this problem, do not attach drywall near the spot where the trusses rest on partition walls. Instead, use a drywall clip to attach the panel to the wall's top plate instead of to the rafter. Then, set nails or screws 10 in. to 18 in. in from the edge of the panel.

An alternative is to float the ceiling edge and let the wall panel hold it up (as described on p. 79). Keep the first screw back on the rafter approximately 18 in. This floating-corner method helps keep the corner intact during seasonal temperature fluctuations.

Clips prevent uplift To prevent truss uplift, attach ceiling panels with drywall clips instead of screwing them to the ceiling joist. Install the first screw in the ceiling panel as much as 18 in. from the wall.

STRESS CRACKS

Stress cracks, which typically occur above a doorway or window, are caused by structural movement or settling. If a crack occurs at a seam, the tape may blister or come loose. But stress cracks can also occur where there is no joint in the drywall. It may run along the panel face, or it may go all the way through to the other side. As I discussed in Chapter 3, a seam located next to the edge of a header is more likely to crack than one located 8 in. or more from the edge.

To repair a stress crack, first cut out any loose drywall tape or joint compound with a utility knife or the corner of a taping knife. The V-groove formed provides a wider area for filling with joint compound. Next, apply hand pressure around the crack to check for movement. If the panel moves in and out, fasten it to the framing member closest to the crack. This makes the drywall more solid and less likely to crack again. Fill any large cracks with joint compound, and then cover with mesh or paper tape. Smooth the area with two or three coats of compound and then sand it.

WATER DAMAGE

On drywall, water damage is usually confined to ceilings. Roof problems and leaky plumbing in an upstairs bathroom are two common causes of water damage. Usually, water runs along the top of the drywall until it finds a seam or corner. Once the joint compound on the seam or corner becomes wet enough, the water breaks through and runs down the wall or onto the floor. This type of leak does not usually cause extensive drywall damage, because the water found an exit and didn't pool on top of the drywall or cause it to sag.

Before repairing the drywall, you must first fix the roof or the plumbing to prevent further damage. Next, remove any loose tape and joint compound. If the drywall has come loose, allow it to dry completely before refastening it. To prevent sagging, which is difficult to correct when reattaching a dried-out panel, prop up the drywall with a T-support or temporary furring strips. It's a good idea to go into the attic and remove and dry out any insulation that may be wet. Removing wet insulation allows the drywall to dry faster, and it may also prevent further

REPAIRING STRESS CRACKS

As homes age and settle, stress cracks often turn up. They can occur along seams or on the actual face of drywall—especially over windows and doors. Before repairing stress cracks, let them cycle through the seasons to insure that further cracking won't occur.

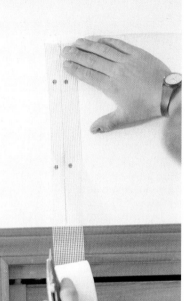

1. Cut along the crack
In this case, the wall cracked along a seam. Cut along each side of the crack with a utility knife to form a V-groove.

2. Secure and tape
If the drywall is loose around a crack, nail it along the closest framing member, and then cover the nails with tape.

3. Add joint compound
Whether along a seam or through a solid piece of drywall (as seen here), cover the tape with compound and sand it smooth.

MOLD DAMAGE

Under the right heat and humidity conditions, mold can grow on any drywall surface. It usually occurs after the drywall has gotten wet. To correct a mold problem, you must first eliminate the source of the moisture. If the problem occurs in a bathroom (the most common location), you may need to decrease the room's humidity with an exhaust fan, a dehumidifier, or a better supply of heat.

Once the humidity problem has been corrected and the drywall has dried out thoroughly, wash off the mold stain with bleach and water (¼ cup of bleach to 1 gal. of water). Repair any damaged areas and repaint the drywall with a mold-resistant paint. Maintain low-humidity conditions to prevent mold from recurring.

THINK AHEAD

Wait at least six months to a year before repairing stress cracks in new construction; this is usually enough time for a structure to finish settling.

REPAIRING WATER DAMAGE

Small stains from water damage can be sealed with a stain blocker and simply repainted. Larger areas of damage, whether from a leaking roof or a burst water pipe, need to be removed, cleaned, thoroughly dried, and then repaired.

Conceal the damage

There are a number of stain-blocking paints available. If the area will be painted, opt for water-based stain blockers, which are easy to work with. Oil- or alcohol-based paints work best if you're applying a texture over the stained area.

1. Clean off the damage

To repair a water-stained ceiling, make sure that the damaged area is dry, and then remove any loose material.

2. Seal off the damage

Apply a coat of stain-killing paint over the stained area.

3. Patch and repaint

After the stain-killing paint has dried, patch the damaged areas, and then repaint the entire ceiling.

damage. When the drywall is thoroughly dry, it will return to its original strength and can be refastened. Re-tape any damage using the techniques described in Chapter 4.

If a section of drywall has bowed excessively between the ceiling joists because it has soaked up too much water, the effected area will need to be removed and the opening patched in the same way as for large holes. If you're removing drywall in a contaminated area, be sure to wear safety gear to protect against airborne dust and mold. Drywall exposed to water should be replaced unless *all* of the following conditions are met:

- Water source or moisture is eliminated.

- Water was *not* contaminated.

- Drywall can be thoroughly dried out before mold grows.

- Drywall is structurally sound.

If there is ever any doubt about whether to keep or replace drywall that has been exposed to moisture, replace it.

WATER STAINS

Along with water damage, there will inevitably be some staining, and the stains will likely extend over a much larger area than the damage itself. Whether you're working on drywall or old plaster walls, the repair work is the same. Refasten or replace the damaged areas as described above. Then, before taping, seal all the stained areas with a good-quality stain-killing paint. I prefer to use an oil-based rather than a latex stain killer because it better prevents water stains from bleeding through joint compound. For small areas when you don't want to dirty a roller or brush, the spray cans come in handy.

Once the paint is thoroughly dry, patch the damaged and repaired areas, blending them into the ceiling. Before repainting, check the ceiling for any stains that may have bled through and reseal them, if necessary.

REDUCING DRYWALL CALLBACKS

Since this chapter deals with drywall repairs, it is fitting to end it with a list of ways to reduce drywall callbacks.

- **Use screws instead of nails to attach drywall. Screws should penetrate wood $\frac{5}{8}$ in., metal $\frac{3}{8}$ in.**
- **Do not force panels into place; cut them for a loose fit.**
- **Use the floating corner technique explained on p. 79.**
- **Create a tighter bond by using panel adhesives, as explained on p. 74.**
- **Make sure you use the appropriate compounds and tape (see Chapter 2 for more information).**
- **Whenever possible, install a back-blocking device for butted seams (see pp. 144–145).**
- **Select glue-on or tape-on corner beads, as well as special tapes and beads for off-angle corners.**
- **Use control (expansion) joints, if necessary.**
- **Use the appropriate grit of sandpaper or sanding screen and don't oversand.**

WORK SMART

Use oil-based stains or blocking paint rather than latex-based products to seal water stains. They do a better job.

CHAPTER

8

Decorating Drywall

O nce all the drywall work is done, the final step is to decorate the surface. Drywall can be finished with paint, textured coatings, or wall coverings. For satisfactory results, this step must be done properly. A poor finishing job can ruin even the most meticulous taping job.

PAINTING

Painting is a little more complicated than just using some cheap primer and rolling on a heavy coat of paint. Proper preparation makes an obvious difference. Surfaces should be dry, clean, sound, and free from oil or grease. Drywall manufacturers recommend dusting walls and ceilings prior to painting to remove the fine residue left from sanding, but in my experience there are no obvious benefits to this practice. I usually sand the walls lightly with fine sandpaper (200 grit works well) after the prime coat is dry.

Choose your finish Drywall can be painted or finished with a textured coating.

HOW TO PREVENT PHOTOGRAPHING

Chapter 4 discussed the problem of photographing, or taped seams and fasteners that are visible through paint in normal light. Photographing is always a concern if gloss paint (or even eggshell or satin finish) will be applied as a top coat. Even if you plan to coat with latex flat-finish paint, it's a good idea to prepare the drywall to even out the porosity and texture of the surface and the taped seams. There are three ways to do this: by skim-coating with joint compound, by spraying on a primer-surfacer, and by applying a quality priming.

The best way to avoid the problem is to finish the wall to a level 5 finish (see Appendix on p. 212). You can do this by skim-coating the entire surface after the third coat of joint compound has dried (see p. 109). Skim-coating helps to equalize the porosity and texture of the surface. After the skim coat is complete, apply a good-quality primer-sealer or latex flat-finish wall paint before finishing with a top coat. Another way to achieve the level 5 finish is to spray on a primer-surfacer which does the above in one easy step (see p. 110).

Although achieving a level 5 finish is a time-consuming process, it is effective against photographing and becoming more common. If left up to me, I would apply a level 5 finish on any area that will be painted with gloss paint or that will receive a lot of direct light, such as a large, open ceiling.

At the very least, prime all taped surfaces with a quality interior latex flat-finish wall paint. Flat finishes have a very low sheen because of the fillers used to formulate the paint, and these fillers help even out the variations among the drywall face paper, the taped seams, and the fasteners. A light sanding before finish painting also helps.

Proper prep prevents photographing Photographing, the term used to describe taped seams and fasteners that are still visible after painting, can be a problem if drywall isn't adequately prepared.

This light sanding removes small chunks of paint or drywall and knocks down raised fibers on the paper face, leaving a very smooth surface.

If you're working in a room with a finished floor, cover the floor with drop cloths to protect it from paint spatters; cover windows, doors, tubs, showers, and other fixtures with 1-mil plastic (known in the trade as "painter's plastic").

While actually applying the primer or paint it is easier to keep a wet edge if there is not much air movement and excessive heat. This applies not only in cold climates where the heat is on but also in hot climates where the temperature is high and windows are open. After painting, make sure there is good air circulation in the room to help the paint dry properly. And be sure to wait the specified time before recoating.

The prime coat

It usually takes two coats of paint to finish drywall—one prime coat and one top coat. There's a confusing assortment of products that are advertised as prime coats, and it's important to understand the differences among them.

The terms "primer" and "sealer" are commonly used to refer to the first coat of paint applied before a top coat, but these two terms do not refer to the same product. A primer is mainly made of fillers and pigments that are designed to even out textural variations and provide a good adhesion surface for the finish paint. Primers often do not contain enough resin to even out the porosity of the different surfaces on taped drywall; when used as the first coat over drywall, photographing of the seams and fasteners may be a problem (see the sidebar at left).

Sealers have a high resin content, which is good for evening out the porosity of taped surfaces, but they usually cannot correct variations in surface textures. Again, photographing may result after top coats are applied over sealers. Primer-sealers, which combine the qualities of both products, do an adequate job as a prime coat, but they are not my first choice, either.

I find that I get the best results when I prime with a good-quality interior latex flat-finish wall paint. It provides good coverage as a prime coat and minimizes the problem of photographing. If I'm working on walls that will be painted a color other than white, I usually have the flat latex paint tinted to the same color as the top coat to avoid having to apply two top coats. Some manufacturers make a primer designed as a first coat for unfinished drywall. It works great and produces results very similar to those I obtain with flat paint.

A relatively new product on the market is the primer-surfacer that I mentioned on p. 111. I highly recommend this type of finish in larger, very visible areas that are to have a paint with any kind of shine. Remember that these types of products are a primer and a surfacer, so there is no need for an additional prime coat.

The top coat

As with prime coats, there's a bewildering array of products that can be used as top coats. These include paints with flat, egg-shell, satin, semigloss, gloss, and high-gloss finishes. Flat-finish paints are less prone to photographing, but they are harder to maintain. Gloss paints (including eggshell and satin finishes) are easier to wash than flat paints and are less likely to smudge and mark up; they are commonly used in bathrooms, kitchens, and other areas that need frequent cleaning. Gloss paints are primarily wall paints. They are seldom used on ceilings because photographing, which is often a problem with gloss paints, is more pronounced on the large exposed surfaces of a ceiling.

Gloss paints are harder to apply than flat paints and may require two coats for a quality finish. Roller marks or lapped areas that dried slightly before they were blended in become quite obvious on glossy surfaces. Whereas flat paint can be applied as a prime coat, gloss paint should not be applied directly over a taped drywall surface. Always apply a prime coat first.

WORK SMART

Before painting, vacuum or dust out electrical boxes and make sure that there is no dust on top of door and window trim.

WORK SMART

Flat latex wall paint works well as a primer for finishing drywall.

HOW TO PREVENT YELLOWING

After the drywall has been taped and sanded, don't let it sit for too long before painting it. Timely painting is especially important when the surface will be exposed to direct sunlight for any length of time. Sunlight can cause the face paper to yellow or fade. If the face paper becomes too yellow, the color may bleed through slightly when painted; because the taped seams and fasteners will not bleed through, the finish will look streaked. If the face paper has turned yellow, seal the drywall with a good-quality latex stain-killing paint before applying a latex flat-finish prime coat. For bad cases use an oil- or alcohol-based stain blocker.

Priming prevents yellowing Drywall that goes unprimed for a long period of time will turn yellow. This yellow color can bleed through the compound, prime coat, and paint when finally finished.

ABOVE: Choose the right roller Rollers are available in a variety of nap thicknesses for applying different types of paint and for achieving different textured finishes.

BELOW: Thick nap leaves a rough finish Using a roller with a too-thick nap (more than ¼ in.) to apply glossy paint can result in a pocked finish caused by air bubbles.

Painting techniques

There are three ways to apply paint to a wall or ceiling: with a brush, a roller, or a sprayer. Brushes are used mainly for cutting in around trim and painting inside corners. Rollers are used to fill in large areas between brushed edges. Sprayers, which are used to paint an entire surface, are used primarily for large jobs in new construction.

Rolling Paint rollers come in a variety of widths and nap thicknesses. A 9-in.-wide roller, which is the most common size used, is excellent for painting small areas and narrow sections. Other roller widths include 12 in., 18 in., and 24 in. The larger widths work well for bigger jobs, not only because they cover more area with each stroke, but also because they leave fewer roller marks, which are more evident on large, open surfaces.

The nap refers to the thickness of the fibers on the roller. Nap thicknesses range from 1/8 in. to 1/2 in. for regular painting; thicker naps are available for applying and painting textured finishes (see the top photo at left). For best results, apply gloss paints with a 1/4-in.-nap (or thinner) roller. If the nap is too thick, small bubbles will appear on the painted surface. These bubbles soon pop, but they usually leave a small mark or thin spot on the surface that is still evident when the paint dries.

It's best to use a 3/8-in.-nap roller for flat paints. A roller with a shorter nap does not cover the surface as well, and a longer nap leaves a slight texture. Longer-nap rollers (1/2 in. and greater) are used for light texturing and for painting textured surfaces.

For the best results when painting with a roller, apply the final coat by rolling on the paint perpendicular to the taped seams. Each coat should be applied in the opposite direction to the one before it. For example, if two coats will be applied, the prime coat should be applied parallel to the seams and the final coat perpendicular to the seams. This system applies the paint more evenly and there is less chance of missing any spots. The roller flows over minor ridges or crowns along the seams, covering them with paint.

Spraying If you use a sprayer to apply paint, use one that applies undiluted paint, like the model shown on p. 180. Paint is pumped directly from a 1-gal. or 5-gal. pail and applied with a handheld spray gun that is fed through a hose.

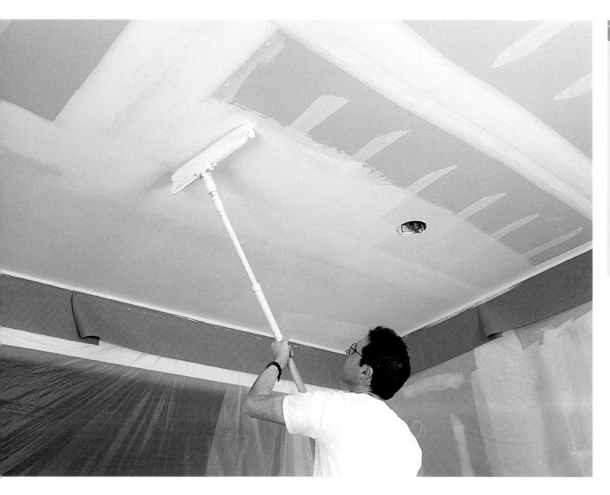

Use the right technique When painting with a roller, apply the prime coat parallel to the taped seams and the top coat perpendicular to the seams.

Using a paint sprayer produces a certain amount of overspray and some airborne paint, so wear a respirator or a dust/mist mask. You'll also need to mask off walls and other areas that you don't want to paint. Follow the same procedure as you would when painting with a roller. Apply a prime coat and then a top coat. It may be tempting to spray on a good heavy coat of paint and be done with it, but the paint will just drip or run. For best results, apply thin, even coats (usually one prime and one top coat for flat paint, one prime and two top coats for gloss).

Spraying paint is much faster than rolling paint, mainly because paint is always available at the nozzle. Most rollers must be dipped into the roller pan repeatedly (although there are now rollers with an automatic feed). For finish painting, I prefer the look of paint that has been rolled on—it just seems to be more uniform and consistent. In order to achieve both the speed of a sprayer and the finish of a roller, use a method called backrolling—apply paint with a sprayer and then have a helper follow close behind and roll it out into a smooth, even finish.

TEXTURING

Decorating ceilings and walls with a textured finish is a very popular alternative to a flat, painted surface. Textured finishes, which can be produced in a wide variety of patterns, add beauty and contrast to drywall surfaces. They are excellent at hiding minor surface

SPRAY SMART

For large areas, spraying saves a lot of time over rolling. When done properly, it also leaves a near-flawless finish. Just be sure to do the proper prep work and follow all safety precautions.

Protect the room, protect yourself
Wear a respirator when using a paint sprayer; cover walls and other surfaces to protect them from overspray.

For a flawless finish
To save time and achieve a smooth, even finish, apply paint with a sprayer and then roll it out.

> ## WORK SMART
>
> Texture surfaces using a drying-type compound—it goes on easily, dries quickly, and has no odor.

imperfections and irregularities and, in their coarser forms, provide a certain degree of sound control.

There are a variety of textured finishes that can be created with a regular or an irregular pattern. The texture can be applied with a brush, roller, trowel, sprayer, or combination of these tools. The surface is usually primed before texturing and sometimes painted after texturing. My favorite method of texturing is to apply the texture either by spraying or by hand and then use a knockdown knife to smooth over the texture and create a more uniform and easier-to-maintain texture. I usually use a drying type compound as my texture material because they go on easy, dry fast, and don't leave a bad smell in the room.

Preparation

Applying textures reduces the amount of surface preparation required, but the surface must still be clean, dry, and sound. Textured finishes are only as good as the surfaces to which they are applied. Always apply a prime coat to new drywall and to any area where repairs have been made. If the surface is not new but has a clean, flat, painted surface, a prime coat is not necessary.

Seal any stains with an oil-based stain-killing paint. Apply texture to a small test area to check for stain bleed-through. Most textures have a high water content and take about 24 hours to dry. If a stain is not properly sealed, it will quickly bleed through and discolor the texture.

Ceilings that have yellowed after years of exposure to smoke, particularly cigarette smoke, need special preparation prior to texturing. The surfaces should be washed before any necessary repairs are made and then primed with latex flat-finish wall paint. Once again as an extra precaution, texture a small test area to check for stain bleed-through. If the texture in the test area is still white after an hour or so, then it should be safe to texture the entire surface.

Water-based textures may cause ceiling drywall to sag between joists if the maximum o.c. spacing for joists has exceeded the requirements for the thickness of the drywall (see Chapter 1). For example, 3/8-in. drywall is not recommended on ceilings, especially if the ceiling will be textured. If you're texturing 1/2-in. drywall, the spacing of the joists should not exceed 16 in. o.c.; for 5/8-in. drywall, the spacing can be up to 24 in. o.c. Both thicknesses of drywall should be attached perpendicular to the joists. Controlling the humidity by providing a good heat source and proper ventilation is also very important.

Application

Textures are usually applied with special spray equipment. For smaller residential jobs, they are most commonly sprayed on with a hand-

Use the right tools This simple compressor and handheld hopper, which apply textured finishes, are available at rental tool centers.

GENERAL GUIDELINES FOR TEXTURING

- Make sure the surface is clean and seal any stains. If stains are a concern, texture a test area to check for bleed-through.

- Fill any cracks or holes in the surface and taped areas to create a smooth finish.

- Allow taped areas to dry completely before texturing.

- Use latex flat-finish wall paint as a prime coat to give the surface a low-luster appearance.

- Maintain a temperature of at least 55°F before, during, and after the texture is applied. Keep the area well ventilated while the texture is drying.

- For ceiling textures, make sure the joists' o.c. spacing meets maximum recommended guidelines to avoid potential sagging problems.

- Cover areas that are not going to be textured or clean up overspray promptly.

- Dull or roughen glossy surfaces to help the prime coat adhere better.

PROTECTING SURFACES FROM OVERSPRAY

In new construction, overspray from the ceiling can be scraped off the walls with a wide trowel; when dry, it can be sanded before the walls are decorated. If a wall texture will be applied, very little sanding is necessary.

If the walls are already sanded or decorated, they must be protected from overspray. I like to use a 12-in.-wide strip of paper masked around the perimeter of the ceiling. A paper roller machine, which applies tape to the paper's edge as it is unrolled, works great for this purpose. The tool and paper can be purchased at auto-body supply stores.

When a ceiling is sprayed, a certain amount of texture settles to the floor and lower walls. Protect floors with drop cloths and walls with 1-mil painter's plastic. Tuck and tape the plastic underneath the 12-in.-wide paper along the ceiling. Taking the time to cover everything before texturing makes for a quick and easy cleanup at the end of the job.

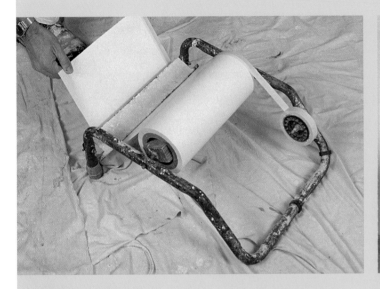

Roller machine speeds work A paper roller machine applies tape to paper as the paper is unrolled. Use the paper to protect the top edge of walls, light fixtures, and so on.

Protect the fixtures Tape 12-in. strips of paper around fixtures using masking tape.

Cover up Cover floors with drop cloths and walls and furniture with painter's plastic.

held hopper (see the bottom right photo on the facing page) and an air compressor. On larger residential and commercial jobs, larger texturing machines feed the material through a hose and into a spray gun. Spray equipment can be rented.

The air, surface, and texture temperatures should all be at least 55°F during and after application. Once the texture has been applied, the room should be properly ventilated to help the texture dry. In an unventilated room, there is a greater risk of the drywall sagging as the moisture is absorbed into the drywall panels. Under very hot and dry conditions, the texture may dry too quickly, causing cracking and a poor bond.

Sprayed-on acoustical ceiling textures

Sprayed-on acoustical textures, often referred to as popcorn ceilings, were once one of the most common textures applied. They're also one of the easiest to apply. The texture comes in a dry form containing solid particles made of either vermiculite (puffed mica) or polystyrene.

After mixing the dry texture with the recommended amount of water, use a handheld hopper or spray gun to apply the material. Spray the texture by holding the applicator 2 ft. to 4 ft. away from the surface (see the bottom right photo on the facing page). Move the sprayer from side to side, applying a thin, even layer as you walk around the room. Then apply another layer, moving around the room in the opposite direction. Working this way helps avoid streaks or patterns that may result from applying the texture from a single direction. Finish the entire ceiling in one session.

Painting a popcorn ceiling is not usually necessary, because the texture is white and will stay white unless it is exposed to smoke from cigarettes, kerosene heaters, or fireplaces. However, popcorn ceilings can be

painted if a more durable and easier-to-clean surface is required (an unpainted popcorn ceiling is not washable) or if a different color is desired. It may also be necessary to paint over the texture if it is stained or discolored for any reason.

An airless paint sprayer can be used to apply latex paint to a popcorn ceiling, but care must be taken to move along quickly. Because latex paint is water based, it will loosen the texture and damage the ceiling if it is oversprayed or if it is applied with a roller or brush. If you want to paint the ceiling with a roller, use a flat oil-based paint with a long-nap roller ($^1/2$ in. or more). Give a freshly textured popcorn ceiling 24 hours to dry before painting it. If you want to decorate with glitter, blow it onto the surface as you apply the paint.

REMOVING A POPCORN CEILING

Styles change. When I first started in business, popcorn ceilings were the rage. Now I rarely apply a new popcorn texture. But I certainly remove a lot of them!

If the ceiling has never been painted the popcorn is easy to remove. It can simply be scraped off with a taping knife and then finish sanded. The drywall will most likely have to be coated and patched with compound here and there because the knife will dig things up a little. Also the original taping job may not be good enough to just be painted over. If a different texture is going to be applied, you can usually just patch bad spots and prime the ceiling before texturing.

Scraping off the texture is a very dusty job, and even the most careful sealing-off is not enough. Because popcorn texture is water soluble, spraying the ceiling with a fine mist of water or rolling water on with a paint roller not only loosens up the texture but also helps cut down on dust. Don't get things so wet that the face paper of the drywall is damaged—just dampen the texture a little ahead of the person scraping. To help protect the room, I usually put another layer of drops over the floor and leave everything covered until the new texture or painting is finished.

WORK SMART

When texturing with hand-held tools, don't be afraid to experiment—just because you've never seen the pattern you create doesn't mean it won't look good. But be sure you can replicate the techniques over the entire area.

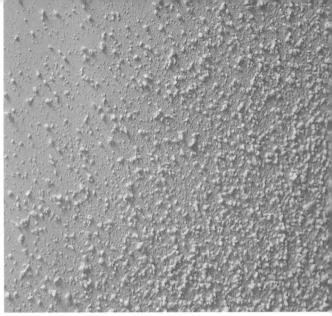

ABOVE: Choose your finish Popcorn ceiling textures are available in coarse, medium, and fine grades.

LEFT: Mix paint and texture A hopper holds the texture before it is mixed with paint and applied to surfaces.

Sprayed-on wall textures

Textures add a beautiful effect to walls; however, because walls are exposed to more wear and tear than ceilings, the texture must be durable and easy to wash and paint. Two very popular wall textures (which also make excellent ceiling textures) are orange-peel texture and knockdown texture. Each one is applied with the same spraying equipment that is used to apply popcorn ceilings. To vary the desired pattern, you simply adjust the size of the nozzle opening and the force of the air pressure.

You can buy special texturing compounds to create these textures, but you can achieve excellent results using an all-purpose joint compound that has been watered down and mixed thoroughly. (Setting-type compounds are not recommended because they can set up in the spraying equipment, making removal very difficult.)

Orange-peel texture An orange-peel texture is achieved by thinning joint compound with water. This makes it flow easily through the spraying equipment but, once applied, it stays in place without running or sagging.

An orange-peel texture can be applied directly over a freshly taped drywall surface. However, if orange-peel texturing is part of a redecorating scheme, the surface should be smooth, solid, and first painted with flat-finish latex wall paint.

Make a test area before finishing the entire surface. Hold the spray nozzle at a consistent distance from the wall (2 ft. to 3 ft. works well) and apply the texture evenly. Make sure the texture is consistent by mixing each batch of joint compound to the same thickness and keeping the airflow and nozzle opening at the same settings throughout the job.

Knockdown texture A knockdown texture is typically made from a coarser-consistency compound than an orange-peel texture. Apply the material in the same way, wait about 10 minutes, and then use a large flat trowel with a curved blade to knock down the raised surface of the texture (see the bottom left photo on p. 186). Pull the trowel lightly along the surface, holding the blade almost flat and applying very little pressure. For best results, pull the trowel perpendicular to the drywall seams and in only one direction.

Always prime the surface before applying a knockdown texture. The primer equalizes the absorption rates between the drywall and the taped areas. If you don't prime, the texture will dry faster on the taped surfaces. When you knock down the finish, the drier areas will not smooth out as much as the wetter ones, resulting in a texture that highlights the taped areas. If the surface is irregular and wavy, I don't recommend applying a knockdown texture, because the trowel will just hit the high areas and leave the low areas untouched, resulting in a spotty appearance.

TOP LEFT: Small repairs Texture-repair sprayers are convenient for retexturing damaged areas of textured finishes.

ABOVE: An orange-peel texture To create an orange-peel texture, spray thinned joint compound onto a surface. In this case the walls were not primed ahead of time because there won't be any trowel work.

LEFT: For a different look Vary the appearance of an orange-peel texture by adjusting the air pressure of the compressor and the diameter of the spray nozzle.

REPAIRING TEXTURED SURFACES

If a popcorn ceiling is damaged or badly stained, and it is determined that the best way to fix the ceiling is to retexture it (rather than just repainting it), scrape off the entire ceiling with a wide taping knife. Repair the damaged area, reprime it, and then spray on a new layer of texture. If the majority of the ceiling is still nice and white, you can repair and respray just the damaged areas. Scrape the texture off with a taping knife and feather the edges to avoid creating ridges that may show when the ceiling is retextured. To repair cracks in textured ceilings, scrape off the texture around the crack, patch the crack, and then prime and retexture the area. To touch up small damaged spots, mix a small amount of texture and apply it to the area with a paintbrush.

To blend in the edge where the repair meets the texture I use a sponge to create a gradual transition. This makes the repair less conspicuous when retextured.

KNOCKDOWN TEXTURES

Knockdown textures are achieved by applying compound to the wall using a hopper. To add the knockdown effect, the surface is then smoothed with a knife.

1. Spray on the texture
To create a knockdown texture, spray compound as you would for an orange-peel texture but use a coarser consistency.

2. Knock down the high spots
Wait 10 minutes or so and then use a knife similar to the one shown here to smooth out the tops of the texture. For the best results, pull the knife perpendicular to the drywall seams.

Vary the look
I like to paint the ceiling white before applying the texture to obtain a subtle contrast between the slightly different colors.

Once orange-peel and knockdown textures are dry, they should be painted so the surface will be washable and more durable. These textured finishes can be applied to ceilings as well as walls.

Hand-applied textures

In addition to sprayed-on textures, there are many textures that can be applied by hand. Some of these textures have repeating patterns, which require a very steady hand to perfect. I have better luck with hand-applied textures that have a nice, uniform finish or intentional irregularities. The textures discussed here, which can be created with texturing compounds, all-purpose compounds, or setting-type compounds, are simple to apply and easy to maintain.

Roller textures Roller textures are made by watering down joint compound to a consistency that will hold its shape and not run or sag when rolled onto the drywall surface. Use a short-nap roller (1/2 in. or less) and apply the compound as evenly as possible to the entire surface. Let the compound dry for 10 minutes or until the surface looks dull. Go over the surface again with the roller, leaving the desired textural appearance.

Knockdown roller finishes Knockdown roller finishes are achieved in the same way as roller textures. However, the texture is then flattened with a large, flat, curved-blade trowel. Hold the trowel almost flat against the surface and use very little pressure as you pull it along in the same direction as the rolled-on texture.

Hand-trowel finishes Hand-trowel finishes are best achieved with undiluted joint compound or a texturing material. Apply a thin layer of compound to the entire surface in an irregular, random design using a 6-in. taping knife. The thickness of the compound should vary from some areas that are bare to areas that are 1/8 in. or so thick. Trowel marks, ridges, and low areas are desirable when creating this finish.

Regular paint roller

Stipple roller

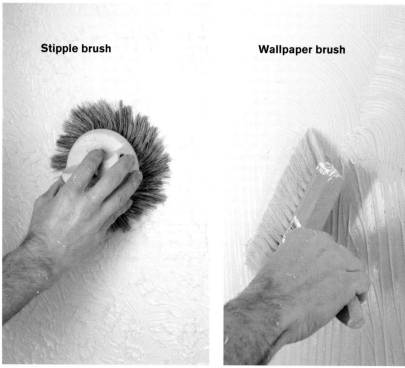

Stipple brush

Wallpaper brush

Hand applied textures By applying diluted compound with a paint roller then texturing with a hand tool, you can create an almost endless variety of finishes. A stipple brush (above left), wallpaper brush (above right), stipple roller (left), and regular paint roller (top left) are used to create different textures.

Once dry, all of these hand-applied textures should be coated with quality paint for easy maintenance and a more durable finish. Usually one coat of paint is sufficient to cover the surface.

WALL COVERINGS

Drywall is an excellent surface for all types of wall coverings, including regular wallpaper, fabric-backed wallpaper, and vinyl-paper-backed cloth. The surface should be sound, as smooth as possible, and free of peeling paint or plaster. If the surface is rough and loose, the wall covering will also be rough and loose, and it will not adhere securely. Thinner, shinier coverings require a smoother finished wall because they hide very few blemishes. Heavier wall coverings do not require nearly as perfect a finish. Also keep in mind that wall coverings are applied

wet, so it is important that stains be sealed properly. Otherwise, moisture from the wall covering's adhesive may cause the stain to bleed through.

Preparation

For most wall coverings, you'll need to prepare the drywall with three coats of joint compound and then sand it smooth, (a level 4 finish). Then apply a prime coat of latex flat wall paint. Once the paint is completely dry, apply a good-quality primer-sizer. This is a water-based product that serves a number of purposes. It helps wall coverings bond to surfaces (even to glossy or vinyl-covered ones), it prevents underlying colors from showing through thin wallpapers, and it minimizes damage to drywall when the wall covering is removed.

WORK SMART

When texturing by hand, it's a good idea to practice the technique on a sample board before committing yourself to the wall or ceiling.

CHAPTER

9

The Basics of Sound Control

Limit noise transmission Installing insulation on interior walls helps prevent sound from bouncing around in the stud cavity and then entering the adjacent room.

Noise is simply unwanted sound that is transmitted by vibration through air, walls, floors, or ceilings. In a home, most people consider noise to be just about any sound other than those made by what they are doing. If my boys are watching television in the living room next to the kitchen, they cannot stand it when my wife Linda is talking on the phone in the kitchen, so they turn the television up and then Linda can't hear because the television is too loud. Of course, that only compounds the problem.

As I sit typing in my home office in the basement, a sliding door opens to the outside and I can hear Linda mowing the lawn. Also, someone has left the door to the laundry room open and I can hear the washing machine spinning and switching from one cycle to the next. On top of that, Christopher, my younger son, is bouncing a basketball in his bedroom. All this unwanted sound is driving me crazy.

RIGHT: Shared walls transmit sound The wall where the vanity is located is a common wall with a bedroom. If this wall is left untreated for sound control, you'll be able to hear most of the bathroom noise from the bedroom.

BELOW: Sound travels through ductwork This air duct feeds not only this office area but also a small factory behind the wall, creating a direct path for transmitting sound.

Buildings are full of noise—from water heaters, dishwashers, and various other appliances. Add to that the noises that occur when people actually live and work in a building and it can become an issue for all of the building contractors to consider. But there are ways to cut down on the noise. With the right planning, sound can be contained and peace restored. Designing structures to control noise effectively makes homes and offices more pleasant places to live and work.

THE DRYWALLER'S ROLE

If acoustic goals are to be achieved, all of the contractors and subcontractors must be part of the team. Because the drywall contractor is right in the middle of things, he can play an important role in sound control. After all, drywall adds mass to a wall or ceiling and mass helps reduce sound transmission. But sound control is a complex issue, and it's not always as easy as choosing and installing the right drywall. In this chapter, I explain the basics of sound control from a drywaller's vantage point.

Sound control means different things to different people. I have worked on a few jobs

where a multifaceted sound control system was designed and everyone involved went to long lengths to contain noise. Other times, I am simply asked to install the insulation and caulk gaps before I hang and finish the drywall. Keep in mind that good acoustic design is a chain that requires each of its component links to be strong—the acoustics of a structure are only as good as the weakest link. For me, the more thorough the design, the better: I enjoy the detailed work that sound control demands. Whether you're aiming for the most thorough sound control or simply making a few tweaks to limit noise transmission, the drywaller plays a key roll in implementing an acoustic design.

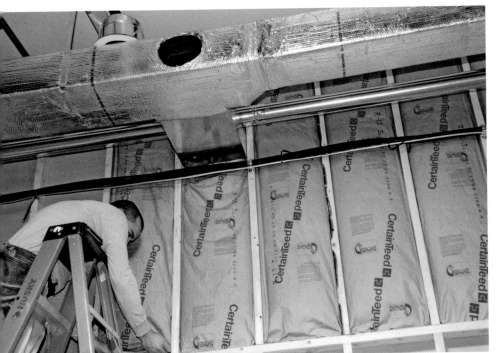

DEVELOP A PLAN

It is far less costly to consider noise control at the design stage and install solutions from the very beginning of construction than it is to retrofit solutions after the building has been built. When my wife and I were designing our house, it was only the two of us so we didn't think too much about noise control. We thought about how we lived and where we wanted things. I hung the bathroom mirror high so that I wouldn't have to duck to see myself. It wasn't until we had kids that I realized it would be another 15 years before they would be able to use the mirror. This was an easy fix; I just bought a larger mirror.

But now this same bathroom shares a common wall with the master bedroom. We didn't treat this wall in any way for sound control. On the bathroom side of the wall there is $1/2$-in. drywall over 2x4 construction. The bedroom side is covered with $3/4$-in. tongue-and-groove pine. Not only is there no insulation in the wall, but there is also a common heat duct in the wall. The vanity is also a problem because of the squeaky faucet handle, the sink drain, and the impact noise that occurs when the drawers and cabinet doors are closed.

Unfortunately, the kids usually go to bed later than I do, so the noise traveling through this wall causes me to lose sleep. It would have been simple to control this noise

25 years ago during construction, but it never occurred to us that noise would be a problem. At this stage, limiting the sound transmission isn't an easy fix.

Measure the sound

The first step in developing a sound control plan is to figure out how much noise will actually be present. You need to know a few terms and formulas before you can determine what steps should be taken.

STC—Sound Transmission Class STC is a rating for airborne noise reduction through walls and partitions. An STC value is a single number rating used to classify the sound insulating value of a partition (a wall, floor, or ceiling, for instance). A partition prevents sound from being transmitted directly from one area to another. The higher the STC rating, the less sound will be transmitted.

NOISE CONTROL MISTAKES TO AVOID

- Thinking sound control is not an issue.
- Not considering noise control before a project begins.
- Not conducting a detailed study of noisy equipment.
- Not using a systematic approach to noise control.
- Not sealing up leaks.

SOUND TRANSMISSION CLASS (STC)

STC	SPEECH AUDIBILITY	NOISE CONTROL RATING
15–25	Normal speech easily understood	Poor
25–35	Loud speech easily understood	Marginal
35–45	Half of loud speech understood	Good
45–55	Loud speech faintly heard but not understood	Very Good
55–higher	Loud speech usually not heard	Excellent

Given a typical background noise level of 30dB on the "listening" side.

Decibel (dB) levels The decibel (dB) is used to express sound intensity or loudness. The more intense a sound, the higher the dB level. An increase of only 10 dB translates into sound that is twice as loud. Any sound more than 5 dB above the background noise level can be distracting or can interfere with sleep.

The easiest way to figure out how these measures and ratings dictate the necessary sound control tactics is to look at an everyday example. Consider someone watching TV. The sound levels within that room vary from 60 dB to 80 dB. On the other side of the wall is a bedroom where someone may be sleeping and where the sound is heard at approximately 30dB. Using simple math: 80dB-30dB = 50dB. We have determined we need a wall with an STC of approximately 50 to reduce the TV noise to an acceptable level in the bedroom. For more on STC ratings, see the chart "Sound Transmission Class," on p. 191.

For residential partition walls, recommended STC ratings depend on the particular type of room: For example, a bedroom with an STC rating between 45 and 55 is considered good; anything above 55 is considered excellent. Living rooms should be a couple of points higher. Bathrooms and kitchens should be about 5 points higher.

Frequency Measured in cycles per second and expressed in hertz (Hz), frequency refers to the number of complete cycles of a vibration that occur in a second. High frequencies, which STC ratings pertain to, are generally easier to deal with than low frequencies (bass). The bass frequency is more of a structure-borne noise, and it is best dealt with by using some form of decoupling, which means disconnecting the vibration path.

It should be noted that the STC does not really take low frequencies into consideration. If you are faced with a situation where you are dealing with low frequencies, such as

Using mass-loaded vinyl The mass-loaded vinyl product covering this entire wall works not only by adding mass to the wall, but it also because it is a nonrigid material that slows vibrations.

a home theater, considering only the STC rating may not be enough. For further sound control measures, see the discussion of impact noise in the section on floors and ceilings on p. 204.

CONTROLLING NOISE

Sound control can actually be thought of as vibration control. Sound is produced when a vibrating object causes air particles around it to vibrate, producing sound waves that can travel through almost any material in your home. These sound waves are either airborne (like the sound of a human voice) or structure borne (like when the sound of a voice hits a wall and causes the wall to vibrate). In most noise control situations both airborne and structure borne sound must be addressed. All structure-borne sound must eventually become airborne in order for us to hear it. Also, keep in mind that sound will always travel through the path of least resistance—any place where air can leak through is a path where sound can leak through.

Sound travels from the source, along a path, and to the listener or receiver. There are four ways to control this movement:

• Replace or treat the sound source.

• Add mass—block the sound with a heavy, solid material that resists the transmission of sound waves.

• Absorb the sound with a light, porous material that soaks up sound waves. This can be done at the source, along the path, and at the location of the receiver.

• Break up the sound waves as they travel through the structure.

Start at the source

As you develop a gameplan for dealing with noise, it is almost always best to start by look-

When designing a sound control system, both direct and flanking paths must be considered.

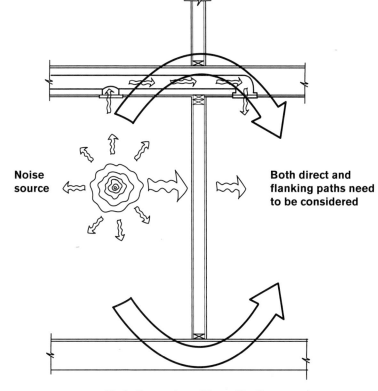

Noise source

Both direct and flanking paths need to be considered

Illustration courtesy of Green Glue Company

ing at the source. Dealing with noise at the source—instead of creating a means by which to contain it—is usually the most cost effective alternative. And it's often the easiest. Can you simply move the source of noise? Does replacing the source alleviate or minimize the problem? Or perhaps the source of noise only needs a small adjustment or repair.

Block the path

If you can't alter the source of the noise, the next option is to block the path along which sound is traveling. Blocking means adding mass; the more mass the sound waves encounter, the shorter the distance they travel. More mass, in other words, equals less

vibration. And less vibration means less noise.
When it comes to blocking, a continuous barrier is best—any points of penetration allow
sound to travel. For this reason, be thorough
and make sure all gaps are sealed up.

Absorb the sound

Sound absorption is the ability of a material to transform acoustical energy into some
other form of energy, most often heat. The
material used for absorption purposes is
usually light and porous, including various
types of objects. Different textures also absorb sound. Installing insulation is the most
common—and often easiest—way to achieve
absorption.

Break up the sound waves

In order to break up sound waves, you need
to break up the vibration path. Anything disconnecting the path of sound waves helps in

sound control. Building separate walls or ceilings (building a room within a room) or installing acoustical furring helps control noise
by breaking up the path where sound wants
to travel. The air spaces separating walls and
ceilings help break up the sound waves, as
does using rubber or similar connectors that
interrupt the travel of sound waves.

TROUBLE SPOTS AND SOLUTIONS

When treating any part of a room—a wall,
ceiling, or door, for instance—for sound
control it is important to remember that
sound will travel through any gap or hole,
so I like to start by sealing up these places.
These small details are often the weakest
link in a sound control plan because they're
easily overlooked or ignored. But even
defects that aren't large enough to be of
structural concern can be large enough to
warrant acoustical concern. Airborne sound
only needs the slightest gap to travel easily
from room to room.

The key to sealing up these gaps is to use
a caulk that stays flexible over a long period

HOW SOUND TRAVELS

Noise causes standard wall construction to vibrate, conduct, and radiate sound.

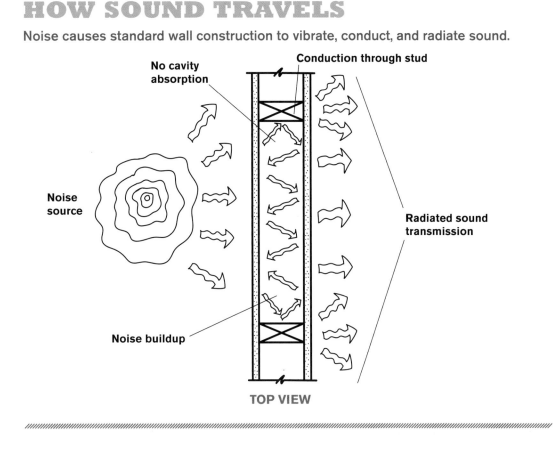

No cavity absorption

Conduction through stud

Noise source

Noise buildup

Radiated sound transmission

TOP VIEW

WORK SMART

To help absorb sound as it travels in a ceiling cavity from room to room, fill the entire cavity with insulation along the perimeter of the ceiling at the path to another room.

NOISE CONTROL ON THE JOBSITE

Working on a construction site can be very noisy. If I'm taping on a nice summer day, I like to have the windows open and maybe the radio on. But the portable electric generator, just outside the house, is noisy and the racket really takes way form the enjoyment of working. What are my options?

- Treat the source: Put the generator far away from the house and run long electric cords.

- Treat the path: You can also block or reflect the sound by standing a sheet of plywood next to the generator between the house and the generator. Or simply close the doors and windows facing the generator.

- Treat the receiver by using ear protection.

The easiest thing to do is to close the doors and windows, but I hate doing it in nice weather. And nobody really likes wearing ear protection. In this situation, treating the source usually works best for me.

The work environment A noisy generator at a job site can be a real annoyance. You can either live with the noise or treat it. It can be treated at the source, along the path, or at the receiver.

A STANDARD FRAMED WALL

A wall free of plumbing, electrical, or heating and air ductwork can be easily treated for sound control.

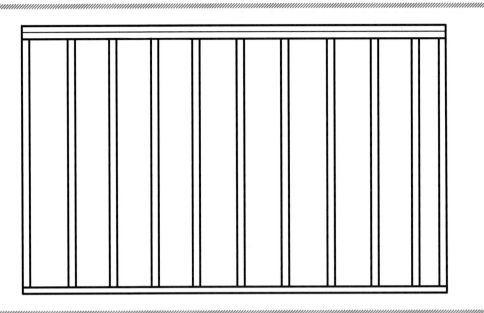

SOUND FOLLOWS MANY PATHS

With most walls in real-world construction—like this common wall between a bedroom and a bathroom—there are numerous spots that make sound control difficult.

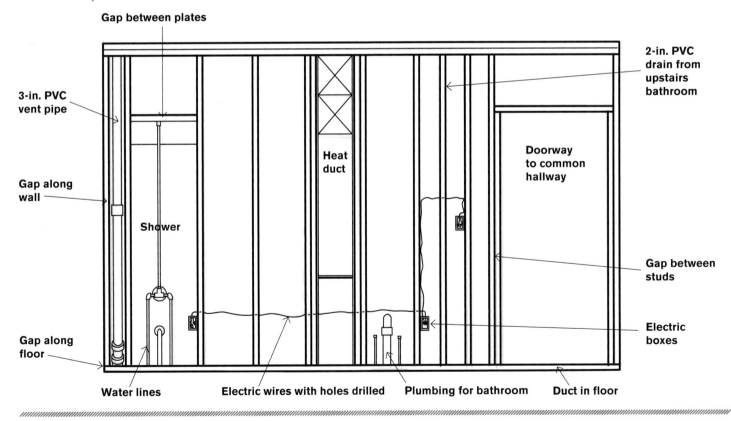

Gap between plates

3-in. PVC vent pipe

Gap along wall

Shower

Gap along floor

Water lines

Heat duct

Electric wires with holes drilled

Plumbing for bathroom

2-in. PVC drain from upstairs bathroom

Doorway to common hallway

Gap between studs

Electric boxes

Duct in floor

BELOW: Fire-resistant sealants Because both sound and fire can travel through gaps and holes–especially ductwork–it is sometimes necessary to close up gaps using a fire-resistant sealant.

of time. There are specialized acoustical sealants made for this purpose, but any caulk that stays flexible and stretches will work.

Electrical boxes create holes

Electrical boxes are a major culprit for transmitting airborne sound. They're full of holes and actually create a hole in a wall or ceiling assembly. When back-to-back electrical boxes are installed, they create an almost direct patch from one room to the next. To limit noise transmission, electrical boxes should be separated by at least a couple of studs bays.

To seal an electrical box, fill all of the holes with caulk, then wrap the fixture with mass-loaded vinyl. After the vinyl is in place, seal any gaps in the vinyl with caulk. Seam tape can be used to tie together any small pieces of vinyl.

Ductwork transmits sound

A run of duct work is like an intercom system when it comes to sound movement. Noise enters through the register openings or by

vibrating through the thin metal wall, travels to other rooms, and broadcasts itself through registers and air returns at various locations throughout the building. For this reason, plan ahead when you're installing ductwork.

A room that is being targeted for noise control may need to have a separate run of ductwork for only that space. Consider using ductwork that is lined with insulation, because insulation absorbs a great deal of the sound before it can travel very far. Many of the flexible ducts work quite well for this purpose.

Empty spaces carry sound

Filling spaces like stud cavities and space between floors with insulation is always a good idea. Simply filling these spaces can increase the STC rating by 5 points or more. These voids need only to be filled, and there is no need to stuff it tight—tighter is no better. Just avoid leaving any gaps in the insulation. The insulation in the cavities does not increase the STC by adding mass, it simply absorbs the sound in the cavity. In addition to filling spaces with insulation, you'll get better results if small holes are filled with caulk or foam.

Minimize plumbing noise

A well-planned plumbing layout helps to minimize the noise of flowing water. Using

ABOVE: Containing sound The high wall in the back of this workshop has an air conditioning register that connects directly to the adjoining office. Though this should have been avoided, lining the duct with insulation will help prevent sound from traveling into the office.

LEFT: Cover the ductwork I cut the sound-deadening material just a bit larger than the stud bay and fasten it to the studs with drywall screws. For a tight seal around the edges we spray foam or some caulk.

DUCTWORK IS A PATHWAY FOR SOUND

In this case, even the most thorough sound control treatments of the walls between these two rooms can be voided out by the air ducts.

Close up the gaps In this wall the owner used 2-in.-thick blue foam board in attempt to reduce noise transmission. It filled in the space but there are large gaps that should be sealed with foam.

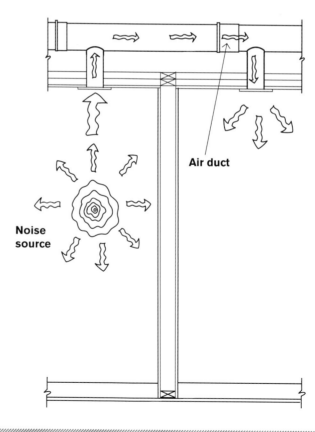

Air duct

Noise source

RIGHT: Sound sources hide in the ceiling These drain pipes from an upstairs bathroom can generate a lot of noise that will be heard in the room below.

FAR RIGHT: Wrap the pipes Wrapping the drain pipes with an insulated, mass-loaded material helps contain noise traveling through the pipes.

THINK AHEAD

PVC drainpipes are very poor at insulating sound, so it's easy to hear through the pipe. But even without water in the pipe, sound travels along the pathway of the pipe, as is the case with ductwork.

oversize pipes and reduced pressure slows the speed of flowing water; in turn, noise is reduced. It also helps to isolate piping from the structure with resilient pads and sleeves, and then seal them up so that they are airtight. Wrapping pipes with a sound absorbing and blocking material provides additional help. All openings cut into the framing need to be caulked. In the walls and cavities containing plumbing pipes, you can also install mass-loaded and absorbing material to contain the noise.

In the drawing of the bathroom/bedroom wall on p. 196, we were trying to stop bathroom noise from entering the bedroom. A good plumbing plan would have helped: It would have been much easier to locate the pipes in different walls or even separated walls. But without a well-thought-out plan, we were left to do the best with what we had.

Wall strategies for sound control

Adding mass is an essential part of an effective sound control system. Typical coverings such as drywall, plaster, or wood are all heavy, dense materials that add mass to the assembly. These dense materials do not vibrate easily and, therefore, help cut down on noise. Adding an extra layer of wall covering on one or both sides of a wall helps improve the sound rating.

A typical, insulated 2x4 wall makes a good example. With the customary single layer of ½-in. drywall on both sides, the wall has an STC rating of 38. Add an extra layer of ½-in. drywall on only one side and you boost the STC rating to 40. By adding an extra layer to both sides, the STC rating jumps to 46.

You can see the increase of STC rating with mass, but it is not dramatic. The main reason is that the added mass does not eliminate the vibration of sound into the 2x4 studs and out the other side of the wall, it simply reduces the vibration. Still, it helps.

Mass-loaded vinyl There are situations when you don't want to add much to the thickness of a wall. Perhaps, for example, the wall has already been built and electrical boxes have been set to accommodate the thickness of ½-in. drywall. When this happens, adding an extra layer of drywall would mean calling in the electrical contractors. Still, you're looking for an easy way to create a higher STC rating. In these cases, use a product called mass-loaded vinyl behind the drywall. The vinyl that I typically use is 1/8 in. thick and weighs about 1 lb. per sq. ft. It is very effective because of its high density and flexibility.

Use sound board to dampen sound

Sound board is a commonly used product installed as a substrate behind the finish material. It's usually a lower density material designed to go up on the walls against the framing. Sound board has an absorbing and damping effect on the movement of sound. (Damping, as it pertains to sound control, means reducing the vibration that travels through the material.) Sound board helps control noise transmission between living spaces by trapping and diffusing frequencies

Adding mass The dense vinyl material helps prevent noise transmission. It can be easily attached to the studs before the drywall is hung.

DOUBLE UP THE DRYWALL

With only one layer of drywall on each side of a conventional 2x4 stud wall the STC rating is 38. By adding a second layer of drywall to one side of the wall, the STC rating moves to 40, but by adding an extra layer to each side of the wall, the STC rating jumps to 46.

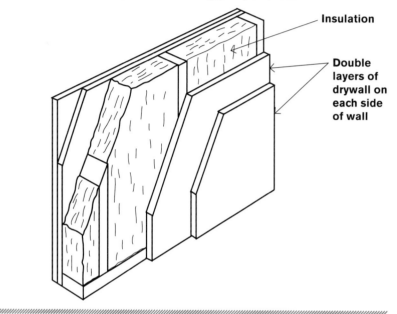

Insulation

Double layers of drywall on each side of wall

USING MASS-LOADED VINYL

This 2x4 wall is treated with both insulation and a dense vinyl mat to prevent sound transmission. Regular 1/2-in. drywall is installed directly over the vinyl. Not only is the vinyl thinner (1/8 in.) than an additional layer of drywall, but it also does a better job controlling sound. This wall has an STC rating of 55.

Dense vinyl mat

Insulation

1/2-in. drywall

SINGLE WOOD STUDS WITH A RESILIENT CHANNEL

Over a 2×4 stud wall, resilient channel can be installed before ½-in. drywall is attached. If you add resilient channel to one side, the wall jumps from an STC rating of 38 to 47. If you add a second layer of drywall to each side, the STC rating jumps to 55.

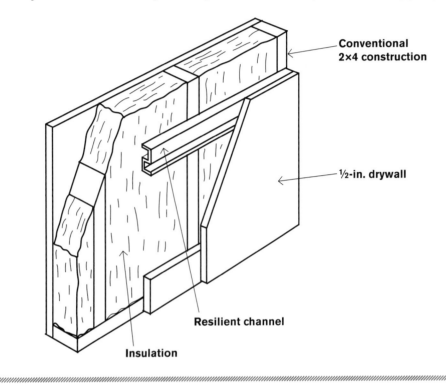

Conventional 2×4 construction

½-in. drywall

Resilient channel

Insulation

that mass-loaded covering doesn't. It can also be attached to the resilient channel and sound clips (explained later).

Breaking eliminates vibration Other ways to decrease sound vibration is to eliminate the direct connection of materials. Constructing staggered stud walls (essentially, building rooms within rooms) and applying resilient channel strips and sound clips, are all common techniques. For more on these techniques, see the drawings on pp. 202, 203, and 205.

Shared floors and ceilings

Floor/ceiling assemblies (surfaces in multi-floor buildings that are floors on top and ceilings on the bottom) create their own set of problems. The main difference between walls

and floor/ceilings is that with a floor/ceiling assembly you are usually dealing with both impact and airborne noise. To visualize the problem, think of a ball bouncing on the second floor of a house (see the bottom drawing on p. 205): Not only does the ball create the impact noise when it hits the floor, but it also creates airborne structural noise—noise passing through the air cavity and then the ceiling below.

Many of the materials and techniques used to retrofit a wall for sound control also apply to floor/ceiling assemblies. Just as with walls, pay attention to details, caulk and seal gaps, add more mass, and add products that isolate or dampen sound. After you study the drawing on p. 205, you'll notice that the noise

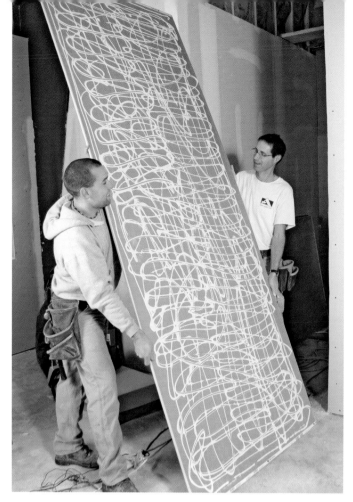

ABOVE: Absorbing sound Sound board is often installed behind drywall for its absorbing and damping qualities.

LEFT: Use damping materials A damping material is applied to the back of a sheet of drywall that will be attached over another layer of drywall or soundboard.

STAGGERED WOOD STUD WALLS

Studs can be staggered along the wall, creating a larger cavity and more opportunity for sound control. Here, insulation is installed between each stud, with wider, continuous lengths installed between every other stud. Once insulated and covered on both sides with ½-in. drywall, this wall has an STC rating of 50.

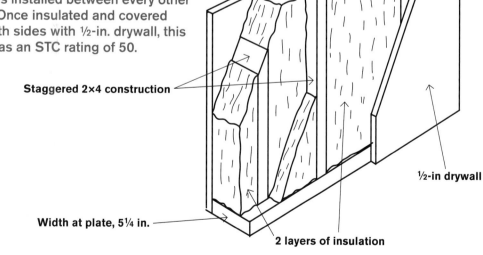

Staggered 2×4 construction

Width at plate, 5¼ in.

2 layers of insulation

½-in drywall

ABOVE: Sound overhead Having multiple utilities in a ceiling is very common. The result is the potential for a lot of noise to travel from room to room.

RIGHT: Reducing impact noises The padding seen here, called acoustipad, helps reduce impact noise without adding a great deal of mass to the assembly. Photo courtesy of Sound Sense

can travel freely through the structure. The solution becomes obvious: Treat the noise at the floor.

Treat impact noise at the floor One of the best products available for controlling impact noise is carpet with a thick pad. The soft carpet and thick pad cushion the impact so that far less energy is delivered to the floor and therefore to the structure. Carpets and pads, however, have little effect on airborne sound, like voices traveling from one floor to the next.

Use resilient underlayments The use of underlayments means installing a surface material over a resilient layer. Resilient layers come in many forms, including the following:

• Rubber or vinyl mats

• Rigid fiberglass

• Foams of various sorts

• Low-density sound board

• Cork

These resilient underlayments can be covered with plywood and then hardwood or concrete flooring, cement board and tile, or any other floor covering. Because resilient underlayments work to keep energy away from the structure, they are an effective means of sound control on both sides of the floor/ceiling. They also contribute more mass than carpets, so they work better to reduce airborne sound.

Damping material reduces impact noise
Earlier I discussed damping and its ability to reduce airborne sound. But damping also works well at reducing impact noise. In a floor/ceiling assembly, damping material—a soft sticky substance that dampens sound—can be placed between a layer of sound board and a layer of plywood on the floor or between layers of drywall on the ceiling below. (Plywood and drywall with a dampening material already attached is also available.) The damping material reduces impact noise by dissipating vibration quickly as it moves through the plywood, drywall, or sound board.

DOUBLE WOOD STUD WALLS

Building two separate walls is better than building staggered stud walls because the plates are also separate. With ½-in. drywall installed on each side of this wall, the STC rating is 57. Add an second layer of drywall to each side to boost the STC rating to 64.

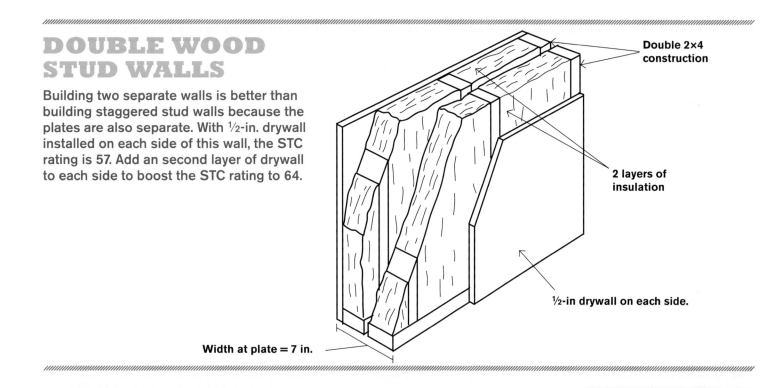

Double 2×4 construction

2 layers of insulation

½-in drywall on each side.

Width at plate = 7 in.

IMPACT SOUND

This diagram shows that when we think about impact noise, we have to think about structural noise as well as noise passing through the air cavity and then the ceiling below.

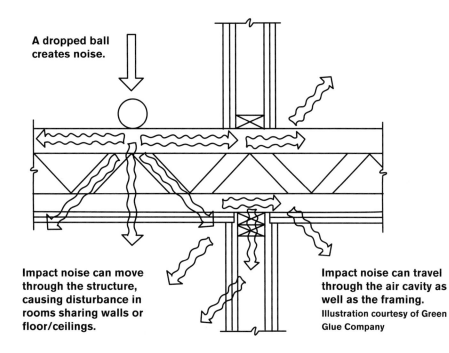

A dropped ball creates noise.

Impact noise can move through the structure, causing disturbance in rooms sharing walls or floor/ceilings.

Impact noise can travel through the air cavity as well as the framing.
Illustration courtesy of Green Glue Company

WORK SMART

Carpets and pads have only a minimal effect on airborne sound isolation, (keeping downstairs voices from going up and upstairs voices from going down, for example).

ADDING A RESILIENT LAYER TO THE FLOOR

When the floor shares framing with a ceiling below, it's a good idea to lay a resilient layer over the subfloor, then install your floor covering over the top.

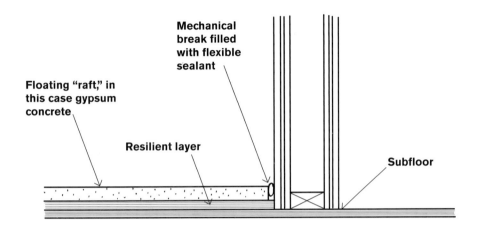

Mechanical break filled with flexible sealant

Floating "raft," in this case gypsum concrete

Resilient layer

Subfloor

Treating impact noise in the receiving area Resilient mounts—products such as RCI, sound clips, and spring ceiling hangers—work well on impact noise by breaking the structural path from the floor to the ceiling below. But because some of the structure-borne sound will travel through the walls, some of the benefit will be lost. To remove the noise from the flanking path, you may have to use resilient mounts on all sides of the room below. In extreme cases, you can even try building a "room within a room" where two stud rows are used in walls and separate joists are used for the ceiling, this more thoroughly breaks the structural path.

Damping and mass Using a damping material between layers of drywall on the ceiling helps to reduce impact noise. For additional sound control (and for the same reasons discussed earlier) you can further limit sound transmission by treating all the walls in the room with a damping material between the layers of drywall.

Mass is more valuable at stopping airborne noise than it is at stopping impact noise. So mass alone won't really do the job—it must be used in combination with the methods described earlier.

Insulation It is also important that you use some sort of absorbing material in the areas between framing. R-19 insulation works well, and there's no need to fill the entire ceiling area—to absorb sound along its path to another room, simply fill the cavities around the perimeter of the room's ceiling and any gaps or holes.

SOUND TRANSMISSION THROUGH CEILING FIXTURES

If not properly treated, ceiling fixtures on shared floor/ceiling assemblies create a pathway for sound to travel upstairs. Baffles and spring mountings help cut off this common pathway for sound.

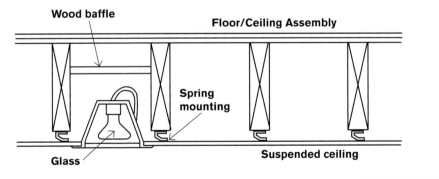

Wood baffle

Floor/Ceiling Assembly

Spring mounting

Glass

Suspended ceiling

Just like when treating walls, all gaps and holes that will become paths for movement of sound have to be filled with a flexible caulk or an expandable foam.

Ceiling fixtures create a pathway for sound Just as electrical outlets in walls create openings from one room to the next, ceiling fixtures in multifloor buildings create pathways for sound to travel from one floor to the next. To limit the transmission of sound through ceiling fixtures, do the following:

• Try to surface mount ceiling fixtures on resilient mounted ceilings. This will avoid shorting out the system.

• Make sure openings around the boxes are sealed tight.

• Seal holes in the electrical box and wrap the box in the same way an outlet box is wrapped.

• Don't use recessed or hi-hat type fixtures without boxing in the fixture.

• Use lights approved for insulation.

Mass-loaded insulation blankets are also available for containing noise that travels into the fixture. Whether isolating with a wooden box or the blanket material, be sure to give the fixture some space to avoid overheating problems. Also, remember to caulk and seal all of the gaps in the box.

Doors open for sound too

Doing all the right things to control noise and then installing a loose-fitting hollow-core door can easily void out all your hard work. But there are doors made specifically for sound control situations, and many of them work well. When installing doors, remember the following:

DON'T LET DOORS BE THE WEAK LINK

Interior doors keep out sound in much the same way that exterior doors keep out hot and cold air. If the doors are not properly treated for sound control, it makes little difference what measures are taken with the walls, ceilings, and floors.

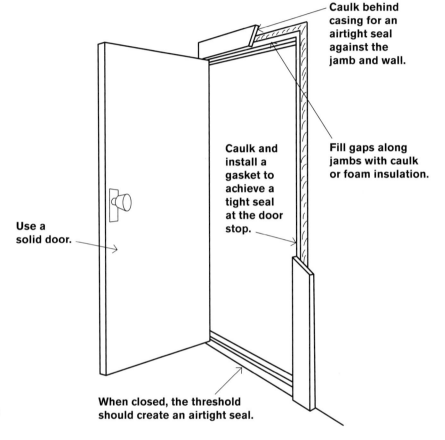

Caulk behind casing for an airtight seal against the jamb and wall.

Fill gaps along jambs with caulk or foam insulation.

Caulk and install a gasket to achieve a tight seal at the door stop.

Use a solid door.

When closed, the threshold should create an airtight seal.

• Two doors aligned are a straight path for sound—stagger doors across hallways.

• When possible, position doors so that they face away from noisy areas.

• Use doors made of solid wood or doors with insulated cores.

• Treat an interior door as you do an exterior door—you are trying to stop the transmis-

Retrofitting a church hall
When this church hall was built, the walls were treated for sound control, but the doors were not. Casings had to be removed, and all the gaps filled. A sound board panel was attached to the door and exterior door stops, and a door sweep was also installed. If an exterior door had been used in the first place, the door would not be such a weak link.

Also, be careful with replacement windows. They are sometimes poorly insulated along the jambs and fit too loosely. Using quality windows helps to reduce sound.

SOUND CONTROL FOR EXISTING STRUCTURES

When it comes to sound control, retrofitting walls, ceilings, and floors offers a different set of obstacles than new construction. Still, the same problems exist, and the solutions are based on the same fundamentals of sound transmission used to develop any sound control plan. Here are a few of the techniques you can use to reduce noise transmission on existing walls:

• Blow in insulation.

• Add drywall for mass.

• Apply a dampening or breaking material between the new layer and the existing.

• Seal perimeter with caulk.

• Caulk outlets and switches.

• Treat or upgrade doors and windows by insulating, sealing and adding mass.

• Don't assume a problem, such as back-to-back closets, is too small to address or good enough as it is.

sion of sound just as you're trying to stop the transmission of hot or cold air with an exterior door.

Windows let in more than light

Sound control for windows is kind of obvious, because most of the same things you consider for keeping the cold out have to be considered for sound.

• Insulate and caulk along jambs.

• Caulk casing as it is installed, just like when treating doors.

• Windows can be purchased that have better sound control qualities and are labeled for sound control applications.

• Avoid windows facing noisy areas or at least reduce their size.

RESOURCES

AUTOMATIC TOOLS
Ames Tools
3305 Beckinridge Boulevard
Suite 122
Duluth, GA 30096
800-241-2771
www.amestools.com

Apla-Tech®
W2024 Industrial Drive #3
Kaukauna, WI 54130
800-827-3721
www.apla-tech.com

Better-Than-Ever Tools
8106 Highland Place
Vernon, BC V1B 3S2
800-444-7908
www.betterthanevertools.com

Can-Am Tool Co.
Box 14
St. Albert, AB TBN 1N2
780-458-2116
www.canamtool.com

Columbia Taping Tools
250 H Street
Blaine, WA 98230
800-663-8121
www.columbiatools.com

Wilco Tools
1122 Siddonsburg Road
Mechanicsburg, PA 17055
888-292-1002
www.wilcotools.com

CORNERBEADS AND TAPES
FibaTape®
Saint-Gobain Technical Fabrics
1795 Baseline Road
Grand Island, NY 14411-0390
585-589-4401
www.fibatape.com

Flannery, Inc.
300 Parkside Drive
San Fernando, CA 91340
800-765-7585
www.flannerytrim.com

No-Coat®
Structus Building Technologies
PO Box 5937
Bend, OR 97708-5937
888-662-6281
www.no-coat.com

Phillips Manufacturing
4949 South 30th Street
Omaha, NE 68107
800-822-5055
www.phillipsmfg.com

Strait-Flex Cornerbead
Con Form International, Inc.
11644 Fair Grove Industrial
Boulevard
Maryland Heights, MO 63043
314-692-8999
www.straitflex.com

Trim-Tex®
3700 Pratt Avenue
Lincoln, IL 60712
800-874-2333
www.trim-tex.com

USG Corporation
125 South Franklin Street
Chicago, IL 60606-4678
800-874-4968
www.usg.com

DRYWALL COMPANIES
BPB Celotex®
800-235-6839
www.bpb-celotex.com

Georgia-Pacific Corporation
133 Peachtree Street, N.E.
Atlanta, GA 30303
800-225-6119
www.gp.com

James Hardie Gypsum
26300 La Alameda, Suite 250
Mission Viejo, CA 92691
800-426-3669
www.hardirock.com

LaFarge North America Inc.
12950 Worldgate Drive
Suite 400
Herndon, VA 20170-6001
703-480-3600
www.lafargenorthamerica.com

National Gypsum Company
2001 Rexford Road
Charlotte, NC 28211
800-628-4662
www.nationalgypsum.com

Raised Panel Designer Drywall
Pittcon Industries, Inc.
6409 Rhode Island Avenue
Riverdale, MD 20737-1098
800-637-7638
www.pittconnindustries.com

USG Corporation
125 South Franklin Street
Chicago, IL 60606-4678
800-874-4968
www.usg.com

DRYWALL ROUTERS
DeWalt®
PO Box 158
626 Hanover Pike
Hampstead, MD 21074
800-732-4447
www.dewalt.com

Porter-Cable® Professional
Power Tools
PO Box 2468
4825 Highway 45 North
Jackson, TN 38302-2468
800-487-8665
www.porter-cable.com

RotoZip® Tool Corporation
1861 Ludden Drive
Cross Plains, WI 53528
800-521-1871
www.rotozip.com

HAND TOOLS

E-Z Trowel®
4505 West Hacienda
Las Vegas, NV 89118
866-397-6657
www.eztrowel.com

Hyde Manufacturing Co.
54 Eastford Road
Southbridge, MA 01550
800-331-5569
www.hydetools.com

Johnson Abrasives Co., Inc.
49 Fitzgerald Drive
Jaffrey, NH 03452
800-628-8005
(603-628-8005 in New
Hampshire)
www.johnsonabrasives.com

Kraft Tool Co.
8325 Hedge Lane Terrace
Shawnee, KS 66227
800-422-2448
www.krafttool.com

Marshalltown Trowel Company
104 S. 8th Avenue
Marshalltown, IA 50158
515-753-0127
www.marshalltown.com

Sheetrock Tools
130 South Jefferson Street
Suite 250
Chicago, IL 60661
312-454-6731

Stanley® Goldblatt® Tools
The Stanley Works
1000 Stanley Drive
New Britain, CT 06053
(860) 225-5111
www.stanleyworks.com

Warner Tool
Warner™ Manufacturing
Company
13435 Industrial Park Boulevard
Minneapolis, MN 55441

877-927-6372
www.warnertool.com

MISCELLANEOUS TOOLS

All-Wall
12700 NE 124th Street, #8
Kirkland, WA 98034-8304
800-929-0927
www.all-wall.com

Back-blocking device

Wilco Tools
1122 Siddonsburg Road
Mechanicsburg, PA 17055
888-292-1002
www.wilcotools.com

BeadBoxers™
1405 Cannon Circle
Faribault, MN 55021
507-334-0552
www.beadboxers.com

Bench step

Mack's Step™
4686 Eagle Circle, NW
North Canton, OH 44720
888-586-8650
www.macksstep.com

Calculator

Calculated Industries
4840 Hytech Drive
Carson City, NV 89706
800-854-8075
www.calculated.com

Caulk gun

Rigid Tools
Highway 8
Pickens, SC 29671
866-539-1710
www.rigid.com

C. H. Hanson
3630 North Wolf Road
Franklin Park, IL 60131
800-827-3398
www.chhanson.com

Curved wall track

Flex-Ability Concepts
PO Box 7145
Edmond, OK 73083
405-715-1799
www.flexc.com

Drywall clips

The Nailer®
2300 W. Eisenhower Boulevard
Loveland, CO 80537
800-280-2304
www.thenailer.com

Prest-on Company
312 Lookout Point
Hot Springs, AR 71913
800-323-1813
www.prest-on.com

Drywall lift

Telpro, Inc.
7251 South 42nd Street
Grand Forks, ND 58201
800-448-0822
www.telproinc.com

Sanders

Dustless Technologies
43980 Mahlon Vail Circle
Temecula, CA 92592
800-568-3949
www.dustlesstechnologies.com

Full Circle International
1820 Flag Avenue
St. Louis Park, MN 55426
866-675-2401
www.fullcircleinternational.com

Porter-Cable®
PO Box 2468
4825 Highway 45 North
Jackson, TN 38302-2468
800-487-8665
www.porter-cable.com

Wilco Tools
1122 Siddonsburg Road
Mechanicsburg, PA 17055
888-292-1002
www.wilcotools.com

Dust mask

3M®
3M Center, Building 275-6W-01
PO Box 33275
St. Paul, MN 55133-3275
800-265-1840
www.3M.com/occsafety/

Electric box protectors

Mark N Guard
984 Ridge Road
Broadalbin, NY 12025
888-480-8531
www.thatdrywallguy.com

Light

Wobblelight®
www.wobblelight.com

Stilts

Dura-Stilt® Sales
Limited Partnership
PO Box 271313
8316 SW 8th Street
Oklahoma City, OK 73128
800-225-2440
www.durastilts.com

Skywalker Stilts
104 S. 8th Street
Marshalltown, IA 50158
641-753-5999
www.marshalltown.com

Temporary wall supports

Curtain Wall Company
490 Wellington Avenue
Cranston, RI 02910
800-424-8251
www.curtain-wall.com

ZipWall®
2464 Massachusetts Avenue
Cambridge, MA 02140
617-499-9966
www.zipwall.com

Texturing tools

Sherwin-Williams®
www.sherwin-williams.com

Spraytex, Inc.
28430 W. Witherspoon Parkway
Valencia, CA 91355
800-234-5979
www.spraytex.com

Tex Master Tools
175 S. Columbus Street
Sunbury, OH 43074
800-852-8355
www.texmaster.com

Tool bags
Veto Pro Pac®
PO Box 2072
Norwalk, CT 06852-2072
877-847-1443
www.vetopropac.com

SCAFFOLDING
Bil-Jax®
125 Taylor Parkway
Archbold, OH 43502
419-445-9675
www.bil-jax.com

Falcon Ladder and Scaffold
Manufacturing Ltd.
222 Adams Road
Kelowna, BC V1X 7R2
Canada
800-522-3313
www.falconscaffold.com

Telpro Inc.
7251 South 42nd Street
Grand Forks, ND 58201
800-448-0822
www.telproinc.com

SCREWGUNS
Bosch® Tools
877-267-2499
www.boschtools.com

DeWalt
PO Box 158
626 Hanover Pike
Hampstead, MD 21074
800-732-4447
www.dewalt.com

Grabber® Construction Products
205 Mason Circle
Concord, CA 94520
800-477-8876
www.grabberman.com

Makita®
14930 Northam Street
La Mirada, CA 90638
800-462-5482
www.makita.com

Senco Products, Inc.
8485 Broadwell Road
Cincinnati, OH 45244
800-543-4596
www.senco.com

SOUND CONTROL PRODUCTS AND INFO
Greenglue Company
989-832-1602
www.greengluecompany.com

Owens-Corning®
800-438-7465
www.owenscorning.com

Sound Sense
29 Gann Road
East Hampton, NY 11937
631-324-2266
www.soundsense.com

DRYWALL ASSOCIATIONS AND FURTHER READING
Associations
AWCI
Association of the Wall and
Ceiling Industries
803 West Broad Street, Suite 600
Falls Church, VA 22046
703-534-8300
www.awci.org

Gypsum Association
810 First Street N
Suite 510
Washington, DC 20002
202-289-5440
www.gypsum.org

Further reading
Construction Dimensions
803 West Broad Street, Suite 600
Falls Church, VA 22046
703-534-8307
www.awci.org

Jobsite Magazine
PO Box 550
Newburg NY 12551-9968
609-397-5601
www.jobsitemagazine.com

USG Handbook
USG Corporation
125 South Franklin Street
Chicago, IL 60606
800-874-4968
www.usg.com

Walls & Ceilings
2401 W. Big Beaver Rd
Suite 700
Troy, MI 48084
248-362-3700
www.wconline.com

Education
Building Event Solutions
888-480-8531
www.buildingeventsolutions.com

Plaster Man
www.plasterzone.com

That Drywall Guy
888-480-8531
www.thatdrywallguy.com

Toronto School of Drywall
905-270-0443
www.torontoschoolofdrywall.com

APPENDIX

RECOMMENDED LEVELS OF GYPSUM BOARD FINISH

In an effort to prevent misunderstandings about the quality of drywall finishing, four major trade associations developed a document that does a great job of explaining the levels of finishing and where a specific finish would be best suited. Known as "Recommended Levels of Gypsum Board Finish," it was developed by the Association of the Walls and Ceilings Industries International, Ceiling Interior Systems Construction Association, Gypsum Association, and Painting and Decorating Contractors of America.

The following information is taken from document GA-214-96:

LEVEL 0

No taping, finishing, or accessories required. This level of finish may be useful in temporary construction or whenever the final decoration has not been determined.

LEVEL 1

All joints and interior angles shall have tape set in joint compound. Surface shall be free of excess joint compound. Tool marks and ridges are acceptable.

Frequently specified in plenum areas above ceilings, in attics, in areas where the assembly would generally be concealed, in a building's service corridors, and in other areas not normally open to public view. Accessories are optional at specifier discretion in corridors and other areas with pedestrian traffic.

Some degree of sound and smoke control is provided: In some geographic areas this level is referred to as fire taping. Where fire-resistance rating is required for the gypsum board assembly, details of construction shall be in accordance with reports of fire tests of assemblies that have met the fire-rating requirement. Tape and fastener heads need not be covered with joint compound.

LEVEL 2

All joints and interior angles shall have tape embedded in joint compound and wiped with a joint knife with a thin coating of joint compound left over all joints and interior angles. Fastener heads and accessories shall be covered with a coat of joint compound. Surface shall be free of excess joint compound. Tool marks and ridges are acceptable. Joint compound applied over the body of the tape at the time of tape embodiment shall be considered a separate coat of joint compound and shall satisfy the conditions of this level.

Specified where water-resistant gypsum backing board (ASTM C 630) is used as a substrate for tile; may be specified in garages, warehouse storage, or other similar areas where surface appearance is not of primary concern.

LEVEL 3

All joints and interior angles shall have tape embedded in joint compound and one additional coat of joint compound applied over all joints and interior angles. Fastener heads and accessories shall be covered with two separate coats of joint compound. All joint compound shall be smooth and free of tool marks and ridges. Note: It is recommended that the prepared surface be coated with a drywall primer prior to the application of final finishes. See painting/wallcovering specification in this regard.

Typically specified in appearance areas that are to receive heavy- or medium-texture (spray- or hand-applied) finish before final painting, or where heavy-grade wallcoverings are to be applied as the final decoration. This level of finish is not recommended where smooth-painted surfaces of light to medium wallcoverings are specified.

LEVEL 4

All joints and interior angles shall have tape embedded in joint compound and two separate coats of joint compound applied over all flat joints and one separate coat of joint compound applied over interior angles. Fastener heads and accessories shall be covered with three separate coats of joint compound. All joint compound shall be smooth and free of tool marks and ridges. Note: It is recommended that the prepared surface be coated with a drywall primer prior to the application of final finishes. See painting/wall covering specification in this regard.

This level should be specified where flat paints, light textures, or light to medium wallcoverings are to be applied.

In critical lighting areas, flat paints applied over light textures tend to reduce joint photographing. Gloss, semigloss, and enamel paints are not recommended for use over this level of finish.

The weight, texture, and sheen level of wallcoverings applied over this level of finish should be carefully evaluated. Joints and fasteners must be adequately concealed if the wallcovering material is lightweight, contains limited pattern, or has a gloss finish, or if any combination of these finishes is present. Unbacked vinyl wallcoverings are not recommended over this level of finish.

LEVEL 5

All joints and interior angles shall have tape embedded in joint compound, two separate coats of joint compound applied over all flat joints, and one separate coat of joint compound applied over interior angles. Fastener heads and accessories shall be covered with three separate coats of joint compound. A thin skim coat of joint compound or material manufactured especially for this purpose shall be applied to the entire surface. The surface shall be smooth and free of tool marks and ridges. Note: It is recommended that the prepared surface be coated with a drywall primer prior to the application of finish paint. See painting specification in this regard.

This level of finish is highly recommended where gloss, semigloss, enamel, or nontextured flat paints are specified or where severe lighting conditions occur. This highest quality finish is the most effective method of providing a uniform surface and minimizing the possibility of joint photographing and of fasteners showing through the final decoration.

INDEX